Rockmo

THE FORGOTTEN HUME

DAVID HUME, *le bon David,* 1766
FROM THE PAINTING BY ALLAN RAMSAY IN THE SCOTTISH
NATIONAL PORTRAIT GALLERY, EDINBURGH

*Allan Ramsay painted a portrait of David Hume, dressed in scarlet with rich
gold lace. George III thought the picture very like, but thought the dress rather
too fine. "I wished," said Ramsay, "posterity should see that one philosopher
during your Majesty's reign had a good coat upon his back."*—BOSWELLIANA

THE FORGOTTEN HUME

Le bon David

By ERNEST CAMPBELL MOSSNER

AMS PRESS, INC.
NEW YORK
1967

ACKNOWLEDGMENTS

THIS INTIMATE biography of David Hume was made feasible at the present time by the grant of a fellowship on the John Simon Guggenheim Memorial Foundation for 1939-40. During that year of freedom from academic duties I was able to pursue research abroad and at home. It is most gratifying to return thanks to the sponsors of the Foundation, its trustees, and its genial and able secretary, Dr. Henry Allen Moe.

In Edinburgh my investigations at the National Library of Scotland—the Advocates' Library of Hume's day—were pleasantly facilitated by the interest of Dr. Henry W. Meikle in his distinguished predecessor in the keepership. At Edinburgh University Library, Dr. Lauriston W. Sharp was untiring in bringing to my attention documents relating to the most famous of that institution's long line of eminent philosophers. The Robert Wallace manuscript collection there provided the substance for Chapter 5. To Dr. W. G. Maclagan and Dr. R. Klibansky of Oriel College, Oxford, I am profoundly grateful. Engaged in editing a supplementary volume of Hume's unpublished letters, they generously placed all of their findings at my disposal. The little that I have been able to return in kind still leaves me deeply in their debt.

In the United States the Harvard College Library and the Huntington Library proved most fruitful for research. An early version of Chapter 3 was published in the *Huntington Library Quarterly* for July, 1940. To Professors Katherine G. Hornbeak of Smith College, W. Powell Jones of Western Reserve University, and R. Morrell Schmitz of Washington University, St. Louis, I am obligated for the location of certain materials inaccessible to me. I am further obligated to the Rev. L. Humphrey Walz of New York City for his dexterous reconstruction from my rather vague specifications of Hume's personal seal, which appears as tailpiece.

Acknowledgment is also to be made to the Viking Press for permission to quote from the *Private Papers of James Boswell from Malahide Castle* as originally published in a limited edition by William Rudge (New York, 1928-34, 18 vols.) and to be published eventually in an unlimited edition by the Viking Press under the editorship of Professor Frederick A. Pottle. The excerpts appear chiefly in Chapter 7.

In the helpful and sympathetic criticisms of several authorities I have been exceedingly fortunate: Professors Gerald E. Bentley of the University of Chicago, James M. Osborn of Yale University, Frederick A. Pottle of Yale University, Harold W. Thompson of Cornell University, Dixon Wecter of the University of California at Los Angeles, and Ernest Hunter Wright of Columbia University. To these philosophers and scholars, my sincere thanks. For the basic positions taken in this book, however, the responsibility is mine alone, and what defects still remain are doubtless due to my reluctance to follow good advice.

Finally, I am happy to express gratitude to three persons upon whose coöperation I have presumed most of all. Professor James L. Clifford of Lehigh University and Dr. Allan Evans of the Huntington Library performed the friendly service of reading the manuscript in its entirety. By their sound judgment and good taste I have greatly benefited. As for my wife, had *le bon David* himself encountered similar zeal and industry, I am persuaded that he would not have expressed himself entirely as he did in a letter of 1753: "What would you have more? Independence? I have it in a supreme degree. Honour? that is not altogether wanting. Grace? that will come in time. A wife? that is none of the indispensable requisites of life. Books? that *is* one of them; and I have more than I can use."

E. C. M.

Syracuse University
September 15, 1942

CONTENTS

FOREWORD   xi

PART I: HUME'S HUME

1. MY OWN LIFE   3

PART II: THE SCOTTISH POETS

2. HUME AND THE SCOTTISH PINDAR   13

3. HUME AND THE SCOTTISH SHAKESPEARE   38

4. HUME AND THE SCOTTISH HOMERS   67
   The Homer of the Lowlands (68); The Homer of the
   Highlands (82)

PART III: THE CONTROVERSIALISTS

5. HUME AND WALLACE   105

6. HUME AND ROUSSEAU   132

PART IV: THE JOHNSONIANS

7. HUME AND BOSWELL   169

8. HUME AND JOHNSON   189

9. AFTERWORD   210

DISCURSIVE NOTES   213

AUTHORITIES   223

INDEX   237

ILLUSTRATIONS

DAVID HUME, *le bon David,* 1766   *Frontispiece*

JEAN-JACQUES ROUSSEAU, HUME'S
    "PUPIL" IN 1766   148

HUME'S PERSONAL SEAL: TRUE TO
    THE END   212

FOREWORD

THE HERO of this book is David Hume—not as philosopher, or historian, or economist, or political scientist, or skeptic —but simply as a human being, *le bon David*. This is a study in personality, in the humanity of a profound thinker, an Inquirer after truth. A kindly person, Hume occasionally found friendship and patriotism at war with critical judgment. A temperate person, Hume disliked controversy but, when forced into it, strove to keep it amicable. Opponents of the thinker were not infrequently disarmed by the man; those who came to contemn remained to admire, and those who came to hate remained to love. Kindly, temperate, and lovable, Hume made a more congenial friend than some of his famous contemporaries. Two of them found him literally a man to dream about, Rousseau dreaming that he was villainous, Boswell that he was pious. In reality, he was neither villainous nor pious; he was simply *le bon David*. Yet this Hume, unlike the Inquirer, is little known today—is, in fact, the forgotten Hume.

The purpose of this book is to revitalize the most stimulating of modern philosophers by observing him as friend and as foe, as critic and as patron, as man and as Scot. The picture drawn here is of a Hume deeply rooted in the eighteenth century, of a Hume who is not merely the symbol of certain ideas but a living man. The stock Hume of the professional handbooks is that mythical creature described by Thomas Carlyle, a man without national affiliations. "Hume was too rich a man to borrow," Carlyle was willing to concede; "and perhaps he reacted on the French more than he was acted on by them: but neither had he aught to do with Scotland; Edinburgh, equally with La Flèche, was but the lodging and laboratory, in which he not so much morally *lived*, as metaphysically *investigated*." This sad philosopher-without-a-country remains acceptable only because the historical Hume has been forgotten.

Yet the historical Hume was a colorful figure. Those who knew him personally testify that what impressed them most was character. To them, as also to candid opponents of his philosophy, he was always *le bon David*. The agreement is of import because it attests what has frequently been disputed—his moral sincerity and his intellectual integrity. But actions reveal character even more cogently than testimony. In the study of Hume they are especially valuable when they exhibit signs of conflict between the Inquirer and *le bon David*, between the thinker and the social being. Such strife arises when ideals come up against facts because the world of ideas does not necessarily coincide with the world of society. Indications of internal conflict, painstakingly read, are thus important clues toward the resolution of the enigma of Hume that has for so long intrigued the modern world.

I

The middle and late career provide ample materials for this inquiry into character. That was the time when Hume was less the spectator and more the actor, less the formal metaphysician and more the broad philosopher.

"I am surprised, Mr. Hume," said Thomas White, a decent rich merchant of London, "that a man of your good sense should think of being a philosopher. Why, I now took it into my head to be a philosopher for some time, but tired of it most confoundedly, and very soon gave it up."

"Pray, sir," said Mr. Hume, "in what branch of philosophy did you employ your researches? What books did you read?"

"Books?" said Mr. White; "nay, sir, I read no books, but I used to sit you whole forenoons a-yawning and poking the fire."

There is much in the following chapters that may legitimately be called new. For it is a fact that although articles and books on Hume have been appearing at the rate of more than two a year for the past two hundred years, they have with few exceptions been devoted to Hume the philosopher, or the historian, or the economist, or any of the other Humes, but not to the man. Important exceptions number only two: J. H. Burton's *Life and Correspondence of*

David Hume in 1846 and J. Y. T. Greig's *David Hume* in 1931. The first, though unreliable in its scholarship according to modern standards, is still the fullest available biography; for Greig, brilliant and entertaining as he is, and editor of the best collection of Hume's letters, disappointingly fails to round his picture.

The specialists have naturally been preoccupied with their specialties; and quantities of documents relating to Hume's career have hardly been turned over. It was my good fortune to examine many of them just before the outbreak of World War II. Indeed, that unhappy event necessitated my leaving Edinburgh when the manuscript collections were placed in safekeeping "for the duration." But, fortunately, I left with a trunkful of notes. From Scotland to California was somewhat more than a sea change, but it was not unproductive of Humiana. Several libraries throughout the United States have contributed unexpected treasures to the collections of one who is interested in everything relating to Hume. This wealth of materials, I hope some day to employ in a full-scale treatment of "David Hume, Man of Letters," for which *The Forgotten Hume* will have provided the basis, inasmuch as the intent of the written word may sometimes be clarified by knowledge of the character of the writer.

II

The present portrayal of *le bon David* opens with his autobiography. An ingenuous and charming self-analysis, *My Own Life* certainly bears reprinting and is especially valuable in providing the setting for the remaining three parts. In Part II Hume is depicted in his relations with certain Scottish poets: Thomas Blacklock, John Home, William Wilkie, and James Macpherson. These chapters dwell upon a neglected aspect of Hume's lifework—his interest in fine letters and his patronage of national talent. Here, already, the conflict between heart and head, desire and integrity, is quite apparent.

In Part III Hume is depicted in controversy, both pleasant and disagreeable. That with Wallace, transcending all pettiness, attained the highest ideals of the Age of Enlightenment and established Hume's reputation throughout Europe as *le bon David*. The quarrel

with Rousseau, "literary tragi-comedy" that it was, is the acid test
of the character so established. In Part IV Hume is depicted in his
contacts, personal and literary, with the Johnsonians. The ceaseless
effort of James Boswell to fathom the enigma of Hume illuminates
not only Hume, but incidentally Boswell himself. The intense
nationalistic rivalry between Hume and Johnson, leaders of the
Scottish and the English literary coteries, has never been recognized
in its full extent; yet it demands a sweeping review. The Afterword
speculates briefly as to why it was Samuel Johnson and not David
Hume who lent his name to that era. The question was not merely
of production and of influence; nationalism and the time spirit were
involved—also character.

III

Several months before his death in 1776, Hume read with pleasure the first volume of Gibbon's *Decline and Fall* and hailed it as
epoch making. He remarked, however, certain mechanical defects.
"One is . . . plagued with the Notes according to the present Method
of printing the Book," he wrote the publisher. "When a note is
announced, you turn to the End of the Volume; and there you often
find nothing but the Reference to an Authority: All these Authorities ought only to be printed at the Margin or the Bottom of the
Page."

Following Hume's own usage as befits a book on him, the distinction is drawn between referential and discursive notes. Abbre-
viated referential notes, consecutively numbered throughout each
chapter, are placed at the bottom of the page. To reduce their number, references are omitted to the most indispensable source of all,
Letters of David Hume, edited by J. Y. T. Greig (Oxford, 1932,
2 volumes); all important quotations, however, may be verified by
means of the dates. Discursive notes are referred, in turn, from the
bottom of the page to a separate section at the end of the volume.

Through this distinction in notes, it is to be hoped that the three
classes of potential readers may each be satisfied: the general reader,
who wishes to follow the course of the narrative without undue
mechanical interference; the scholar, who wishes to know the source
of all important statements; and the special student of Hume, who

wishes to know why one authority or interpretation is preferred to others.

English works are cited as in the originals. Foreign citations, except where otherwise indicated, are the translations of the present writer.

PART I

HUME'S HUME

You will find among my Papers a very inoffensive Piece, called My own Life, *which I composed a few days before I left Edinburgh, when I thought, as did all my Friends, that my Life was despaired of. There can be no Objection, that this small piece should be sent to Messrs Strahan and Cadell and the Proprietors of my other Works to be prefixed to any future Edition of them.*—HUME TO ADAM SMITH, MAY 3, 1776

CHAPTER I

MY OWN LIFE[1]

18 of April 1776

I T IS difficult for a man to speak long of himself without Vanity: Therefore I shall be short. It may be thought an Instance of Vanity, that I pretend at all to write my Life: But this Narrative shall contain little more than the History of my Writings; as indeed, almost all my Life has been spent in literary Pursuits and Occupations. The first Success of most of my writings was not such as to be an Object of Vanity.

I was born the 26 of April 1711, O.S. at Edinburgh. I was of a good Family both by Father and Mother. My Father's Family is a Branch of the Earl of Home's or Hume's; and my Ancestors had been Proprietors of the Estate, which my Brother possesses, for several Generations. My Mother was Daughter of Sir David Falconar, President of the College of Justice: The Title of Lord Halkerton came by Succession to her Brother.

My Family, however, was not rich; and being myself a younger Brother, my Patrimony, according to the Mode of my Country, was of course very slender. My Father, who passed for a man of Parts, dyed, when I was an Infant; leaving me, with an elder Brother and a Sister under the care of our Mother, a woman of singular Merit, who, though young and handsome, devoted herself entirely to the rearing and educating of her Children. I passed through the ordinary Course of Education with Success; and was seized very early with a passion for Literature which has been the ruling Passion of my Life, and the great Source of my Enjoyments. My studious Disposition, my Sobriety, and my Industry gave my Family a Notion that the Law was a proper Profession for me: But I found an unsurmountable Aversion to every thing but the pursuits of Philosophy and general

[1] Hume, *Letters*, I, 1-7.

Learning; and while they fancied I was poring over Voet and
Vinnius, Cicero and Virgil were the Authors which I was secretly
devouring.

My very slender Fortune, however, being unsuitable to this plan
of Life, and my Health being a little broken by my ardent Application, I was tempted or rather forced to make a very feeble Trial for
entering into a more active Scene of Life. In 1734, I went to Bristol
with some Recommendations to eminent Merchants; but in a few
Months found that Scene totally unsuitable to me. I went over to
France, with a View of prosecuting my Studies in a Country Retreat;
and I there laid that Plan of Life, which I have steddily and successfully pursued: I resolved to make a very rigid Frugality supply
my Deficiency of Fortune, to maintain unimpaired my Independency, and to regard every object as contemptible, except the Improvement of my Talents in Literature.

During my Retreat in France, first at Reims, but chiefly at
La fleche in Anjou, I composed my *Treatise of human Nature.*
After passing three Years very agreeably in that Countrey, I came
over to London in 1737. In the End of 1738, I published my
Treatise; and immediatly went down to my Mother and my Brother,
who lived at his Countrey house and was employing himself, very
judiciously and successfully, in the Improvement of his Fortune.

Never literary Attempt was more unfortunate than my Treatise
of human Nature. It fell *dead-born from the Press;* without reaching such distinction as even to excite a Murmur among the Zealots.
But being naturally of a cheerful and sanguine Temper, I very soon
recovered the Blow, and prosecuted with great Ardour my Studies
in the Country. In 1742, I printed at Edinburgh the first part of
my Essays: The work was favourably received, and soon made me
entirely forget my former Disappointment. I continued with my
Mother and Brother in the Countrey; and in that time, recovered
the Knowledge of the Greek Language, which I had too much
neglected in my early Youth.

In 1745, I received a Letter from the Marquess of Annandale,
inviting me to come and live with him in England: I found also,
that the Friends and Family of that young Nobleman, were desirous of putting him under my Care and Direction: For the State of

his Mind and Health required it. I lived with him a Twelvemonth: My Appointments during that time made a considerable Accession to my small Fortune. I then received an Invitation from General St clair to attend him as Secretary to his Expedition, which was at first meant against Canada, but ended in an Incursion on the Coast of France: Next Year, to wit 1747, I received an Invitation from the General to attend him in the same Station in his military Embassy to the Courts of Vienna and Turin. I there wore the Uniform of an Officer; and was introduced at these courts as Aide-de-camp to the General, along with Sir Harry Erskine and Capt Grant, now General Grant. These two Years were almost the only Interruptions which my Studies have received in the Course of my Life: I passed them agreeably and in good Company: And my Appointments, with my Frugality, had made me reach a Fortune, which I called independent, though most of my Friends were inclined to smile when I said so: In short I was now Master of near a thousand Pound.

I had always entertained a Notion, that my want of Success, in publishing the Treatise of human Nature, had proceeded more from the manner than the matter; and that I had been guilty of a very usual Indiscretion, in going to the Press too early. I therefore cast the first part of that work anew in the Enquiry concerning human Understanding, which was published while I was at Turin. But this piece was at first but little more successful than the Treatise of human Nature. On my return from Italy, I had the Mortification to find all England in a Ferment on account of Dr. Middletons Free Enquiry; while my Performance was entirely overlooked and neglected. A new Edition, which had been published at London of my Essays, moral and political, met not with a much better reception.

Such is the force of natural Temper, that these disappointments made little or no Impression on me. I went down in 1749 and lived two Years with my Brother at his Country house: For my Mother was now dead. I there composed the second Part of my Essays, which I called Political Discourses; and also my Enquiry concerning the Principles of Morals, which is another part of my Treatise, that I cast anew. Mean-while, my Bookseller, A. Millar, informed me, that my former Publications (all but the unfortunate Treatise) were beginning to be the Subject of Conversation, that the Sale of them was gradually encreasing, and that new Editions were demanded. Answers, by Reverends and Right Reverends, came out two or three in a Year: And I found by Dr Warburtons Railing that the Books were beginning to be esteemed in good Company. However, I had fixed a Resolution, which I inflexibly maintained, never to reply to any body; and not being very irascible in my Temper, I have easily kept myself clear of all literary Squabbles. These Symptoms of a rising Reputation gave me Encouragement as I was ever more disposed to see the favourable than unfavourable Side of things; a turn of Mind, which it is more happy to possess than be born to an Estate of ten thousand a Year.

In 1751, I removed from the Countrey to the Town; the true Scene for a man of Letters. In 1752, were published at Edinburgh, where I then lived, my Political Discourses, the only work of mine, that was successful on the first Publication: It was well received abroad and at home. In the same Year was published at London my Enquiry concerning the Principles of Morals, which, in my own opinion (who ought not to judge on that subject) is of all my writings, historical, philosophical, or literary, incomparably the best: It came unnoticed and unobserved into the World.

In 1752, the Faculty of Advocates chose me their Librarian, an Office from which I received little or no Emolument, but which gave me the Command of a large Library. I then formed the Plan of writing the History of England; but being frightened with the Notion of continuing a Narrative, through a Period of 1700 years, I commenced with the Accession of the House of Stuart; an Epoch, when, I thought, the Misrepresentations of Faction began chiefly to take place. I was, I own, sanguine in my Expectations of the Success of this work. I thought, that, I was the only Historian, that had at once neglected present Power, Interest, and Authority, and the Cry of popular Prejudices; and as the Subject was suited to every Capacity, I expected proportional Applause: But miserable was my Disappointment: I was assailed by one Cry of Reproach, Disapprobation, and even Detestation: English, Scotch, and Irish; Whig and Tory; Churchman and Sectary, Free-thinker and Religionist; Patriot and Courtier united in their Rage against the Man, who had pre-

sumed to shed a generous Tear for the Fate of Charles I, and the
Earl of Strafford: And after the first Ebullitions of this Fury were
over, what was still more mortifying, the Book seemed to sink into
Oblivion. Mr Millar told me, that in a twelvemonth he sold only
forty five Copies of it. I scarcely indeed heard of one Man in the
three Kingdoms, considerable for Rank or Letters, that cou'd endure
the Book. I must only except the Primate of England, Dr Herring,
and the Primate of Ireland, Dr Stone; which seem two odd Exceptions. These dignifyed Prelates separately sent me Messages not to
be discouraged.

I was, however, I confess, discouraged; and had not the War
been at that time breaking out between France and England, I had
certainly retired to some provincial Town of the former Kingdom,
have changed my Name, and never more have returned to my native
Country. But as this Scheme was not now practicable, and the subsequent Volume was considerably advanced, I resolved to pick up
Courage and to persevere.

In this Interval I published at London, my natural History of
Religion along with some other small Pieces: Its public Entry was
rather obscure, except only that Dr Hurd wrote a Pamphlet against
it, with all the illiberal Petulance, Arrogance, and Scurrility, which
distinguishes the Warburtonian School. This Pamphlet gave me
some Consolation for the otherwise indifferent Reception of my Performance.

In 1756, two Years after the fall of the first Volume, was published the second Volume of my History, containing the Period
from the Death of Charles I, till the Revolution. This Performance
happened to give less Displeasure to the Whigs, and was better
received. It not only rose itself; but helped to buoy up its unfortunate Brother.

But though I had been taught by Experience, that the Whig
Party were in possession of bestowing all places, both in the State
and in Literature, I was so little inclined to yield to their senseless
Clamour, that in above a hundred Alterations, which farther Study,
Reading, or Reflection engaged me to make in the Reigns of the
two first Stuarts, I have made all of them invariably to the Tory

Side. It is ridiculous to consider the English Constitution before that Period as a regular Plan of Liberty.

In 1759 I published my History of the House of Tudor. The Clamour against this Performance was almost equal to that against the History of the two first Stuarts. The Reign of Elizabeth was particularly obnoxious. But I was now callous against the Impressions of public Folly; and continued very peacably and contentedly in my Retreat at Edinburgh, to finish in two Volumes the more early part of the English History; which I gave to the public in 1761 with tolerable, and but tolerable Success.

But notwithstanding this Variety of Winds and Seasons, to which my Writings had been exposed, they had still been making such Advances, that the Copy Money, given me by the Booksellers, much exceeded any thing formerly known in England: I was become not only independant, but opulent. I retired to my native Country of Scotland, determined never more to set my Foot out of it; and retaining the Satisfaction of never having preferred a Request to one great Man or even making Advances of Friendship to any of them. As I was now turned of fifty, I thought of passing all the rest of my Life in this philosophical manner; when I received in 1763 an Invitation from Lord Hertford, with whom I was not in the least acquainted, to attend him on his Embassy to Paris, with a near Prospect of being appointed Secretary to the Embassy, and in the mean while, of performing the functions of that office. This Offer, however inviting, I at first declined; both because I was reluctant to begin Connexions with the Great, and because I was afraid that the Civilities and gay Company of Paris woud prove disagreeable to a Person of my Age and Humour: But on his Lordship's repeating the Invitation, I accepted of it. I have every reason, both of Pleasure and Interest, to think myself happy in my Connexions with that Nobleman; as well as afterwards, with his Brother, General Conway.

Those who have not seen the strange Effect of Modes will never imagine the Reception I met with at Paris, from Men and Women of all Ranks and Stations. The more I recoiled from their excessive Civilities, the more I was loaded with them. There is, however, a real Satisfaction in living at Paris from the great Number of sensible, knowing, and polite Company with which the City abounds above all places in the Universe. I thought once of settling there for Life.

I was appointed Secretary to the Embassy, and in Summer 1765, Lord Hertford left me being appointed Lord Lieutenant of Ireland. I was *chargé d'affaires*, till the Arrival of the Duke of Richmond towards the End of the Year. In the beginning of 1766, I left Paris and next summer, went to Edinburgh, with the same view as formerly of burying myself in a philosophical Retreat. I returned to that place, not richer, but with much more money and a much larger Income by means of Lord Hertford's Friendship, than I left it; and I was desirous of trying what Superfluity coud produce, as I had formerly made an Experiment of a Competency. But in 1767, I received from Mr Conway an invitation to be Under-Secretary; and this Invitation both the Character of the Person, and my Connexions with Lord Hertford, prevented me from declining. I returned to Edinburgh in 1769, very opulent (for I possessed a Revenue of 1000 pounds a year) healthy, and though somewhat stricken in Years, with the Prospect of enjoying long my Ease and of seeing the Encrease of my Reputation.

In spring 1775, I was struck with a Disorder in my Bowels, which at first gave me no Alarm, but has since, as I apprehend it, become mortal and incurable. I now reckon upon a speedy Dissolution. I have suffered very little pain from my Disorder; and what is more strange, have, notwithstanding the great Decline of my Person, never suffered a Moments Abatement of my Spirits: Insomuch, that were I to name the Period of my Life which I shoud most choose to pass over again I might be tempted to point to this later Period. I possess the same Ardor as ever in Study, and the same Gaiety in Company. I consider besides, that a Man of sixty five, by dying, cuts off only a few Years of Infirmities: And though I see many Symptoms of my literary Reputation's breaking out at last with additional Lustre, I know, that I had but few Years to enjoy it. It is difficult to be more detached from Life than I am at present.

To conclude historically with my own Character—I am, or rather was (for that is the Style, I must now use in speaking of myself;

which emboldens me the more to speak my Sentiments) I was, I say, a man of mild Dispositions, of Command of Temper, of an open, social, and cheerful Humour, capable of Attachment, but little susceptible of Enmity, and of great Moderation in all my Passions. Even my Love of literary Fame, my ruling Passion, never soured my humour, notwithstanding my frequent Disappointments. My Company was not unacceptable to the young and careless, as well as to the Studious and literary: And as I took a particular Pleasure in the Company of modest women, I had no Reason to be displeased with the Reception I met with from them. In a word, though most men any wise eminent, have found reason to complain of Calumny, I never was touched, or even attacked by her baleful Tooth: And though I wantonly exposed myself to the Rage of both civil and religious Factions, they seemed to be disarmed in my behalf of their wonted Fury: My Friends never had occasion to vindicate any one Circumstance of my Character and Conduct: Not but that the Zealots, we may well suppose, wou'd have been glad to invent and propagate any Story to my Disadvantage, but they coud never find any which, they thought, woud wear the Face of Probability. I cannot say, there is no Vanity in making this funeral Oration of myself; but I hope it is not a misplac'd one; and this is a Matter of Fact which is easily cleard and ascertained.

PART II

THE SCOTTISH POETS

Really it is admirable how many Men of Genius this Country produces at present. Is it not strange that, at a time when we have lost our Princes, our Parliaments, our independent Government, even the Presence of our chief Nobility, are unhappy, in our Accent & Pronunciation, speak a very corrupt Dialect of the Tongue which we make use of; is it not strange, I say, that, in these Circumstances, we shou'd really be the People most distinguish'd for Literature in Europe?
—HUME TO GILBERT ELLIOT OF MINTO, JULY 2, 1757

CHAPTER 2

HUME AND THE
SCOTTISH PINDAR

B LACKLOCK to posterity will seem a fable, as to the present
age he is a prodigy. It appears altogether a fiction that a man,
absolutely deprived of sight, from three years of age, besides having
acquired a surprising knowledge of Greek, Latin, Italian, and French,
should at the same time be a great poet, and, without having almost
even seen the light, should notwithstanding be singularly happy in
his descriptions." So wrote Carlo Giovanni Maria Denina [1] in 1764;
and the prophecy of the learned Professor of Eloquence and Belles-
Lettres at the Royal School of Turin has been duly fulfilled, although not entirely as anticipated. For while the prodigy has become
a fable, the fable has been forgotten. Nor does the disappearance
from literature of this curiously pathetic figure, undeservedly called
a great poet by the Italian critic and the Scottish Pindar by his
fellow countrymen, constitute a serious loss. In point of fact, Thomas
Blacklock was a diminutive poet of an age not prolific of first-rate
poetry.

Yet Blacklock has a value far surpassing his dreary odes. He
provides a notable commentary upon the state of Scottish culture
from the high philosophic age of Hume to the high romantic age
of Burns and Scott. Moreover, it was his good fortune to attract the
attention and to engage the sympathy of those greater than himself.
In particular, his friendship with Hume is a virtually unknown
chapter that sheds light upon the humanity of *le bon David*. Chrono-
logically, this is the first of the episodes which reveal the efforts of
Hume to inspire in Scottish poetry the exalted qualities already
attained by Scottish prose. The conflicts between critical integrity,

[1] Quoted in *Scots Magazine*, XXVI (1764), 467.

on the one hand, and benevolence, friendship, and nationalism, on the other, which arose in this campaign of Hume's among the Scottish poets provide instructive materials for the reading of character.

I

The blindness of the bard fascinated a period engrossed in philosophy, for Locke himself had speculated over the hypothetical "man born blind and now adult," who is suddenly "made to see." [2] Leibniz and Berkeley set their minds to the question and arrived at contrary solutions; Voltaire, Condillac, and Diderot also entered into the controversy. The case of Blacklock, therefore, was immediately recognized by the mid-eighteenth century as a variant of the Lockian problem; and psychologists, amateur and professional, spiritedly advanced hypotheses to account for the man blind from early infancy who could accurately and vividly describe external nature— and that, too, in verse. "I think he is the greatest Curiosity in the World," observed Hume, and all the world concurred.

Certain it is that the early accounts of Blacklock consistently emphasized the sources of his knowledge of external nature. Metaphysics and psychology in the Age of Enlightenment overshadowed poetical criticism. This predilection is apparent not only in Hume and Denina, but also in Spence, Burke, Johnson, and even Blacklock himself. Like the incomparable Milton, the Scottish poet had much to say concerning his sad affliction and his poetic verve:

> Nature, when scarce fair light he knew,
> Snatch'd heav'n, earth, beauty from his view;
>   And darkness round him reigns:
>
> The muse with pity view'd his doom;
> And, darting thro' th' eternal gloom
>   An intellectual ray,
> Bade him with vocal sounds inspire
> The plaintive flute, the sprightly lyre;
>   And tune the feeling lay. [3]

[2] Locke, *Essay*, Book II, chap. ix, par. 8.
[3] "To a Young Gentleman, Bound for Guinea: an Ode," in *Poems* (1746).

Stimulated by the inquisitive prodding of well-intentioned friends, however, he soon expressed dissatisfaction with a simple "intellectual ray" and began to propound a more devious philosophy.

In contrast to Locke's blind man who had learned to associate colors with sounds, scarlet being like the blare of a trumpet, Blacklock now described his color-associations in intellectual or moral terms: "To *red* he had connected the idea of courage; and called it, 'a very bold colour.'—He gave a mixed character of *yellow*, partly good, and partly bad. . . . To *green* he had annexed the ideas of peace and serenity.—*Blue*, he said, must be pleasing, because it was the colour of the Heavens; and *purple*, because it was like the dawn of day. . . .—To *white* (he said) he had annexed the idea of joy; and to *black*, that of melancholy." [4] All of which was sufficiently abstruse to elicit a sagacious assent from Joseph Spence, formerly Professor of Poetry and, at the time, Professor of Modern History at Oxford. Spence also introduced the equally ambiguous suggestion that Blacklock may have taught himself to distinguish colors by touch! The young Edmund Burke, however, in his precocious *Philosophical Inquiry into the Origin of Our Ideas of the Sublime and Beautiful* employed Blacklock to illustrate the contention, "that a man may hear words without having any idea of the things which they represent, and yet afterwards be capable of returning them to others, combined in a new way, and with great propriety, energy, and instruction." [5]

Gently skeptical of Blacklock's pretentious system of psychology, David Hume remarked with characteristic understatement, "It was not altogether easy for me to understand him." But Samuel Johnson disposed of the issue with customary brusqueness. "We may be absolutely sure," he pronounced, that the descriptive passages in Blacklock are "combinations of what he has remembered of the works of other writers who could see." The Doctor added by way of example: "Suppose, I know a man to be so lame that he is absolutely incapable to move himself, and I find him in a different room from that in which I left him; shall I puzzle myself with idle conjectures, that, perhaps, his nerves have by some unknown change all at once become

[4] Spence, *Account of Blacklock*, prefixed to *Poems* (1756), p. xlvi.
[5] Burke, *Works*, I, 174.

effective? No, Sir; it is clear how he got into a different room: he was *carried*." [6] This salutary common sense may be taken as having finally clinched the matter.

Apparently the "ingenious Gentleman in England" who, Hume was informed, intended to write "a Book, in order to solve the Phaenomenon" of Blacklock's poetical genius, had found the competition too keen. Or possibly he had an inkling of Johnson's protest against Spence's vacuous theorizing: "That foolish fellow, Spence, has laboured to explain philosophically how Blacklock may have done, by means of his own faculties, what it is impossible he should do." At any rate, the promised study was not forthcoming; and the Age of Enlightenment had to be satisfied with the Burkean-Johnsonian exposition of Blacklock's unique version of *ut pictura poesis*. For in the end the poet himself acquiesced. In an article on blindness in the second edition of the *Encyclopaedia Britannica*, Blacklock makes plain that a sightless person, through a retentive memory, may correctly use descriptive words, "but as he never had a sensation of colour, however accurately he may speak of coloured objects, his language must be that of a parrot—without meaning, without ideas."

A second explanation of why Blacklock attracted an attention incommensurate with his endowments is afforded in the rebirth of nationalism. After the middle of the century, Scotland had settled down to a period of relative political tranquillity and unprecedented intellectual activity. Deliberately choosing to ignore the Rising of 1745, that ill-fated attempt of the Jacobites to restore the Scottish line of Stuarts to the English throne, Scotland now wisely elected to conquer from within and shortly was rivaling English historians, novelists, philosophers, and political scientists. The Edinburgh circle of David Hume, William Robertson, and Adam Smith deeply influenced all Europe intellectually and brought a greater glory to politically mute Scotland. Their age has since—and with perfect propriety —been called the Augustan Age of Scottish literature.

That Augustan Age was not long content to remain an age of prose, even of superior prose. Zealously it searched for a poetical counterpart. And as the Scottish intellectuals had abjured the vernacular in favor of a language purged of dialect, so they now de-

[6] Boswell, *Life of Johnson*, I, 466.

manded that Scottish poetry conform to their Attic standards in continuance of the all-English tradition of William Drummond of Hawthornden and James Thomson. If Scotland was enjoying a genuine classical age—and who could doubt it in the realm of the intellect?—where were its poets? Who was its Homer? Who was its Shakespeare? Who was its Pindar?

The desire, not unnaturally, became father to the poets; and within a half-dozen years all the classical Scottish progeny requisite to this vigorous program had been identified. In that happy event, the circle of Hume ultimately derived some little embarrassment from its precipitous enthusiasm, yet had the fortitude to stand by its godchildren. It did not, however, convince this unbelieving world of the verity of its findings. There always remained the suspicion that for Pindar, Shakespeare, and Homer the Caledonian climate was too inclement.

A third and equally notable factor which contributed to the receptive attitude toward Blacklock was the high moral character of that bard himself. Not only was it an age of philosophy, but it was also an age of humanity—of enlightened humanity, it professed. What more fitting object of enlightened humanity than a poet at once impecunious (like Hesiod and Dryden), blind (like Homer and Milton), philosophical (like Lucretius and Pope), and good (like all great poets)? Whatever difference of opinion there might be about Blacklock's poetry, there could be no two opinions about his goodness. That was recognized and acclaimed by everybody: "I looked on him with reverence," acknowledged Dr. Johnson.[7] The "good" Mr. Blacklock was his customary epithet. Indeed, if goodness implied genius, Blacklock would still be the unchallenged Pindar of Scotland!

I I

The title of Thomas Blacklock as "Scottish" Pindar, in point of fact, was not perfectly valid. For although he was born at Annan, Dumfriesshire, on November 10, 1721, both of his parents were English from just south of the border in Cumberland. To his credit, Blacklock did the utmost to improve his right to the "Scotian lyre"

---

[7] Johnson, *Works*, XII, 351.

by never setting foot outside of Scotland. His father, a bricklayer by trade and a man of some education, was deeply devoted to the unfortunate infant who had been blinded by smallpox before reaching six months. Permanently debarred from active life, the child was early indulged with books and found the greatest pleasure in poetry. He must have lisped in numbers, for the numbers came—came from Spenser, Milton, Pope, Addison, Prior, and Scotland's own Thomson and Ramsay. One of his poetical exercises composed at the age of twelve has, according to Spence, "something very pretty in the turn of it." *Tatlers*, *Spectators*, and *Guardians* filled out his readings, but he was never entirely at ease in prose.

After the death of his father when Blacklock was nineteen, things went so poorly for a while that he seriously contemplated becoming an itinerant flute-player. But in 1741 he was taken from Dumfries to Edinburgh to live under the protection of the eminent physician, Dr. John Stevenson, who had been attracted by accounts of the destitute poetical prodigy. For the next four years Blacklock attended a Latin grammar school and later became a student of divinity at Edinburgh University.

It was about 1742 that David Hume first became acquainted with the poet.[8] Ten years his senior, the philosopher was then living alternately at his family home in Ninewells and at Edinburgh. In the country he studied Greek and in the city wrote and published essays, devoting free hours to society. The meeting with Blacklock, Hume describes in a letter of 1754: "The first time I had ever seen or heard of Mr Blacklock was about twelve years ago, when I met him in a visit to two young ladies. They informed me of his case, as far as they could in a conversation carried on in his presence. I soon found him to possess a very delicate taste, along with a passionate love of learning. Dr. Stevenson had, at that time, taken him under his protection; and he was perfecting himself in the Latin tongue. I repeated to him Mr Pope's Elegy to the Memory of an unfortunate Lady, which I happened to have by heart: and though I be a very bad reciter, I saw it affected him extremely. His eyes, indeed, the great index of the mind, could express no passion: but his whole body was thrown into agitation. That poem was equally

[8] See Note A, below.

qualified to touch the delicacy of his taste, and the tenderness of his feelings."

The scene provides a study in sentiment. There was the brilliant, young, and already somewhat corpulent philosopher, painfully but earnestly declaiming in a rich brogue the famous lines from Pope:

> What can atone (oh ever-injur'd shade!)
> Thy fate unpity'd, and thy rites unpaid?
> No friend's complaint, no kind domestic tear
> Pleas'd thy pale ghost, or grac'd thy mournful bier;
> By foreign hands thy dying eyes were clos'd,
> By foreign hands thy decent limbs compos'd,
> By foreign hands thy humble grave adorn'd,
> By strangers honour'd, and by strangers mourn'd!

There was the shy and somewhat uncouth little blind poet, whose every nervous reaction was painstakingly remarked by the others. There were the two bright young ladies in delighted rapture at this unexpected double potation of literature, surreptitiously wiping with the tip of a dainty handkerchief the tears that could not be withheld. A sentimental era was at hand. Only the previous year Henry Mackenzie had been born in this same Edinburgh; and it was no accident that as part of his cultural training the Scottish Man of Feeling was to act as literary page to David Hume and his coterie.

The friendship between Hume and Blacklock was temporarily disrupted between 1745 and 1750 by Hume's absence from Scotland. At the outbreak of the Rebellion in 1745, Blacklock fled the insecurity of the capital city for the peace of Dumfries; and, at the insistence of his Maecenas, Dr. Stevenson, he prepared for publication a volume of *Poems on Several Occasions*. Brought out at Glasgow in 1746 with an unsigned Preface briefly recounting the hardships of the blind author, this modest eighteen-pence octavo attracted little attention.

Upon his return to Edinburgh soon afterwards, Blacklock resumed his studies at the University, where he continued for the next six years. In Scotland again in 1750, after much adventurous travel but still far from affluent, Hume shortly removed "from the Countrey to the Town; the true Scene for a man of Letters." And upon his election to the keepership of the Advocates' Library early in 1752, he began concerted work upon the long projected *History of England*. Blacklock was too diffident, at first, to call upon the philosophical historian; but friends who knew Hume well convinced him that he would be courteously received. He was; and Hume soon professed to consider Blacklock "a very elegant genius, of a most affectionate grateful disposition, a modest backward temper, accompanied with that delicate pride, which so naturally attends virtue in distress."

Virtue's distress was, of course, poverty; and a welcome opportunity to alleviate Blacklock's troubles presented itself with the new edition of his poems issued privately at Edinburgh early in 1754. This volume, of which Hume had somehow been ignorant until its publication, was a reprint of the Glasgow edition with corrections and with "several new pieces." The author was now designated on the title page as "Student of Philosophy in the University of *Edinburgh*"; and a prefatory "To the Publisher" by Gilbert Gordon of Dumfries, presented a few more biographical facts. The price was raised to three shillings.

With great vigor Hume entered upon a personal sales campaign, dunning his friends with letters. That to Adam Smith [9] was typical:

DEAR SIR

I am writing kind of circular Letters, recommending Mr Blacklock's Poems to all my Acquaintance, but especially to those, whose Approbation wou'd contribute most to recommend them to the World. They are, indeed, many of them very elegant, and wou'd have deserv'd much Esteem, had they come from a Man plac'd in the most favorable Circumstances. What a Prodigy are they, when considered as the Production of a man, so cruelly dealt with, both by Nature and Fortune? When you add to this, that the Author is a Man of the best Dispositions, that I have ever known, and tho of great Frugality, is plac'd in the most cruel Indigence, you will certainly think his Case more deserving of Pity & Regard than any you have almost met with. Mr Foulis has Copies to dispose of, which I have sent him; & which he will disperse without expecting any Profit. I must entreat you, not only to take a Copy yourself, but also to take a few more & dispose of among your Acquaintance. I trust at least

---

[9] Hume, MS letter, Harvard College Library, insertion in T.P. 2050.50.2.

to have half a dozen disposd of by your means. I have sold off above fifty in a few days. The Price is three Shillings. That you may recommend them with a safer Conscience, please read the Ode to a young Gentleman going to the Coast of Guinea, that on Refinements in metaphysical Philosophy, that to a Lady on the Death of her Son; the Wish, an Elegy; the Soliloquy. I am much mistaken, if you do not find all these very laudable Performances; & such as would be esteemd an Ornament to Dodesley's Miscellanies or even to better Collections. . . .

My Compliments to Mr & Mrs Betham. If that Lady can be engagd to have an Esteem of Mr Blacklock's Productions, she woud be of great Service in dispersing them. Tho born blind, he is not insensible to that Passion, which we foolish People are apt to receive first by the Eyes; and unless a man were both blind & deaf, I do not know how he cou'd be altogether secure of Impressions from Mrs Betham. I am Dear Sir

Yours sincerely

DAVID HUME

Edinr. 27 of Feby. 1754

In a letter to Matthew Sharp, Hume specified the issues involved in the patronage of Blacklock. First, the manner of publishing the volume. Blacklock, wrote Hume, "has printed a collection of poems, which his friends are endeavouring to turn to the best account for him. Had he published them in the common way, their merit would have recommended them sufficiently to common sale; but, in that case, the greatest part of the profit, it is well known, would have redounded to the booksellers. His friends, therefore, take copies from him, and distribute them among their acquaintances. . . . I must, therefore, recommend it to you to send for a cargo of these poems, which the author's great modesty will prevent him from offering to you, and to engage your acquaintance to purchase them." Second, Scottish nationalism: "I would fain presume upon our friendship (which now begins to be ancient between us) and recommend to your civilities a man who does honour to his country by his talents, and disgraces it by the little encouragement he has hitherto met with." Third, Blacklock's own future: "He is a man of very extensive knowledge and of singular good dispositions; and his poetical, though very much to be admired, is the least part of his merit. He is very well qualified to instruct youth, by his acquaintance both with the languages and sciences; and possesses so many arts of supplying the want of sight, that that imperfection would be no hindrance."

Among other known recipients of such avowed special pleadings are John Clephane, Robert Dodsley, the Abbé Le Blanc, John Stewart, and John Wilkes. The appeal to Dodsley, the poetical bookseller in Pall Mall, proved highly successful. Hume's letter of March 12, 1754, accompanied with the present of six copies of Blacklock's poems of which Dodsley was instructed "to keep one, and to distribute the rest among men of taste of his acquaintance," is not extant. The letter had done good work, however, as Dodsley, acting on Hume's suggestion, forwarded it and a volume of the poems to Spence.

Of Spence, Dr. Johnson has provided the seemingly reliable estimate: "a man whose learning was not very great, and whose mind was not very powerful. His criticism, however, was commonly just; what he thought, he thought rightly, and his remarks were recommended by his coolness and candour." [10] With equal reliability, Johnson might have added that Spence was both charitable and narrow-minded. Of his charity, there is an abundance of evidence; an example of his narrow-mindedness will appear in the sequel with Blacklock and Hume.

Taking an immediate fancy to the blind Scottish bard, Spence introduced him to the English reading public in a small shilling pamphlet, *An Account of the Life, Character, and Poems of Mr. Blacklock; Student of Philosophy, in the University of Edinburgh,* published by Robert and James Dodsley in November, 1754. The sources for this pamphlet were the "To the Publisher" of the latest edition of *Poems on Several Occasions* and Hume's letter to Dodsley. Identifying Hume as the "Author of the Moral Essays," Spence made seven different references to his letter, including three direct quotations, and appeared to be as well disposed toward the patron of Blacklock as toward that indigent poet himself. How well disposed he was to the latter is evident from the final paragraph: "What an Object, what a happy Opportunity is here, for any one who is capable of it, (either from his Affluence or his Power,) to acquire a good deal of solid and unenvied Reputation, by raising a Person

[10] *Lives of the Poets,* III, 142-43.

of this Turn, and of such extraordinary Desert, to some Situation where he may be above Want; or rather by which he may be enabled, in some degree, to exert and enjoy the beneficent and noble Dictates of his Soul!"

Needless to say, Hume was delighted with the advertisement afforded his protégé, not only by Spence's *Account of Blacklock* itself, but also by generous reviews in the periodicals. He was also pleased with the proposed new edition of the poems to be sold by subscription, for which Dodsley had already opened the lists in his shop at a guinea for the large paper printing and half a guinea for the small. On first learning of these benevolent intentions, Hume, on October 15, had addressed a long letter to Spence. This was received too late to be of any direct use in the composition of the *Account of Blacklock* except to grant the permission, evidently requested by Dodsley, to use Hume's name. Largely repetitive of the now familiar facts about Blacklock, the letter also discussed the new projects for his relief. It is this personal appeal that makes Spence's later treatment of Hume the more unaccountable:

SIR,
The agreeable productions, with which you have entertained the public, have long given me a desire of being known to you: but this desire has been much increased by my finding you engage so warmly in protecting a man of merit, so helpless as Mr Blacklock. I hope you will indulge me in the liberty I have taken of writing to you. . . .

As you are so generous to interest yourself in this poor man's case, who is so much an object both of admiration and compassion, I must inform you entirely of his situation. He has gained about one hundred guineas by this last edition of his poems, and this is the whole stock he has in the world. He has also a bursary, about six pounds a year. I begun a subscription for supporting him during five years; and I made out twelve guineas a year among my acquaintance. That is a most terrible undertaking; and some unexpected refusals I met with, damped me, though they have not quite discouraged me from proceeding. We have the prospect of another bursary of ten pounds a year in the gift of the Exchequer; but to the shame of human nature, we met with difficulties. Noblemen interpose with their valet-de-chambres or nurses' sons, who they think would be burdens on themselves. Could we ensure but thirty pounds a year to this fine genius and man of virtue, he would be easy and happy: for his wants are none but those which nature has given him, though she has unhappily loaded him with more than other men. . . .

Your scheme of publishing his poems by subscription, I hope will turn to account. I think it impossible he could want, were his case more generally known, I hope it will be so by your means. Sir George Lyttleton, who has so fine a taste, and so much benevolence of temper, would certainly, were the case laid before him in a just light, lend his assistance, or rather indeed quite overcome all difficulties. I know not, whether you have the happiness of that gentleman's acquaintance. . . .

I shall be very glad if the employing my name in your account of Mr Blacklock can be of any service. . . .

Mr Blacklock is very docible, and glad to receive corrections. I am only afraid he is too apt to have a deference for other people's judgment. I did not see the last edition till it was printed; but I have sent him some objections to passages, for which he was very thankful. I also desired him to retrench some poems entirely; such as the *Ode on Fortitude*, and some others, which seemed to me inferior to the rest of the collection. You will very much oblige him, if you use the same freedom. I remarked to him some Scotticisms; but you are better qualified for doing him that service. I have not seen any of his essays; and am afraid his prose is inferior to his poetry. He will soon be in town, when I shall be enabled to write you further particulars.

The letter was sent to Dodsley with the added explanation:

SIR

I have us'd the Freedom of sending under Cover to you a Letter to Mr Spence; because I did not know how to direct to that Gentleman. All the Contents of it regard Mr Blacklocke, and are equally your Concern, as Mr Spence's & that of every Lover of Ingenuity. I have therefore left the Letter open, that, if you have Leizure, you may read it. I esteem myself very much beholden to you for the Pains you have taken upon my Recommendation. I own, that I still regard Sir George Lyttleton as our Sheet Anchor; and am infinitely desirous to have him better acquainted with Mr Blacklocke's Case.

Your Criticisms on his Poems might also be of great Service to him. I am Sir

Your most obedient Servant
DAVID HUME

19 Octr 1754 [11]

[11] Hume, MS letter, Victoria and Albert Museum, London.

Before bringing out the new edition, Spence made a trip to Scotland. Though he did not meet Hume, he enjoyed a visit of some weeks from Blacklock, gaining information which necessitated revision of his biographical remarks. But other changes were also made, the full story of which comes out in an amusing letter of April 20, 1756, from Hume to John Clephane. The philosopher chides his friend for not subscribing to the new quarto edition of *Poems by Mr. Blacklock*, "To Which Is Prefix'd, an Account of the Life, Character, and Writings, of the Author, by the Reverend Mr. Spence, Late Professor of Poetry, at Oxford":

I do not find your name [writes Hume] among the subscribers of my friend Blacklock's poems; you have forgot; buy a copy of them and read them; they are many of them very elegant, and merit esteem, if they came from any one, but are admirable from him. I commend Spence's industry in so good a work, but there is a circumstance of his conduct that will entertain you. In the Edinburgh edition there was a stanza to this effect:

> The wise in every age conclude,
> What Pyrrho taught and Hume renewed,
> That dogmatists are fools.

Mr. Spence would not undertake to promote a London subscription, unless my name, as well as Lord Shaftesbury's (who was mentioned in another place) were erased: the author frankly gave up Shaftesbury, but said that he would forfeit all the profit he might expect from a subscription, rather than relinquish the small tribute of praise which he had paid to a man whom he was more indebted to than to all the world beside. I heard by chance of this controversy, and wrote to Mr Spence, that, without farther consulting the author, I, who was chiefly concerned, would take upon me to empower him to alter the stanza where I was mentioned. He did so, and farther, having prefixed the life of the author, he took occasion to mention some people to whom he had been obliged, but is careful not to name me; judging rightly that such good deeds were only *splendida peccata*, and that till they were sanctified by the grace of God they would be of no benefit to salvation.

The offending ode "On the Refinements in Metaphysical Philosophy" is an indication that Blacklock was an admirer of Hume, described in a footnote as the "Author of a Treatise on Human

Nature." Always devoutly religious, nevertheless, and timorous that the poem might possibly be misconstrued, he added a second note by way of apology for his philosophical convictions. Both notes were suppressed by Spence, who also substituted his own verses, following Hume's authorization, for those deleted. The reference is to "letter'd Pride":

> The wise in ev'ry age conclude
> Thy fairest prospects, rightly view'd,
> The Paradise of Fools.

Any lingering doubts of Blacklock's religious fidelity were finally dispelled by a new prose essay, *On the Immortality of the Soul,* also included in the poetical volume.

By long practice, Hume had become inured to the rudeness of zealots; but even he was momentarily nonplused by the extraordinary reward meted out for his efforts on behalf of Blacklock. Consider the situation. Blacklock had been brought to the attention of Spence through Hume's plea to Dodsley. Hume had then written Spence at least twice: first, telling of his efforts to raise the annuity fund; and, second, overriding Blacklock's refusal to delete his name from the poem. In return Spence deliberately expunged all previous references to the philosopher.

Nor is that all. For Spence both refused to give any credit whatsoever to Hume and actually quoted from his letter of October 15, 1754, without indicating the source. Hume had written of Blacklock: "He is a very good philosopher, and in general possesses all branches of erudition, except the mathematical." Spence's variation is but the slightest: "he is a very good philosopher, and in general, possesses all the branches of erudition, except the mathematics." There can be little question that Spence had revised his *Account of Blacklock* with the letter open before him.

Hume's benignity was too inbred to be discommoded by such ill will, and he refused to make an issue of it. Urging all his circle to purchase copies of the poems, he continued to act as a sort of literary agent. One transaction of this nature, dated "20 of March 1756," involved the sale of twenty-seven copies, presumably the remainders of the 1754 edition, at two shillings and sixpence apiece.[12] Appar-

---

[12] Hume, MS receipt, Edinburgh University Library, MSS Laing, II, 508.

ently Spence later regretted his discourtesy to Hume, for he expressed the opinion [13] that the *History of England* was a masterpiece
and, on several occasions, inquired after its author. On June 15,
1762, he was informed by Sir Alexander Dick that "David Hume
is well, as is Dr. Robertson; and they will be both glad to see you
when you come." If Spence actually met Hume, it is safe to assume
that the reconciliation was completed, as few could resist *le bon
David* in person. But whatever may be said about Spence's earlier
rudeness, it must be universally acknowledged that Hume had acted
the part of honor, swallowing his pride for the welfare of a friend.

I I I

In the winter of 1754, an otherwise regrettable episode gave
Hume the opportunity of doing considerably more for Blacklock
than he had anticipated. This was the dispute with the curators of
the Advocates' Library, a tempest-in-a-teapot which was, none the
less, taken seriously by all concerned. In his capacity of Keeper,
Hume had included in an order of some seventy-four books, three
items that several curators who were anxious to discountenance him
ruled indecent and ordered returned. They also prohibited the
Keeper from buying books thereafter on his own authority.

Justly indignant, Hume protested on November 20 to the Lord
Advocate, Robert Dundas of Arniston: "As to the three books themselves, your Lordship has little leizure from more grave and important occupations to read them; but this I will venture to justify
before any literary society in Europe, that if every book not superior
in merit to *La Fontaine* be expelled the Library, I shall engage to
carry away all that remains in my pocket. I know not indeed if any
will remain except our fifty pound Bible, which is too bulky for me
to carry away. If all worse than *Bussi Rabutin,* or *Crebillon,* be expelled, I shall engage that a couple of porters will do the office. By
the bye, *Bussi Rabutin* contains no bawdy at all, though if it did,
I see not that it would be a whit the worse. For I know not a more
agreeable subject both for books and conversation, if executed with
decency and ingenuity. I can presume, without intending the least
offence, that as the glass circulates at your Lordship's table, this topic

[13] Spence, *Anecdotes,* pp. 461, 464.

of conversation will sometimes steal in, provided always there be no ministers present. And even some of these reverend gentlemen I have seen not to dislike the subject."

The upshot of stubbornness on both sides was that Hume partially withdrew from the library. "But being equally unwilling to lose the Use of the Books & to bear an Indignity," he explained to Adam Smith; "I retain the Office, but have given Blacklock, our blind Poet, a Bond of Annuity for the Sallary. I have now put it out of these malicious Fellows power to offer me any Indignity; while my Motives for remaining in this Office are so apparent. I shou'd be glad that you approve of my Conduct: I own I am satisfy'd with myself." By this expedient, Hume continued to have the library for historical research until he finally resigned in January, 1757. In the meanwhile, the stipend of £40 a year accrued as a sinecure to the needy Blacklock.

As usual, Hume's counsel to his ward continued to be both wise and practical, unlike that of Spence who pressed the susceptible poet into the composition of a tragedy, which, he said, he had interest enough with David Garrick to get produced. Though this drama has long been lost, one feels confident that it would hardly have shown Blacklock to be the Scottish Sophocles as well as the Scottish Pindar. Hume's opinion of it is unknown. In another instance, his advice was so practical and timely as to head Blacklock off from certain failure when, in 1757, he aspired to the study of oratory in order to instruct candidates for the bar and the pulpit. Blacklock's interest in preaching, indeed, never abated; and in later years he translated two French sermons as desirable specimens of a high pulpit ardor. But at last in desperation at ever finding a livelihood, he turned, with the approval of Hume, to a career in the church. In 1759 he was licensed to preach.

There is no indication, however, that Hume or anyone else was consulted in 1762 when Blacklock married Miss Sarah Johnston of a well-known Dumfries family. In his famous letter to Spence of October 15, 1754, Hume had revealed something of the poet's amatory propensity:

Apropos to this passion [he wrote], I once said to my friend, Mr Blacklock, that I was sure he did not treat love as he did colours; he did not speak of it without feeling it. There appeared too much reality in all his expressions to allow that to be suspected. 'Alas!' said he, with a sigh, 'I could never bring my heart to a proper tranquillity on that head.' Your passion, replied I, will always be better founded than ours, who have sight: we are so foolish as to allow ourselves to be captivated by exterior beauty: nothing but the beauty of the mind can affect you. 'Not altogether neither,' said he: 'the sweetness of the voice has a mighty effect upon me: the symptoms of youth too, which the touch discovers, have great influence. And though such familiar approaches would be ill-bred in others, the girls of my acquaintance indulge me, on account of my blindness, with the liberty of running over them with my hand. And I can by that means judge entirely of their shape. However, no doubt, humour, and temper, and sense, and other beauties of the mind, have an influence upon me as upon others.'

You may see from this conversation [continued Hume] how difficult it is even for a blind man to be a perfect Platonic. But though Mr Blacklock never wants his Evanthe, who is the real object of his poetical addresses, I am well assured that all his passions have been perfectly consistent with the purest virtue and innocence. His life indeed has been in all respects perfectly irreproachable.

Of the good Mrs. Blacklock, herself, not much is known beyond her undying devotion to the blind bard. Though she was actually not the Evanthe of his verses, she has a more certain claim to a small niche in literary story through her excess of hospitality to Dr. Johnson, when that dignitary visited Edinburgh in 1773 and interpreted for her husband the subtleties of Bishop Butler's *Analogy of Religion*. Too awed to converse with the literary dictator, Mrs. Blacklock strove to maintain her dignity as hostess by plying him with cups of tea. A final polite invitation after the twenty-second cup brought about her trembling ears the terrifying roar, "I tell thee, no, woman!" [14]

Possibly it was this display of bad manners to his wife that offended Blacklock. At any rate, he was long resentful of Johnson's condescending air and, in an article written early in 1784, finally gave vent to his feelings. "Doctor Johnson," wrote Blacklock, "will be universally acknowledged to have united a great genius with profound and extensive learning; but these qualities, however eminent,

[14] Thompson, *A Scottish Man of Feeling*, pp. 139-40.

are not only disfigured but almost counterbalanced by his hateful and incorrigible affectation." [15]

Shortly after his wedding in 1762, Blacklock had been ordained minister in the parish of Kirkcudbright but, instead of thereby acquiring a sanctuary as well as a livelihood, was plunged into a welter of litigation. For two years the questions were acrimoniously debated as to whether a local congregation was required to accept the minister named by the patron and whether a blind man might be a minister at all. The first was already of national scope, the whole Church of Scotland being divided into two warring camps. The second, however, might have been expected to be decided with charity and restraint—but it was not; and the poor clergyman was rudely treated by irate parishioners.

During this grim period, Blacklock was unfortunately deprived of his chief moral support through the absence of Hume, who in 1763 had gone to Paris as Secretary to the British Embassy. Yet Hume did not leave Edinburgh without deep misgivings even while taking the precaution of presenting Blacklock "as a Legacy" to Baron Mure of Caldwell. Appeals continued to reach him from the unwelcome minister of Kirkcudbright; and ever solicitous of Blacklock's welfare, Hume wrote the Rev. Alexander Carlyle on September 15, 1763:

The Case of poor Blacklocke gives me great Distress; and so much the more, as, I am afraid, it is not in the Power of any human Being to relieve him: His unhappiness seems to proceed from the Infirmity of his Body and the Delicacy, not to say, Weakness of his Mind. He has wrote to me Letters, full of the Bitterest Anguish, on account of the Treatment he meets with from his Parishioners: I believe it is not good; but it is impossible not to think it exaggerated by his Imagination; and I am of your Opinion, that the same Persecution, partly real, partly imaginary, woud follow him in every other Settlement. I had concerted with Baron Mure a very likely Scheme for his Removal; but to what purpose wou'd this Serve, if the same Complaints must return in his new Situation? I agree with you, that a small Pension, could it be obtain'd, might bestow on him some Degree of Tranquillity; but how to obtain it, I profess

[15] Quoted by Miller in "Dr. Blacklock's Manuscripts," *Scottish Historical Review*, X (1913), 371.

I do not know, as I suppose you will readily believe. That Door was never wide for men of Letters; and is become still narrower than ever.

The pessimism of Hume proved to be all too well founded; and in 1764 Blacklock resigned his country living for a small annuity and retired permanently to the cosmopolitan atmosphere of Edinburgh. One of his first literary efforts in that city was "Pistapolis: an Hyperpindaric Ode with Notes by Scriblerus Redivivus," a pungent lampoon of those citizens of Kirkcudbright who had opposed his ministry. Although actually prepared for the press in 1765, this bitter indictment happily remained unpublished during his lifetime.

In Edinburgh, Blacklock's financial situation, though slightly less acute because of the annuity, still necessitated the taking in of boarders and pupils. Hume did not fail to encourage this new enterprise by enrolling his own nephew, Joseph Home, for whose education he had assumed personal responsibility. From 1766 to 1768, before Joseph proceeded to the University to study under Professor Hugh Blair, Blacklock wrote glowing accounts to the fond uncle. In a letter of this nature in 1766, the poet-clergyman-schoolmaster, after recounting his persecution at Kirkcudbright and his humiliation at not being better received in Edinburgh, paid homage, rhetorical but real, to his benefactor: "For these reasons, as well as the private and disinterested attachment of my heart, you will naturally imagine the pleasure I feel from the prospect of your arrival in Edinburgh, and from my promised intercourse with one, who, though he might do honour to the republic of letters in any period, yet descends to honour me with the name of a FRIEND." A letter of the following year warned that the boarding school, though progressing well enough, held no guarantee for the future. In a despondent mood, Blacklock was certain that he could never reassume ministerial duties after "the ten thousand hardships and disagreeable things which I met with in my short but dear-bought experience of that kind of life." Mrs. Blacklock, in a postscript, hoped that Hume might induce Edinburgh University to establish a chair of poetry which her husband would be content to accept for "a moderate salary." [16]

[16] Burton, II, 399-401*n*.

Recurring fits of depression characterized Blacklock during this period. His facility in composing verses was impaired, and his mind was in continual turmoil. A diagnosis of nervous instability might, indeed, have been made as early as 1762 on the day of his ordination. Having fallen into sound slumber after dinner, the new minister was visited by a friend several hours later. Still asleep, he rose, welcomed his guest, joined the party for supper, and partook of an egg and wine. Finally, on beginning to display conspicuous signs of absent-mindedness, he was forcibly roused, only to profess complete ignorance of what had happened since dinner. This extraordinary and well authenticated instance of sleepwalking was so widely discussed that in 1783 it was incorporated into Dr. Cleghorn's treatise *De Somno*. Yet even in that learned work, the mysterious case of the somnambulant poet remains unexplained.

I V

The long and praiseworthy friendship between Hume and Blacklock ended sometime before 1769. The estrangement took place at just about the period of Hume's return from triumphs in Paris and London to settle down permanently in Edinburgh as one of her most distinguished citizens. Perhaps it is futile to speculate about such a delicate point when all the facts can never be ascertained, yet it is clear that from 1767 Blacklock had begun to feel cool toward Hume. Two events of that year may be considered symptomatic. First, Blacklock was granted the honorary degree of D.D. by the Marischal College of Aberdeen University. Second, he dedicated the first part of a new book "To Mr James Beattie, Professor of Morals in the Marischall College, Aberdeen." That the two events were not unconnected is proved by the dedicatory letter to Beattie:

SIR,
    The following sheets were written at a time when it became absolutely necessary to lead my mind out of herself. Had I been so happy then as to have known you, or could have had an opportunity of conversing with you, it is more than probable, that neither the world nor you would have had the trouble of what is here offered. I am glad, however, of having it in my power, in this public manner, to testify my esteem for a person, whose character in the literary world is so deservedly dis-

tinguished, and whose friendship, though a late acquisition, I shall always reckon one of my most valuable. Give me leave here to return you, and the learned and respectable body of which you are a member, my warm acknowledgments for the late honour they conferred upon me.

I am

Sir,

With every sentiment of esteem and regard which friendship can inspire, your most humble servant,

THOMAS BLACKLOCK

Edinburgh, Aug. 10. 1767

The full work, of which the first part was so honored, was *Paraclesis; or, Consolations Deduced from Natural and Revealed Religion: in Two Dissertations. The First Supposed to Have Been Composed by Cicero: Now Rendered into English: the Last Originally Written by Thomas Blacklock, D.D.* If the first dissertation was distinguished by its association with the name of Beattie, the second was equally distinguished by its association with the name of Spence. This second dedication, dated Edinburgh, October 9, 1767, opens:

REVEREND SIR,

How agreeable to me is this public opportunity of expressing the sentiments of a heart overflowing with gratitude for the many favours it has received from you. It is to your kind patronage that I owe my introduction into the republic of letters, and to your benevolence, in some measure, my present comfortable situation.

Through the twin dedications to Beattie and to Spence, Blacklock had, in a manner, renounced Hume as his patron. This signal ingratitude becomes comprehensible, if not condonable, only through an understanding of his peculiar state of mind. An emotional upheaval induced by prolonged years of persecution, real and imagined, had ultimately rendered him myopic to the virtues of *le bon David*. To Blacklock's own intensified religious feelings were added the illiberal principles inculcated by his new-found friend, Beattie; and both conspired against any continued appreciation of Hume. For to Blacklock, Hume was no longer *le bon David;* he was now the Great Infidel. The embracing of Beattie at the very moment when that worthy had announced his intention of demolishing Hume could hardly have been pure coincidence, particularly as the first overtures had come from Blacklock himself.

As early as 1760 the names of Blacklock and Beattie had been associated in *A Collection of Original Poems. By the Rev. Mr Blacklock, and Other Scotch Gentlemen,* a small volume published at Edinburgh seemingly to rival Dodsley's famous English collection. The venture was undistinguished; and Blacklock did not contribute to a second volume which appeared in 1762 under the sponsorship of that rising young literary star, James Boswell. But attracted by a congenial spirit, whom he first met in the summer of 1765, Blacklock penned a poetical epistle "To Dr. Beattie, with the Author's Poems," the last stanza of which is an open bid for friendship:

> O could my thoughts with all thy spirit glow;
> As thine harmonious, could my accents flow;
> Then, with approving ear, might'st thou attend,
> Nor in a Blacklock blush to own a friend.

Duly flattered, the uninspired versifier of *The Judgment of Paris* responded in kind, accepting the proffer in "An Epistle from Dr. Beattie to the Rev. Mr. Thomas Blacklock."

By profession, Dr. James Beattie was not a poet but the Professor of Moral Philosophy and Logic at Aberdeen University, occupying a chair that had been tendered him at the ripe age of twenty-five when, by his own account, he had never so much as inquired into the subject of metaphysics. Within a very few years, however, he had inquired so relentlessly as to convince himself that the great succession of British philosophers (Locke, Berkeley, and above all, Hume) were wrong—perniciously wrong—and that he, Beattie, was right— gloriously right. The more learned attempted to dissuade him from publication, but to no avail. The *Essay on the Origin and Immutability of Truth in Opposition to Sophistry and Scepticism* appeared in 1770, ironically through "a species of pious fraud" on the part of Beattie's friends after it had been turned down by the publishers.[17]

Unlike his poetical pinion, Beattie's philosophy *was* highflying. Never, perhaps, did petulance cover so much ignorance and display

[17] M. Forbes, *Beattie and His Friends*, p. 45.

so much conceit. The distinguished ministerial friends of Hume—William Robertson, Alexander Carlyle, and Hugh Blair—were grieved that the philosopher, no matter how possibly mistaken, should be subjected to a contumely exceeded only by the previous railings of that colossus of controversy, Bishop Warburton. Nevertheless, Beattie had hit precisely the right tone for popularity; and the work sold as metaphysics never could. Dr. Johnson and Edmund Burke immediately proclaimed it true philosophy. Immanuel Kant, on the other hand, objected that, "Hume suffered the usual misfortune of metaphysicians, of not being understood. It is positively painful to see how utterly his opponents, Reid, Oswald, Beattie, and lastly Priestley, missed the point of the problem; for while they were ever taking for granted that which he doubted, and demonstrating with zeal and often with impudence that which he never thought of doubting, they so misconstrued his valuable suggestion that everything remained in its old condition, as if nothing had happened." [18]

Beattie's vaunted reduction of metaphysics to common sense was in reality the reduction to polemics; and one of the legitimate features of polemics is invective. A letter to Blacklock, with whom he was now intimate, makes this clear. Incensed by the politeness and respect hitherto shown Hume by many of his antagonists—several of them ministers and professors at Aberdeen—Beattie acknowledged:

I could not approve that extraordinary adulation which some of them paid to their arch-adversary. I could not conceive the propriety of paying compliments to a man's *heart*, at the very time one is proving that his aim is to subvert the principles of truth, virtue, and religion; nor to his *understanding*, when we are charging him with publishing the grossest and most contemptible nonsense. . . .

You are sensible, that . . . it is absolutely necessary for me to use great plainness of speech. My expressions must not be so tame as to seem to imply either a diffidence in my principles, or a coldness toward the cause I have undertaken to defend. . . . One gentleman, a friend of yours, I shall have occasion to treat with much freedom. . . . But I trust I shall never depart from the Christian and philosophic character. [19]

[18] Introduction to *Prolegomena*.
[19] Wm. Forbes, *Life of Beattie*, pp. 131-132, 134-135.

The superficial philosophic character of James Beattie would be little remembered today if Sir Joshua Reynolds had not imparted to it a certain vicarious immortality through his allegorical painting of the "Triumph of Truth over Error." [20] Hume complained to friends over the ungentlemanly conduct of "that bigotted silly Fellow, Beattie"; but Blacklock was no longer numbered among his friends. A late convert to Beattie's school of abuse, Blacklock privately advised his new preceptor that he had parted company with Hume [21] and, accepting the author's suggestion to puff the work, publicly applauded the *Essay on Truth* in the *Edinburgh Evening Courant* for January 2, 1770. This act may be taken as the finale in the long relationship between *le bon David* and the Scottish Pindar. It does not provide a happy ending.

V

In protecting Thomas Blacklock through so many years, David Hume was nurturing Scottish poetry better than he could possibly have known. It is perfectly apparent that Hume's solicitude for that "strange creature"—to use the description of the robust John Home —"a small, weakly under thing—a chilly, bloodless animal, that shivers at every breeze. . . . the most flagrant enthusiast I ever saw," [22] was excited more by benevolence than by taste. Yet the literary import of Blacklock does not cease with his publications. In later years until his death in 1791 he was the old Edinburgh master before whom all aspiring young poets were paraded; and he played his part with distinction. Robert Burns he saved for Scotland; and Walter Scott he set on the path of the national heritage through Ossian. Along with John Home, Adam Ferguson, and Henry Mackenzie, Blacklock forms the literary link between the Augustan Age of Hume and the Golden Age of Burns and Scott.

Be it to the credit of the aged Thomas Blacklock that when he came into contact with the genius of *Poems, Chiefly in the Scots Dialect, by Robert Burns,* he dropped all prepossessions and antipathies and at once hailed its greatness. The story, though well known, bears repetition; and if in 1786 it seemed to be an overture

---

[20] See Chapter 8, sec. II, below.   [21] See Note B, below.
[22] Mackenzie, *Life of Home*, p. 131.

from a poet to a peasant, the modern world holds a directly inverse opinion. Be that as it may, Blacklock's letter of September 4, addressed to the Rev. George Lawrie of Loudoun, was forwarded to the despairing Burns just as he was packing up to leave Scotland for the West Indies. The warm appreciation of the blind bard was a much needed stimulant: "Many instances have I seen of nature's force and beneficence, exerted under numerous and formidable disadvantages; but none equal to that, with which you have been kind enough to present me. There is a pathos and delicacy in his serious poems; a vein of wit and humour in those of a more festive turn, which cannot be too much admired, nor too warmly approved; and I think I shall never open the book without feeling my astonishment renewed and increased." Immediately posting to Edinburgh in high hopes of bringing out a second edition, Burns humbly acknowledged that, "The Doctor belonged to a set of Critics for whose applause I had not even dared to hope." [23]

Blacklock's unstinted recognition of the "heaven-taught ploughman" proves that, if he was not the Scottish Pindar, he at least followed the honorable tradition of Hume and his circle in their quest for native talent. Though Blacklock may not live for posterity in his own odes, he lives in the letters of Hume, of Burns, and of Scott. And the man who could charm that distinguished triumvirate must have shone with abounding grace. To Hume, Blacklock was the "Man of the best Dispositions, that I have ever known"; to Burns, the "Man whom I not only esteem but venerate"; to Scott, "the worthiest and kindest of human beings." And Burns's Scottish— yet Horatian—epistle "To Dr. Blacklock" is by all odds the best poetry associated with that name and, rather than the unclassical Latin inscription of Beattie, his most fitting epitaph:

> Wow, but your letter made me vauntie!
> And are ye hale, and weel, and cantie?
> I kenn'd it still your wee bit jauntie
>   Wad bring ye to:
> Lord send you aye as weel's I want ye,
>   And then ye'll do.

[23] Blacklock's letter is quoted by Snyder, *Life of Burns*, p. 154. Burns's acknowledgment is in *Letters*, I, 115.

CHAPTER 3

HUME AND THE
SCOTTISH SHAKESPEARE

DAVID HUME was justly proud of his close friendships with the Moderates of the Scottish clergy. As the Rev. Alexander Carlyle expressly testifies, "He took much to the company of the younger clergy, not from a wish to bring them over to his opinions, for he never attempted to overturn any man's principles, but they best understood his notions, and could furnish him with literary conversation." [1] The well-known names of Hugh Blair, Alexander Carlyle, Adam Ferguson, John Home, William Robertson, and Robert Wallace are among those most closely associated with his. This association of clergy with infidel was the more seemly in a day when all were professed men of letters. There was the Rev. John Home, for instance, whose tragedy of *Douglas* won him the enviable title of the Scottish Shakespeare. It was Hume's intimacy with that cheerful cleric that involved him in a literary controversy surpassed in intensity only by the later more famous personal controversy with Rousseau.

The friendship that drew Hume into the defense of *Douglas* was deeply founded. "John Home," according to Carlyle, "was an admirable companion, and most acceptable to all strangers who were not offended with the levities of a young clergyman, for he was very handsome and had a fine person, about 5 feet 10½ inches, and an agreeable catching address; he had not much wit, and still less humour, but he had so much sprightliness and vivacity, and such an expression of benevolence in his manner, and such an unceasing flattery of those he liked (and he never kept company with anybody else)—the kind commendations of a lover, not the adulation of a

[1] Carlyle, *Autobiography*, p. 288.

sycophant—that he was truly irresistible, and his entry to a company was like opening a window and letting the sun into a dark room." [2]

As quasi-cousins, the two Humes shared the same surname, though the philosopher could never induce the poet to spell it as pronounced—with a *u*. They also shared the same generosity of nature and the same high spirits, and their every meeting was occasion for conviviality. A second source of friendly difference lay in the means of conviviality: should the bottle be claret or port? Uncompromisingly Scottish, John refused to sacrifice his country's agelong alliance with France for the recent English alliance with Portugal. His only defense against English preferential tariffs being his pen, however, he wielded that weapon with epigrammatic fury:

> Haughty and fierce the Caledonian stood;
> Old was his mutton, and his claret good.
> Let him drink port, an English statesman cried;
> He drank the poison, and his spirit died. [3]

David, more cosmopolitan, more complaisant, and more judicious, kept a cellar well stocked with both vintages.

The spirit of intimacy between the two Humes has been happily caught in a vignette of Laurence Sterne's in *A Sentimental Journey:*

A prompt French Marquis at our ambassador's table demanded of Mr. H——, if he was H—— the poet? No, said H—— mildly—*Tant pis*, replied the Marquis.

It is H—— the historian, said another—*Tant mieux*, said the Marquis. And Mr. H——, who is a man of an excellent heart, return'd thanks for both.

In 1776 when David, in a last effort to regain fast failing health, journeyed to the curative waters of Bath, he was faithfully accompanied by John, who made the way pleasant and easy with gossip and piquet. "Never was there a more friendly Action, nor better placed," acknowledged the invalid. On the return trip when death was imminent, David wrote to Hugh Blair to make arrangements for a farewell dinner in Edinburgh: "Mr John Hume, alias Home,

[2] *Ibid.*, p. 233.
[3] In *A Collection of Poems by Scotch Gentlemen*, II, 167.

alias the Home, alias the late Lord Conservator, alias the late Minister of the Gospel at Athelstoneford, has calculated Matters so as to arrive infallibly with his Friend in St David's Street on Wednesday Evening. He has ask'd several of Dr Blair's Friends to dine with him there on Thursday, being the 4th of July; and begs the favour of the Doctor to make one of the Number." And as a final gesture of thanks David added a codicil to his will:

I leave to my Friend, Mr John Home of Kilduff, ten dozen of my old Claret at his Choice; and one single Bottle of that other Liquor called Port. I also leave to him six dozen of Port, provided that he attests under his hand, signed John *Hume*, that he has himself alone finished that Bottle at two Sittings. By this Concession, he will at once terminate the only two Differences, that ever arose between us, concerning temporal matters.[4]

I

John Home, born at Leith in 1722 of a well connected though moderately circumstanced family, was educated at the Leith grammar school and at Edinburgh University. In the latter institution his amiable genius won the friendship and the respect of fellow students, of professors, and of the local men of letters including David Hume. Hardly had he left the academic halls in 1745 to begin a career in the church when the Rebellion broke out. The impetuous young clergyman at once enlisted in the volunteer corps to guard the capital against the dreaded hordes of ferocious Highland Jacobites. The first or College Company of volunteers also included William Robertson and William Wilkie, making a literary and clerical trio of no mean power.

The doughty defenders of Edinburgh are facetiously depicted by David Hume [5] as, "a List of Heroes equal to those of which *Homer* has given us a Catalogue, if not in his *Illiad*, at least in his *Batrachomyomachia*, or Battle of the Frogs and Mice." The Town Guards were "rather elderly Men, but pretty well disciplined. . . . The rest were, in a Word, undisciplined *Britons*, which implies just

[4] Hume, *Letters*, II, 333*n*.
[5] *A True Account of the Behaviour and Conduct of Archibald Stewart, Esq*, pp. 14-19.

as formidable an Idea as undisciplined *Romans,* or undisciplined *Indians.* They were nominally divided into the Trained-Bands, the *Edinburgh* Regiment, and the Volunteers. But this Division was really what the Schoolmen call a Distinction without a Difference. For with regard to military Prowess they were much the same." The Trained-Bands were timorous of firing their antiquated muskets which were "so bad, that a very moderate Charge of Powder would have made them burst about their Ears." The Edinburgh Regiment, raised and drilled all within a week, resembled *"Falstaff's* Tatter-demallion Company, which his Friend supposed he had levied by unloading the Gibbets and pressing the dead Bodies." The volunteers were well intentioned, but "as to their Discipline and Experience, it was much the same with that of the others."

Among these raw rookies, John Home took his place; and it was probably he who supplied David with the account of how they first went into action. "A Friend of mine," wrote the philosopher, "who has a poetical Genius, has made a Description of their March from the *Lawn-Market,* to the *West-Port,* when they went out to meet the Rebels; and has invented a very magnificent Simile to illustrate it. He compares it to the Course of the *Rhine,* which rolling pomp-ously its Waves through fertile Fields, instead of augmenting in its Course, is continually drawn off by a thousand Canals, and, at last, becomes a small Rivulet, which loses itself in the Sand before it reaches the Ocean." The ignominious surrender of Edinburgh, how-ever, did not end John's martial career. Rejoining the Loyalist forces, he was subsequently captured at the equally ignominious rout of Falkirk. Imprisoned in Doune castle, he and his intrepid com-panions ultimately managed to escape by knotting blankets into ropes.

After the collapse of the Rebellion John Home was ordained minister of Athelstaneford, a parish recently vacated by the death of the Rev. Robert Blair of the popular "Graveyard School" of poetry. But "The Grave" was not to the taste of the new and san-guine incumbent, who was satisfied with nothing less than a stirring poetical drama based on Plutarch's *Lives,* which he entitled *Agis.* In 1749 he rode horseback all the way to London to present this play to David Garrick, manager of the Drury Lane Theatre; but

Garrick, sad to say, had the temerity to refuse it. In a fine frenzy of poetical indignation, the highstrung parson rushed to Westminster Abbey and apostrophized the statue of Shakespeare in somewhat violent terms:

> Image of Shakespeare! To this place I come
> To ease my bursting bosom at thy tomb;
> For neither Greek nor Roman poet fired
> My fancy first, thee chiefly I admired;
> And day and night revolving still thy page,
> I hoped, like thee, to shake the British stage;
> But cold neglect is now my only meed,
> And heavy falls it on so proud a head.
> If powers above now listen to thy lyre,
> Charm them to grant, indulgent, my desire;
> Let petrefaction stop this falling tear,
> And fix my form for ever marble here.[6]

Unmarbled and unstaged, John Home returned to Scotland and resolutely set to work again. Apparently he also brought back with the rejected drama "An Ode on the Popular Superstitions of the Highlands of Scotland, Considered as the Subject of Poetry," which the English poet William Collins had composed expressly for him. Quite possibly it was this ode that first turned his thoughts to national themes. For Collins, recalling that the dearly beloved Shakespeare had found inspiration in Scottish story, advised his friend:

> Proceed, nor quit the tales which, simply told,
>   Could once so well my answ'ring bosom pierce;
> Proceed, in forceful sounds and colours bold
>   The native legends of thy land rehearse;
> To such adapt thy lyre and suit thy powerful verse.

Whether or not as a result of this good advice from south of the Tweed, John Home within the next five years completed *Douglas; a Tragedy*, framing it in "powerful" blank verse. On October 9, 1754, David announced that, "I have seen John Humes new un-baptized Play; and it is a very fine thing. He now discovers a great Genius for the Theatre." And in his letter of October 15 to Joseph

[6] Mackenzie, *Life of Home*, p. 35.

Spence which gave the account of Blacklock, David could not forbear
exulting over Scotland's new dramatic prodigy: "As you are a lover
of letters, I shall inform you of a piece of news, which will be
agreeable to you: we may hope to see good tragedies in the English
language. A young man called Hume, a clergyman of this country,
discovers a very fine genius for that species of composition. Some
years ago, he wrote a tragedy called *Agis*, which some of the best
judges, such as the Duke of Argyle, Sir George Lyttleton, Mr Pitt,
very much approved of. I own, though I could perceive fine strokes
in that tragedy, I never could in general bring myself to like it: the
author, I thought, had corrupted his taste by the imitation of Shakespeare, whom he ought only to have admired. But the same author
has composed a new tragedy on a subject of invention; and here he
appears a true disciple of Sophocles and Racine. I hope in time he
will vindicate the English stage from the reproach of barbarism."

Emboldened by the implicit faith of the Edinburgh men of
letters, John Home in February, 1755, once more mounted his good
horse, Piercy, for London, carrying with him this time the Scottish
tragedy. Once more he was rebuffed by Garrick with the hateful
reply that the play was unsuited to the stage. But this was unendurable! First Shakespeare had been insulted, and now Scotland.
Shakespeare might not be able to do anything about it, but Scotland
both could and would. The literati of the "Athens of the North"
agreed with the wronged member of the local Select Society; and,
conscious of their national literary superiority, they engaged to revise
the play so that it might grace the Caledonian stage. On April 20,
1756, David Hume proclaimed that, "our friend Hume's 'Douglas'
is altered and finished, and will be brought out on the stage next
winter, and is a singular, as well as fine performance, [steering
clear] of the spirit of the English Theatre, not devoid of Attic and
French elegance." [7] *Douglas* was first presented at the Canongate
Theatre in Edinburgh on December 14, 1756.

Thanks to the efforts of the author's literary friends, almost the
entire city turned out, "and many had the mortification," as the
periodical press reported, "to find the house so full when they came

---

[7] The words in brackets, missing in Hume, *Letters*, are supplied from
Brougham, *Lives of Men of Letters*, I, 241.

to the door, that they could not get in." [8] Thanks also to the genuine theatrical qualities of the play, as well as to the loyalty of the onlookers, it was an immediate and overwhelming success. "The applause was enthusiastic," a spectator [9] bears witness, "but a better criterion of its merits was the tears of the audience, which the tender part of the drama drew forth unsparingly." "There was not, I believe," testifies another spectator [10] more particularly, "one dry eye in the whole house." From high in the gallery floated down the triumphant exclamation that but signalized the common sentiment: "Whaur's your Wullie Shakespere noo!"

II

The unprecedented staging of *Douglas* at Edinburgh instead of at London precipitated a controversy that momentarily rocked the two nations. For when David Hume became involved, as he did shortly, his presence raised the controversial plane from the local to the national. Two important issues were at stake. The first was English prejudice, personified by David Garrick who had had the poor taste, as the Scots thought, and the bad judgment, as later box-office receipts proved, to refuse *Douglas* for the London theatre. The second was religious bigotry, the Edinburgh Presbytery denouncing a clergyman's writing a play and even clergymen's seeing a play.

The Highflying or Wild faction of strict Calvinists took a serious view of the matter, representing all drama, be it ever so moral in tone, as a delusion of Satan. Their official *Admonition and Exhortation* of January 5, 1757, stated explicitly: "The opinion which the Christian church has always entertained of stage plays and players, as prejudicial to the interest of religion and morality, is well known; and the fatal influence which they commonly have on the far greater part of mankind, particularly the younger sort, is too obvious to be called into question." [11] The Glasgow Wild Party on February 2 gratuitously endorsed the action of their Edinburgh confreres in a

[8] *Scots Magazine*, XVIII (1756), 624.
[9] Mackenzie, *op. cit.*, I, 38.
[10] George Wallace, quoted in *Letters of George Dempster*, p. 25.
[11] *Scots Magazine*, XIX (1757), 18.

resolution published in the newspapers: "The presbytery, deeply affected with this new and strange appearance, do think it their duty to declare, as they hereby do, that they agree with the Reverend presbytery of Edinburgh, in the sentiments published by them, with respect to stage-plays." [12] All this narrow-mindedness inspired the Rev. George Ridpath, minister of Stitchel, to complain bitterly in his *Diary:* "These people continue the same fools they have been for a long, long period." [13] An attempt in 1737 by the elder Allan Ramsay to establish an Edinburgh theatre had been suppressed almost immediately. But now in 1757 the general indignation at the arbitrary proceedings of the church against the dramatist and his associated theatre-going clerics was great. It became even greater when David Hume appeared publicly as the champion for the defense.

A suitable occasion being supplied by the impending publication of a volume of dissertations, the philosopher, after conference with the tragedian and with his permission, decided to take the unparalleled step, for him, of a dedication: "To the Reverend Mr. Hume, Author of *Douglas,* a Tragedy." This Dedication [14]—"the only one I ever wrote, or probably shall ever write, during the course of my Life"—was a blow aimed at the twin symbols of intolerance, the Scottish Presbytery and the English critics. In the first place, Hume pleaded the cause of broad-mindedness in religion:

I have been seized with a strong desire of renewing these laudable practices of antiquity, by addressing the following dissertations to you, my good friend: For such I will ever call and esteem you, notwithstanding the opposition, which prevails between us, with regard to many of our speculative tenets. These differences of opinion I have only found to enliven our conversation; while our common passion for science and letters served as a cement to our friendship. I still admired your genius, even when I imagined, that you lay under the influence of prejudice; and you sometimes told me, that you excused my errors, on account of the candor and sincerity, which, you thought, accompanied them.

[12] *Ibid.,* p. 48.
[13] Ridpath, *Diary,* p. 118.
[14] *Four Dissertations,* pp. i–vii. The following quotation is from a MS letter, National Library of Scotland, MS 1810, No. 83.

Second, Hume condemned by indirection the taste, the judgment, and the prejudice that had rejected the play:

I own too, that I have the ambition to be the first who shall in public express his admiration of your noble tragedy of DOUGLAS; one of the most interesting and pathetic pieces, that was ever exhibited on any theatre. Should I give it the preference to the *Merope* of *Maffei,* and to that of *Voltaire,* which it resembles in its subject; should I affirm, that it contained more fire and spirit than the former, more tenderness and simplicity than the latter; I might be accused of partiality: And how could I entirely acquit myself, after the professions of friendship, which I have made you? But the unfeigned tears which flowed from every eye, in the numerous representations which were made of it on this theatre; the unparalleled command, which you appeared to have over every affection of the human breast: These are incontestible proofs, that you possess the true theatric genius of *Shakespear* and *Otway,* refined from the unhappy barbarism of the one, and licentiousness of the other.

Hume was perfectly qualified to combat intolerance, whether religious or literary. The notoriety of his own skeptical philosophy had led to his being investigated the previous year by the Edinburgh Presbytery for ecclesiastical censure and possible excommunication, an investigation that resulted in his being defended by the Moderates.[15] Furthermore, in 1757 Hume's name was without exception preëminent in the republic of letters, overtopping that of any individual English writer. His essays were universally acknowledged to exhibit the most refined taste. His word carried great authority. In short, he could afford, as could few men of letters, to overstate the case.

Hume's overstatement of the case for *Douglas* was heavily weighted by the Scots' nationalistic conviction of their literary superiority over the English. Edinburgh, so Alexander Carlyle records, "was in an uproar of exultation that a Scotchman had written a tragedy of the first rate, and that its merit was first submitted to their judgment." [16] *Douglas* belonged peculiarly to Scotland because it was founded on the Scottish ballad of "Gil Morrice" and because it was written by the scion of an ancient Scottish family. It was not only the first successful Scottish tragedy, but was also far more suc-

---

[15] See Chapter 5, sec. IV, below.   [16] Carlyle, *op. cit.,* p. 327.

cessful than *Irene,* brought out in 1749 by the anti-Scottish Samuel Johnson. Its nearest rival among tragedies of the century, indeed, was Addison's *Cato,* as far back as 1713, a play also successful largely for political reasons.

These facts had to be brought to the attention of the English. By his authority Hume could force the critics to pay to the tragedy the deference he felt it intrinsically merited. Specifically, he might even be able to compel its performance upon the London stage. As leading Scottish man of letters, Hume was well aware that, despite other influential patronage that the dramatist might command, he himself would have to bear the brunt of the ensuing counterattacks. Any possible loss to his reputation incurred in so glorious an exploit as forcing the hand of the English he was willing to risk. By the end of July, 1757, he was happily able to inform the Abbé Le Blanc in Paris of his complete success with *Douglas:* "In order to raise it from Obscurity, I wrote to the Author the Dedication, prefix'd to the Four Dissertations, which had so good an Effect, that the Tragedy was brought on in Covent Garden, and extremely well receivd by the Public."

Hume's partiality to his namesake was by no means uncritical. He had disapproved of the earlier *Agis* and found many minor defects in *Douglas* itself, the very defects later castigated by less friendly critics. His essay *Of Tragedy,* basically Aristotelian in principle, followed the tradition of the French classical school; and his exposition of catharsis confirmed his judgment of *Douglas:* The spectators "are pleased in proportion as they are afflicted; and never are so happy as when they employ tears, sobs, and cries to give vent to their sorrow, and relieve their heart, swoln with the tenderest sympathy and compassion." [17] Hume's general opinion that, in regard to the stage, the French "have excelled even the Greeks, who far excelled the English" [18] is perfectly consistent with his private comment to the author of *Douglas:* "With great pleasure I have more than once perused your tragedy. It is interesting, affecting, pathetic. The story is simple and natural; but what chiefly delights me, is to find the language so pure, correct, and moderate. For God's sake, read Shakespeare, but get Racine and Sophocles by heart. It is

---

[17] *Four Dissertations,* p. 186.   [18] *Phil. Works,* III, 159.

reserved for you, and you alone, to redeem our stage from the reproach of barbarism." That barbarism, it is elsewhere [19] made clear, was the result of a century and a half of unbridled and slavish imitation of Shakespeare.

The redemption of the English stage Hume ardently desired. National pride suggested that the redeemer be a Scotsman. What more natural than that this Scotsman turn out to be John Home writing from a Scottish ballad a play that had been spurned by that English idolator of Shakespeare, David Garrick, "the best Actor, but the worst Critic in the World" [20]—a play, furthermore, that held all enlightened Edinburgh entranced and that was decried only by the bigots? Again the Rev. Alexander Carlyle chimed in appositely: "For when David Hume gave it that praise ['a perfect tragedy'], he spoke only the sentiment of the whole republic of belles-lettres." [21]

For friend and for country, Hume "resolv'd to do what lay in my Power to enable a Youth of Genius to surmount the unaccountable Obstacles, which were thrown in his Way," hoping that "the Goodness of the Intention will apologize for the Singularity of the undertaking." Singularity was the characteristic which the Rev. George Ridpath found in the Dedication when he heard of it. "A very strange phenomenon," he commented in his *Diary*, "and, if there be any sense in it, it is so much in the sublime as to be above the reach of ordinary capacities." [22] But, strange or sublime, Hume was deeply shocked by the animosities stirred up, since he had taken considerable pains to avoid involving the good name of his friend in a book that the fanatics would be sure to brand infidel. Two essays, *Of Suicide* and *Of the Immortality of the Soul*, after having actually been set up in print as part of "Five Dissertations," had been replaced at the last moment by *Of the Standard of Taste*, in what was reëntitled *Four Dissertations*. Yet even this prudential gesture did not suffice.

Actuated by the principle of Cæsar's wife, the Moderates in the church, desirous as they were to help their talented member, feared that the Dedication "wou'd involve him, and them of Consequence,

[19] *History of England*, VI, 192-93.
[20] Hume, MS letter, National Library of Scotland, MS 1810, No. 83.
[21] Carlyle, *op. cit.*, p. 317.   [22] Ridpath, *op. cit.*, p. 118.

in the Suspicion of Infidelity." On the advice of these "Men of very good Sense," Hume temporarily suppressed the Dedication. Though he printed it shortly afterward, he had sufficient reason to complain to William Mure of Caldwell: "Pray, whether do you pity or blame me most, with regard to this Dedication of my Dissertations to my Friend, the Poet? I am sure I never executed any thing, which was either more elegant in the Composition, or more generous in the Intention: Yet such an Alarm seiz'd some Fools here (Men of very good Sense, but Fools in that Particular) that they assaild both him & me with the utmost Violence; and engag'd us to change our Intention. I wrote to Millar to suppress that Dedication: Two Posts after I retracted that Order. Can any thing be more unlucky, than that in the Interval of these four days, he shoud have opend his Sale, & dispos'd of 800 Copies; without that Dedication, whence, I imagin'd, my Friend wou'd reap some Advantage, & myself so much Honor. I have not been so heartily vexd at any Accident of a long time. However, I have insisted that the Dedication shall still be publish'd." Republication in some of the weekly papers in Edinburgh and London, as well as in the *Scots Magazine* for June, must have gone far toward making up for the loss of it in the eight hundred copies of the *Four Dissertations*. Certainly it came early and forcefully to the attention of both the Scottish church and the English critics.

"Did you ever hear of such Madness & Folly as our Clergy have lately fallen into? For my Part, I expect that the next Assembly will very solemnly pronounce the Sentence of Excommunication against me: But I do not apprehend it to be a Matter of any Consequence. What do you think?" So Hume wrote to Adam Smith. But the clergy did not choose to investigate his writings a second time, although it seems unlikely that they took to heart his lesson of toleration. Typical of their "Madness & Folly" was *A Letter to the Reverend the Moderator, and Members of the Presbytery of Haddingtoun. With Animadversions concerning the Play-House.* According to this anonymous Highflyer, John Home, in the "horridly wicked" tragedy of *Douglas,* had set forth, "not for caution, but for example, the cursed principles and doctrine of his intimate acquaintance and beloved friend, David Home the Infidel, concerning the warrantableness of self-murder." Warning that, "We see, by the growth of Infidelity, the fatal effects of thus permitting David and John Homes to go on after the manner they do without being censured," the writer demanded the immediate deposition of the dramatist.

The Rev. John Home, however, found discretion the better part of valor and resigned his ministry at Athelstaneford. He "preached his farewel-sermon to his congregation on Sunday June 5, which drew tears from many of the people." [23] He then took a house for the summer near Braid and in a fit of braggadocio invited David Hume to come and live with him. But the philosopher was too circumspect to accept.[24]

Before the year was over "the late Rev. Mr John Home," as he was dubbed by David, was honored by a gold medal of the value of ten guineas, sent over as a present by Thomas Sheridan, manager of the Theatre-Royal at Dublin, with an inscription acknowledging his great merit in having "enriched the English stage with such an excellent tragedy." [25] This medal may be taken as the symbol of John Home's becoming a professional man of letters subject to all the perils of that calling. For Sheridan adopted the medal as a cheap means of compensation for an unsuccessful author's third night. David Hume, somewhat later, could remark sardonically that, "The Success of all plays, in this Age, is very feeble; and the people now heed the Theatre almost as little as the Pulpit." But John Home was already well established in his new profession, having been taken under the protection of that great political deity of Scotland, Lord Bute, who saw to it that he was given a pension by his Royal Highness, the Prince of Wales. In honor of this event, David rejoicingly proclaimed of his friend: *"Il est le mieux renté de tous les beaux esprits."*

III

On the literary side, the *Douglas* controversy drew serious critiques from both camps, John Witherspoon attacking and Adam Ferguson defending. Ferguson was Hume's successor in the keeper-

[23] *Scots Magazine*, XIX (1757), 274.
[25] *Scots Magazine*, XIX (1757), 662.
[24] Ridpath, *op. cit.*, p. 144.

ship of the Advocates' Library and Witherspoon was later President of Princeton University and only clerical signer of the Declaration of Independence. Alexander Carlyle penned the blisteringly ironical *Argument to Prove That the Tragedy of Douglas Ought to Be Publickly Burnt by the Hands of the Hangman,* and an anonymous upholsterer penned the entirely serious *Players Scourge; or, A Detection of the Ranting Prophanity and Regnant Impiety of Stage Plays, and Their Wicked Encouragers and Frequenters; and Especially against the Nine Prophane Pagan Priests, Who Countenanced the Thrice Cursed Tragedy Called Douglas.* When all the literary town had seen the play, Carlyle also wrote a broadside entitled, *A Full and True History of the Bloody Tragedy of Douglas, as It Is Now to Be Seen Acting in the Theatre at the Canongate,* which had so good an effect as to fill the house with small tradesmen and apprentices for another two nights.

Most attention, however, centered around the Dedication to the *Four Dissertations,* where the dedicator was vulnerable to attack, both serious and humorous. The opponents of *Douglas* satirically seized upon David's exalted praise of the play, his physical appearance, his infidelity, his "conversion" of the reverend dramatist, and the membership of the two in the Edinburgh Select Society. For more than six months, the "paper bullets," as they are called in a contemporary letter,[26] flew fast and furious. Many of them were aimed at Hume.

One of the more important pieces opens by noting that, "It is at present often, and justly observed, that the tragedy of *Douglas* has given birth to more burlesque performances, than any occurrence in *Scotland* ever did. Most of the authors of these pieces lurk as unsuspected as they could wish; but some of them are known." The writer, first brought "into the mouths of the world" (in Ramsay of Ochtertyre's [27] picturesque phrase) by his satires against the defenders of *Douglas,* was John Maclaurin, son of the famous Professor Colin Maclaurin, and himself later raised to the bench as Lord Dreghorn. In the *Apology for the Writers against the Tragedy of Douglas,* Maclaurin displayed all the rancor of an outsider against the Edin-

---

[26] *Letters of George Dempster,* p. 28.   [27] *Scotland and Scotsmen,* I, 443.

burgh Select Society, making no effort whatsoever to understand their literary program. His main attack was directed against Hume, their leading literary light:

Some years ago, a few gentlemen in this town assumed the character of being the only judges in all points of literature; they were and still are styled the *geniuses,* and lately erected what they called a *select society,* which usurps a kind of aristocratical government over all men and matters of learning. The first and fundamental maxim of this dictatorial club is, That a punctilious correctness of style is the *summum bonum* of all compositions: though the greatest genius should shine throughout a work, yet if in it is found an unguarded expression, a slip in syntax, or a peccadillo in grammar, *ad piper et farras* with it. Hence *Shakespear* of late is so much decried, that a noted historian, the *Coryphaeus* of this society, when disapproving of a wretched sentiment, adds, "What could *Shakespear* [28] have said worse?" *Addison,* till those gentlemen appeared, was universally esteemed as the finest writer ever *England* produced; but they

Cast him like an useless weed away.

If you believe them, there are ten errors in every page of his *Spectators;* and the above-mentioned author has a copy of them, in which this decalogue of errors in every page is marked with his own hand. . . . Let the reader compare *Voltaire* and *Hume,* with *Shakespear* and *Addison,* and give the preference to the former, if he can.

The Reverend author of *Douglas* was a worthy member of this society; and his tragedy, long before it appeared in public, was by this society, extolled with all the noise of declamation; and the little merit it has, exaggerated with all the amplifications of bombast. A famous author whom I have mentioned more than once, said, in private, that "he would give the *English* 200 years past, and 200 years to come, and they would not be able to produce such another tragedy:" and the same gentleman has publicly told his namesake, that "he possesses the true theatrical genius of *Shakespear* and *Otway,* refined from the unhappy barbarism of the one, and licentiousness of the other." This author must be forgiven for these rhodomontades; for he frankly owns, that "it is less my admiration of your fine genius, which has engaged me to make this address to you, than my esteem of your character, and *my affection to your person.*" Love, we all know, is blind; and it would be unpolite to blame *Corydon* for running out extravagantly in the praises of *Alexis.*

[28] See Note C, below.

In a second blast, a three-act farce of no little wit, Maclaurin relentlessly pursued the philosopher, the dramatist, and the Select Society, his title of *The Philosopher's Opera* revealing the chief object of ridicule. The leading figures in this piece, "as it ought to be represented at *Edinburgh*," are Satan, Mr. Genius as David Hume, Mrs. Sarah Presbytery, "relict of Mr. John Calvin," and Jacky, dramatist and son of that lady, as John Home. The plot concerns the wooing of the now elderly Mrs. Sarah Presbytery by Mr. Genius and the success of Jacky's play by the puffing of the same swain.

Satan, long notoriously weak in Edinburgh through the dominance of the godly, having had only "a small select society" to stick by him, appears in person on hearing of a Scottish clergyman's writing plays. "I thought," he explains, "the least I could do was to give my countenance to such a bold attempt to serve me." Upon making inquiries about other recent literature, Satan is reliably informed that Mr. Genius is the only author of note. Greatly impressed, Satan meets Genius, observing that he has read his books. "Why, then, Sir," replies that worthy, "you are convinced, I suppose, that there is no God, no devil, no future state;—that there is no connection betwixt cause and effect;—that suicide is a duty we owe ourselves;—adultery a duty we owe to our neighbour;—that the tragedy of *Douglas* is the best play ever was written; and that *Shakespear* and *Otway* were a couple of dunces.—This, I think, is the sum and substance of my writings." Genius departs, leaving Satan a little perplexed: " 'Faith, I don't know well what to think of him. Are you sure he is true blue on our side? I confess, I have some suspicion, that he is a shrewd fellow, endeavouring to convert men to Christianity, by writing nonsense against it."

Following the success of Jacky's drama, the farce ends happily and with great affection:

MRS. PRESBYTERY *sings:*
> Dear Sir, and dear Ladies, my *Jacky* is young,
> And bashfulness hinders the thanks of his tongue,
> For filling his pockets with half-crowns so white,
> He's sensible 'twas not the musical lasses,

Who dance, sing, and play on the top of *Parnassus,*
But you who got him the half-crowns so white.

To thee, noble *Genius,* the knee he shou'd bow;
More than to *Apollo* to thee does he owe:
 Shakespear scoffing,
 Douglas puffing,
You screw'd mens opinions to such a great height,
That they filled his pockets with half-crowns so white.

JACKY: Dear mother, you have very handsomely expressed my gratitude, which a foolish bashfulness would not allow me to do. In return, I must insist on your giving to Mr. *Genius* your hand; which a bashfulness, still more foolish than mine, will not, I hope, make you refuse. I know you love one another; your marriage to-night will consummate my happiness.

MRS. PR.: There, Sir, is my hand; you long have had my heart.

MR. GEN.: Madam, I am so very sensible of the honour you do me, that I here vow and swear never more to write essays, discourses, histories, dissertations; but to make your entertainment the sole study of my life.

The Deposition, or Fatal Miscarriage; a Tragedy continues the ragging. This anonymous piece burlesques mirthlessly the alleged "unfrocking" of John Home by the Edinburgh Presbytery. In disturbed slumber the night before the trial, Poetaster and Atheos are plagued by the ghosts of Shakespeare and Otway. The following day Poetaster is deposed by the General Assembly and, deciding to "earn my bread upon the stage," discovers that the loss of his stipend has cost him the love of Lady Tearsheet.

The catchpenny balladists reaped a rich harvest over *Douglas.* As early as the January issue of 1757, the *Scots Magazine* had commented upon the great number of "pieces, occasioned by the tragedy of Douglas, and the admonition of the presbytery of Edinburgh, most satirical; poems, advertisements, &c. at a penny price or under, and some given gratis." [29] *The First Night's Audience,* for instance, sings about John and David:

When the populace dull you to sermon must call,
Let *Douglas* be quoted instead of *St. Paul.*
I leave to 'Squire DAVID to paint, as he ought,
The Poet's sweet art, and th' effect which it wrought;

[29] *Scots Magazine,* XIX (1757), 56.

How greatly it tickled his fancy to find
The priest and essayist were much of a mind:
However our Bible-believers may rave,
Self-murder's the dernier resort of the brave.

Much the same tone is struck in *The Apostle to the Theatre His
Garland:*

Ye wolves in sheep's clothing I pray you draw near,
Nor lecture, nor sermon, nor psalm shall ye hear;
I sing our *Scotch Shakespear,* that promising youth,
Whose tragedy puts this new song in my mouth.

That DOUGLAS eclipses all other plays, DAVID
Did solemnly swear, as he hop'd to be saved:
A friend of the poet's this oath sharply blam'd,
Your fate, should it share, it would doubly be damn'd.

The Revolution, broader in its satire, castigates also the Select
Society:

Learned men whilom were under no fetters,
But made what was call'd the republic of letters;
Republic of letters! there's now no such thing,
The author of DOUGLAS of poets is king.

The poetical crown on his temples was plac'd
By him who is reckon'd the standard of taste;
But amongst us I hope ther's not one whose heart faints
To tell him with DOUGLAS we are *malecontents.*

. . .

I hope your good spirits will not be cast down,
Tho' those hight the GENIUSES on us shou'd frown:
They indeed have thought proper to style themselves *select;*
But, alas! 'tis too plain they're none of the *elect.*

But the favorite gibe of all, constantly recurring as a minor
theme, is at David's physique. Doubtless, readers were intended to
recall the philosopher's own observation in the *Enquiry concerning
the Principles of Morals:* "Broad shoulders, a lank belly, firm
joints, taper legs; all these are beautiful in our species because signs

of force and vigour." [30] The *Letter from Simon O'Queer, to Mrs Grissel Gray at Edinburgh* gives point to this description:

> I ne'er shall get rest, as I hope to be shaved,
> Till I see *young sire* Adam, and *Scotland's St. David;*
> His shoulder, legs, belly, so large are I hear,
> In all our *three* kingdoms *at once* they appear.

To a similar passage *The Stage or the Pulpit; a Sermon* appends a footnote: "These bodily perfections are the cardinal virtues of a *broad-shoulder'd, taper-legg'd* [with *'belly long'*] modern philosopher, with whom our reverend tragedian lives in Christian fellowship and communion." The same ballad also introduces the "conversion" theme, the dramatist singing:

> Let priests with unrelenting zeal
> At my *conversion* rage;
> *Ye* will not blame me tho' I quit
> The pulpit for the stage.

In Part Two he exults:

> Old *Shakespear, Otway*, and the rest,
> Must fly the concert-hall;
> My play, like *Aaron's* serpent, will
> Devour and swallow all.

Part Three, inspired by the impending publication of *Douglas*, warns:

> Prepare, ye Scottish connoisseurs,
> To criticise THE PLAY:
> This to the pious poet is,
> *Of Judgment the great day.*

> But first attentively peruse
> The dedication,
> Which *dainty Davie* has thought fit
> To write to *jumping John*.

The Infernal Council, in a direct attack upon the philosopher, makes capital of the suppressed essays *Of Suicide* and *Of the Im-*

[30] *Phil. Works*, IV, 227.

mortality of the Soul, of which some copies accidentally got into circulation.[31] Regretting the loss of the friendly Hobbes, Spinoza, and Bolingbroke, "Belzebub" asks for a volunteer to go to earth, only to be reminded by Lucifer that Hume is already there:

"Tho' *these champions of Hell* have from earth all retir'd,
"H[u]me aloft bears our *standard,* whose *breast* I've inspir'd:
"Of *talents* so rare, so acute, so profound,
"Of such *depth,* in your *realms,* there are none to be found.

"His *mind* I have swell'd with *vain-glory* and *pride;*
"*Faint emblem his paunch!*—tho' so vast, and so wide:
"Tho' *wealth* he despises, yet, fond of a name,
"He soars in *new tracts,* to *high glory* and *fame.*

"The *laws* of that *Ruler,* whose *realms* are on *High,*
"He boldly subverts, and has dar'd to defy:
"*In his flights how sublime!*—I am charm'd to behold
"Our *hero,* surpassing all *heroes of old.*

"This *maxim* he wisely *resounds* on the *ear*—
"*Men have nothing to hope, so have nothing to fear*—
"Hence, *dagger, ball, poison,* or *cord*—which you please,
"Each *fool* may practise on *himself*—and find *ease.*"

He ceas'd—when in transport cry'd Belzie, "I find
"*This* DAVID *indeed is a man to my mind:*
"Shallow politic *fiends* might for ages have try'd
"To devise such a plan—and their art been defy'd.

"Directed by H[u]me to the *regions of night,*
"What *troops* of pale spirits shall rush on our *sight!*
"To *him* then assign *we* our *delegate sway,*
"*Who* hath *taught* men the *path,* and will soon *lead the way.*"

All *hell* then resounded with shouts of *applause*
To H[u]me, who hath nobly supported its *cause:*
Io paean to H[u]me now their *transports* loud tell,
While *Echo* responsive—*"Amen,"* cries *all hell.*

This garland of verses may fittingly be terminated with a set of Hudibrastics, *An Epistle to Mr Genius, A[theis]t in Edinburgh:*

[31] See Note D, below.

My dear Sir,

It wou'd most certainly have been odd,
Had J[oh]n been censur'd by the synod:
For personally you before 'em
Appear'd, and plainly *in terrorem.*
I don't mean as a goblin fell,
Who carry'd with you blasts from hell.
Nor as a spirit good, ('tis giv'n,
You never will bring airs from heav'n).
'Twas neither shoulders, legs, nor belly,
The parsons frighted, I can tell ye.
Their secret reasons I o'erheard
From one for wisdom much rever'd:
"If I should vote, C[arlyle] suspend,
"Or what is worse, Depose his friend,
"Observe the consequence, with me
"*Genius* will not keep company;
"*Digges* with such a fanatic sinner
"Will never eat a bit of dinner;
"The actress will not lend to me
"Her *body* of divinity.
"And thus by them, with censure fretted,
"We'll all be excommunicated." [32]

I V

All the ephemera so far noticed arose out of the local reaction to
Douglas in Edinburgh from January to April, 1757. By the middle
of March, however, the controversy had spread to London, as the
play had finally been presented at Rich's Covent Garden Theatre on
March 14, with the great Peg Woffington as Lady Randolph. The
beneficial preparative effects of Hume's Dedication are observable
even before that date. The *London Chronicle* of February 22-24 had
remarked in a notice of the "licentious" Mrs. Aphra Behn's *The
Rover:* "We are glad that the Manager of Covent-Garden Theatre
is shortly to make Amends to the Public, for the Revival of *The
Rover,* by exhibiting on his Stage *The Tragedy of Douglas;* of

[32] Digges played the male lead in the Edinburgh production of *Douglas.*
Carlyle's friend of l. 14 is John Home.

which the Reader may see a Character in Mr. Hume's Dedication prefixed to his *Four Dissertations*, lately published by Mr. Millar."

In London *Douglas* was received with great applause, though without the flowing tears of Edinburgh. The *London Chronicle* for March 22-24 speculated concerning this cooler and more critical reception:

The dedicatory Letter, prefixed by Mr. Hume to his *Four Dissertations*, lately publish'd, raised an Expectation, with respect to this Composition, which perhaps has not been intirely gratified. The very elegant Author of that Address, whose Knowledge and Taste are indisputable in Subjects of Literature, has formed his Sentiments of dramatic Poetry, from those exquisite Models we have derived from Sophocles and Euripides. In the masterly Productions of those Artists, Simplicity of Design appears the essential Beauty. One Action, of sufficient Importance to command the Attention and attach the Affections of an Audience, is at all Times kept in View, and no subordinate Events are introduced, but what immediately tend to the Completion of the principal Design. From this simple Sketch of the Greek Drama, it will be obvious to the Reader, that a Play conducted upon this Plan, which the most able Critics, from Aristotle down to Brumoy, have established as the invariable Standard of the tragic Drama, must want the principal Requisite to take hold of the Minds of an English Assembly of Spectators, who have been so long accustomed to be entertained with an amazing Series of Incidents, thrown together often without any Consistency, and seldom with any Regularity of Design. These few Observations will perhaps explain why *Douglas* has not been received with the same Warmth with which the ingenious Dedicator deservedly speaks of it.

The *Monthly Review* for May, though not hostile, refrained from giving the same complete approbation of Hume:

It may not be improper to observe, before we take our leave of this performance, that it was first acted with great applause in Edinburgh; but made its appearance in England under a peculiar disadvantage. The commendation a man of taste and learning had bestowed on it, previous to its representation here, perhaps raised too much expectation in some, and excited a spirit of envy and critical prejudice in others. Possibly, indeed, that gentleman, in some degree, sacrificed his taste to his friendship. However, if this was the case, he will sustain no great loss with regard to his reputation; since he may gain as much on the one hand, as he can lose on the

other: the worst that can be said, amounting only to this, that the benevolence of his disposition prevailed over the rectitude of his judgment.

The writer of this mildly phrased rebuke, if rebuke it be, was Oliver
Goldsmith.

The *Critical Review* for March, however, had not let Hume off
so lightly. Quoting from his Dedication the passage ending, "I might
be accused of partiality," the reviewer stingingly interjects:

And so indeed, in our opinion, he might, with great justice: for though we
are ready to allow much to the bias of friendship and affection, yet we
would beg leave to put this author in mind, that there is something also
due to truth, taste, and judgment, which we cannot think any man hath
a right to sacrifice, even to the most intimate private connections. We
would gladly admit with Mr. *David Hume*, that there is a great degree
of merit in his friend's performance, which we shall point out by and by;
but at the same time will venture to assert in opposition to him, that the
author of *Douglas* is as far from *Shakespear* and *Otway*, as *London* is
from *Edinburgh*, or the banks of *Avon* from the river *Tweed*, as will
sufficiently appear to any impartial reader, who shall attentively consider
the intrinsic merit of this piece, unseduced by the glare of dress, the force
of action, and every other ornament merely theatrical.

And, after a detailed analysis of the play, the critical reviewer goes
on: "We should not indeed have dwelt so long on the little obvious
faults to be found in this tragedy, had not Mr. *David Hume*, whose
name is certainly respectable in the republic of letters, made it absolutely necessary.—Every addition of praise to any work beyond its
real and intrinsic merit, will always be found in the end prejudicial
to it, as the same moisture which feeds and nourishes the plant, if
poured on it in too great abundance may overwhelm and destroy it."
The editor of the *Critical Review*, that canny Scot, Tobias Smollett,
informally saw fit to deny any connection with the attack on *Douglas*,
which, he told a friend, "I assure you, I did not see until it was in
print." [33]

Two pamphlets appearing in April took opposite views of Hume's
Dedication. *The Tragedy of Douglas Analysed*, subtitled "Amicus
Plato, amicus *Socrates*, sed magis amica *Veritas*. Englished, I Honour
Mr. *David Hume*; but *Truth* More!" offered entire approval:

[33] Smollett, *Letters*, p. 47.

This virtuous glow of friendship, by whose intensity each squinting *Zoilus* affects to be offended, and turn aside from, shall be made appear not to have stretched beyond the bounds of truth; nay, receive additional lustre from a candid examination; in writing which, there is an unspeakable pleasure to herald undoubted merit, and at the same time, silence all malignant dissenters from the respectable authority of Mr. *David Hume;* whose sanction (had any modesty been left among our stage smatterers) ought to have awe-struck unlettered jabberers, and injudicious criticlings, who are ever guiltless of the praise-worthy foible, "T'admire superior sense, and doubt their own."

The pamphlet concluded with the chauvinistic threat taken from the play: "The blood of *Douglas* will defend itself."

The second pamphlet, "by an English Critic," was *A Letter to Mr. David Hume, on the Tragedy of Douglas; Its Analysis: and the Charge against Mr. Garrick,* subtitled *"Sic ais, ast ego contra.* So Thou Sayest; but I Am of a Contrary Opinion." It played a far different tune, and the "English Critic" got to the point immediately:

SIR,

Having for a long time conceived the highest esteem for the variety of your literary merit, a recommendation from you was almost a sanction to pre-engage my implicit approbation. How high were my expectations raised by your dedicatory commendation of *the tragedy of Douglas;* but, alas! how fallen, from seeing its representation: nor has a perusal since won me over as an admirer of it.

Had the tragedy of *Douglas* been ushered into the world as the promise of a dramatic genius, as such it ought to have been received with applause; but its having been forced upon us authoritatively, in competition with all antiquity and the moderns, two obvious effects were produced in the minds of men; to wit, curiosity was excited in some, jealousy provoked in others. I am sorry to inform you, Sir, that in consequence, your *national* judgment has been greatly run upon here, and your critical stocks reduced almost to bankruptcy.

For my part, when I first read your panegyrical paragraph, I for some time hesitated as to the sincerity of it. . . . But, on a second reading of it, I changed opinion, and have moreover been assured, that what is written you meant, to which, in amaze, I used the famous reply of *"Est il possible,"* is it possible?

The four great and revered names, *Maffei, Voltaire, Otway, Shake-spear,* which you have employed as supporters of *Douglas,* put me in mind of the statue of *Lewis* XIV. in *Paris,* where the four nations, *Germany, Spain, Holland,* and *England,* are chained round him as vanquished, and lavishly accompanied with all the tokens of subjection. However this may please the national vanity of the *French,* all foreigners with reason laugh at the folly of the design, and unpardonable foppery of the execution. . . .

According to this just and admirable doctrine [of the standard of taste, quoted from Hume's essay on that subject], what is likely to be the fate of *the tragedy of Douglas?* Neglect and oblivion: however illumined for the present by the flambeau, you (forgive the expression,) too partially, or in the mildest terms, too sanguinely, hold before it.

The "English Critic," however, received no praise from the *Monthly Review,* which commented tersely: "Unless this Critic mends his hand, and very considerably too, it will be of little consequence what country produced him." [34]

After the middle of 1757 the controversy over *Douglas* finally simmered down, but the play was not forgotten. Dr. Johnson could always be aroused by reference to it, as Boswell discovered during their trip through Scotland in 1773:

As we sat over our tea, Mr. Home's Tragedy of *Douglas* was mentioned. I put Dr. Johnson in mind, that once, in a coffee-house at Oxford, he called to old Mr. Sheridan, "How come you, Sir, to give Home a gold medal for writing that foolish play?" and defied Mr. Sheridan to shew ten good lines in it. He did not insist they should be together; but that there were not ten good lines in the whole play. He now persisted in this. I endeavoured to defend that pathetick and beautiful tragedy, and repeated the following passage:

                          —Sincerity,
          Thou first of virtues! let no mortal leave
          Thy onward path, although the earth should gape,
          And from the gulph of hell destruction cry,
          To take dissimulation's winding way.

JOHNSON: "That will not do, sir. Nothing is good but what is consistent with truth or probability, which this is not. Juvenal, indeed, gives us a noble picture of inflexible virtue. . . ." He repeated the lines with great

---

[34] *Monthly Review,* XVI (1757), 454.

force and dignity; then added, "And after this, comes Johnny Home, with his *earth gaping*, and his *destruction crying:*—Pooh!" [35]

Boswell was mightily chagrined over his tactical blunder, yet remained unconvinced: "I am sorry that I was unlucky in my quotation. But notwithstanding the acuteness of Dr. Johnson's criticism, and the power of his ridicule, the Tragedy of Douglas still continues to be generally and deservedly admired."

So far as David Hume was concerned, he had done his best for his friend and compatriot and was quite willing to let well enough alone. In none of the many later editions of his *Essays and Treatises*, into which *Four Dissertations* was incorporated, was the Dedication ever reprinted. It had served its purpose and had no further function. Hume did, however, make some efforts to interest the French literati in *Douglas* and to get it translated; but he only succeeded in eliciting a long and unfavorable comment from Mme de Boufflers.[36] Voltaire, on hearing of the clerical dramatist, had paid him in 1760 the somewhat dubious honor of brazenly fostering on "Mr. Hume, pasteur de l'Église d'Edimbourg," the authorship of his own comedy, *Le Caffé; ou, L'Ecossaise*. The story of the Scottish Shakespeare was told to Rousseau in 1764 by Julie Bondeli: "The Scots, it is said, are about to begin the Republic of Plato. Already they have chased out one of their ecclesiastics because he had the misfortune to write three good tragedies. The English have sheltered the author and his talents; and the moralists are now debating whether they were driven to acclaim Mr. Hume [Home] with so much urbanity from a taste for the beautiful or from a desire to plague the Scots." [37]

The intimacy between the two Humes was long remembered. There was the ardent Wilkesite, Charles Churchill, who, in the savagely anti-Caledonian *The Prophecy of Famine*, ranked John Home among "the meek slaves of prejudice and pride" of Scotland—

> Thence, Home, disbanded from the sons of prayer
> For loving plays, though no dull dean was there—

and in *The Journey*, with scathing irony, linked the two names:

[35] *Boswell and Johnson Tour*, pp. 404-5.
[36] *Eminent Persons*, pp. 223-25, 228-29.
[37] Rousseau, *Correspondance générale*, X, 327.

> Let them forge lies and histories with Hume;
> Let them with Home, the very prince of verse,
> Make something like a tragedy in Erse.

There was Robert Burns, who, loyally composing a *Scots Prologue for Mr. Sutherland's Benefit-night, Dumfries,* called for native dramatic talent—

> What needs this din about the town o' Lon'on,
> How this new play an' that new sang is comin'?
> Why is outlandish stuff sae meikle courted?
> Does nonsense mend like brandy, when imported?—

by echoing the comparison made famous by David Hume:

> O for a Shakespeare or an Otway scene,
> To draw the lovely, hapless Scottish Queen!
> One Douglas lives in Home's immortal page,
> But Douglases were heroes every age.

And Burns also voiced the considered judgment of literary Caledonia when he boasted:

> Here Douglas forms wild Shakespeare into plan.

Finally there was Walter Savage Landor, who in the *Imaginary Conversations* brought the two friends together once more in animated discussion of religion. Landor portrayed *le bon David's* philosophical humanity as ultimately triumphing over John's religious irascibility, and the thinker and the tragedian as ending in renewed harmony and complete understanding.

V

The *Douglas* controversy of 1757, having thrown all Scotland into a ferment and leavened English criticism, was of more than casual import. For the issue was national and symptomatic of the struggle for supremacy between the Scottish and the English intellectuals of the Enlightenment. This particular encounter, one of many, was lent dignity by the presence of David Hume. It was

Hume again, ever alert for the recognition of Scottish genius, who managed to keep on a sober plane the later equally fantastic controversies over the Scottish Homers—both of them.[38]

Today there is perhaps no great reason to quibble over Walter Scott's remark of 1827 that, "David Hume was no good judge of poetry; had little feeling for it; and examined it by the hackneyed rules of criticism; which, having crushed a hundred poets, will never, it may be prophesied, create, or assist in creating, a single one." [39] Yet Hume's comment of 1764 to Mme de Boufflers concerning *Douglas* indicates that Scott did him somewhat less than justice: "The value of a theatrical piece can less be determined by an analysis of its conduct, than by the ascendant which it gains over the heart, and by the strokes of nature which are interspersed through it." This is not far removed from Scott's own opinion of the works of John Home: "Good blank verse, and stately sentiment, but somewhat lukewarmish, excepting *Douglas*, which is certainly a masterpiece. Even that does not stand the closet. Its merits are for the stage; and it is certainly one of the best acting plays going. Perhaps a play to act well should not be too poetical."

When the mind of the Enlightenment has been disengaged from the still surviving romanticisms of the nineteenth century, the acceptance of Hume's opinion by Thomas Gray, the most impeccable critic among "the Barbarians who inhabit the Banks of the Thames," no longer appears merely curious. In a personal letter of August 10, 1757, Gray confessed, somewhat shamefacedly as behooved a loyal Englishman: "I am greatly struck with the Tragedy of Douglas, tho' it has infinite faults. The Author seems to me to have retrieved the true language of the Stage, wch had been lost for these hundred years; & there is one Scene (between Matilda & the old Peasant) so masterly, that it strikes me blind to all the defects in the world." [40] But Gray timidly, and wisely, kept out of the affair and never made his views public.

[38] See Chapter 4, below.
[39] Scott, review of Mackenzie's edition of *Works of John Home* in *Quarterly Review*, XXXVI (1827), 193-94. Scott's remark below is quoted by Lockhart, *Scott*, V, 105.
[40] Gray, *Correspondence*, II, 515.

Douglas has recently been called "the Scottish Declaration of Literary Independence." [41] And there is no denying that in the *Douglas* controversy was found the occasion for that untrammeling of Scottish literature which later made possible the Golden Age of Burns and Scott. But credit for the act of liberation perhaps belongs less to the author of the play than to the Scottish man of letters who had the audacity to proclaim publicly that that play surpassed all English tragedy of the century, and who had the authority to force its acceptance upon unwilling English critics. The true Scottish Declaration of Literary Independence, therefore, is the Dedication to *Four Dissertations*. And its Thomas Jefferson is David Hume.

[41] Thompson, *A Scottish Man of Feeling,* p. 46.

CHAPTER 4

HUME AND THE
SCOTTISH HOMERS

IN 1757 Scottish letters enjoyed a banner year. In January, David Hume published *Four Dissertations*, the Dedication of which to John Home, the Scottish Shakespeare, memorialized the coming of age of the Caledonian Enlightenment. In April, John himself published *Douglas*, the first national tragedy. And in May appeared the first national epic. Here, surely, was reason for rejoicing, for though "deep-brow'd Homer" ruled supreme over the demesne of the epic, to possess a national Homer was the narrower yet eminently laudable ambition of all modern countries. When Dryden wrote in 1697 that "A Heroic Poem, truly such, is undoubtedly the greatest work which the soul of man is capable to perform," [1] he was only repeating common criticism.

In the seventeenth century Milton had brought distinction to England and so, earlier in the eighteenth century, had Pope, translator of Homer. Since Milton, and even since Pope, several painstaking and, unhappily, painful efforts had been made toward composing another epic; but the fame of the Blackmores, the Hills, and the Glovers was deservedly transitory. Scotland, so her lovers of poetry fondly imagined, could hardly be less successful than that English trio, and possibly during her Augustan Age of literature might produce the second epic in the English language.

Milton ranked unsurpassed among the moderns; but even he, the critics were reiterating, had not achieved a Homeric perfection. One of the foremost of the critics, David Hume, in the second volume of his *History of the Stuarts*, also published in 1757, presented a high but qualified estimate of Milton's genius: "It is cer-

[1] *Dedication of the Aeneis*, beginning.

tain that this author, when in a happy mood, and employed on a noble subject, is the most wonderfully sublime of any poet in any language; Homer and Lucretius and Tasso not excepted. More concise than Homer, more simple than Tasso, more nervous than Lucretius; had he lived in a later age, and learned to polish some rudeness in his verses; had he enjoyed better fortune, and possessed leisure to watch the returns of genius in himself, he had attained the pinnacle of perfection, and borne away the palm of epic poetry." [2] The chief advantage offered to a poet during an Age of Enlightenment was a highly cultivated taste. In such an age, a Scottish Milton—so went the argument—might indeed become the Scottish Homer.

How David Hume, the leading Scottish man of letters, came into contact with two candidates for the Homeric title provides a neglected chapter in his biography and one of no inconsiderable import in the history of eighteenth-century literature. The first of these candidates, a Lowlander, was the continuator of Homer and of Homer's Pope—or was it now Pope's Homer? The second, a Highlander, was a Celtic Homer in his own right and like nothing that the world had hitherto known or was likely to know again. With both the name of David Hume is inseparable; for the first would otherwise be totally forgotten today, and the second is remembered almost in his despite.

THE HOMER OF THE LOWLANDS

"Wilkie the minister has turned up from obscurity, and become a very fashionable man, as he is indeed a very singular one." So wrote David Hume in April, 1755, reporting informally to Allan Ramsay on the Edinburgh Select Society. "Singular" is the essence of any description of William Wilkie, the Homer of the Lowlands; and no better account of his singularity exists than Hume's letter of July 2, 1757, to Gilbert Elliot:

You know he is a Farmer's Son, in the Neighbourhood of this Town, where there are a great Number of Pigeon Houses. The Farmers are very much infested with the Pigeons, and Wilkie's Father planted him often as

[2] *History of England*, VII, 343-44.

a Scarecrow (an Office for which he is well qualify'd) in the Midst of his Fields of Wheat. It was in this Situation that he confesses he first conceiv'd the Design of his Epic Poem, and even executed Part of it. He carry'd out his Homer with him, together with a Table, & Pen & Ink, & a great rusty Gun. He compos'd & wrote two or three Lines, till a Flock of Pigeons settled in the Field, then rose up, ran towards them, & fir'd at them; return'd again to his former Station, & added a Rhyme or two more, till he met with a fresh Interruption.

Two or three Years ago, Jemmy Russel put a very pleasant Trick on an English Physician, one Dr Roebuck, who was travelling in this Country. Russel carry'd him out one day on horseback to see the Outlets of the Town, and purposely led him by Wilkie's Farm. He saw the Bard at a small Distance sowing his Corn, with a Sheet about his Shoulders, all besmear'd with Dirt & Sweat, with a Coat & Visage entirely proportion'd to his Occupation. Russel says to his Companion, *Here is a Fellow, a Peasant, with whom I have some Business: Let us call him.* He made a Sign, & Wilkie came to them. Some Questions were ask'd him with regard to the Season, to his Farm & Husbandry, which he readily answer'd; but soon took an Opportunity of making a Digression to the Greek Poets, and enlarging on that Branch of Literature. Dr. Roebuck, who had scarce understood his rustic English, or rather his broad Scotch, immediatly comprehended him, for his Greek was admirable: And on leaving him, he coud not forbear expressing the highest Admiration to Russel, that a Clown, a Rustic, a mere Hind, such as he saw this Fellow was, shou'd be possest of so much Erudition. *Is it usual,* says he, *for your Peasants in Scotland to read the Greek Poets? O yes,* replies Russel, very coolly, *we have long Winter Evenings; and in what can they then employ themselves better, than in reading the Greek Poets?* Roebuck left the Country in a full Perswasion that there are at least a dozen Farmers in every Parish who read Homer, Hesiod & Sophocles every Winter Evening, to their Families; and, if ever he writes an Account of his Travels, it is likely he will not omit so curious a Circumstance.

Wilkie is now a settled Minister at Ratho, within four Miles of the Town: He possesses about 80 or 90£ a year, which he esteems exorbitant Riches. Formerly, when he had only 20£, as Helper, he said that he coud not conceive what Article, either of human Convenience or Pleasure, he was deficient in: Nor what any man coud mean by desiring more Money. He possesses several Branches of Erudition, besides the Greek Poets; and, particularly, is a very profound Geometrician, a Science commonly very incompatible with the lively Imagination of a Poet. He has even made some new Discoveries in that Science; and he told me, that, when a young Man, he threw Cross & Pile, whether he wou'd devote himself chiefly to Mathematics or to Poetry, & fears that he rather crost the Bent of his Genius in taking to the latter. Yet this man, who has compos'd the second Epic Poem in our Language understands so little of Orthography, that, regularly thro' the whole Poem, he always spelt the Word *yield* in this manner, *ealde;* and I had great Difficulty to convince him of his Mistake.

Like the English poet Christopher Smart, the Scottish poet William Wilkie was not overly fond of personal cleanliness. His particular aversion was clean sheets and his pet foible was a huge quantity of bedclothes—twenty-four blankets, it is reputed. The brilliant English statesman, Charles Townshend, when visiting Edinburgh, epitomized that most egregious paradox of the Greek-loving, pigeon-shooting, two-dozen-blanketed, scarecrow-poet by owning to Alexander Carlyle "that he had never met with a man who approached so near the two extremes of a god and a brute as Wilkie did." [3]

I

William Wilkie, the god-brute, exhibits an individualism as rugged as Scotland ever engendered. Born at Echlin, Linlithgow, in 1721, he was given by his father, a hard-working farmer, the advantages of a good education at the local grammar school and at Edinburgh University. In Edinburgh, Wilkie associated with David Hume, Alexander Carlyle, John Home, and William Robertson, and with the last two fought among the unsung heroes defending the city during the '45.

The death of his father necessitated Wilkie's return to the farm before graduating from the University; but continuing his studies privately, he was licensed to preach in 1745 and ordained minister in 1753. As farmer Wilkie was so successful in the new cultivation of tubers as to earn the covetable sobriquet of "potato," being variously known as the "potato minister," the "potato poet," or just plain "Potato Wilkie." As minister he was so eccentric as to be universally loved: sometimes, it is said, he would preach with his

[3] Carlyle, *Autobiography,* p. 413.

hat on; sometimes he would forget to administer the sacrament to himself; sometimes he would walk out of the church without offering the benediction; but always, his congregation felt certain, he was sincere and devout. As poet he composed what that highly reputable critic David Hume named "the second Epic Poem in our Language."

The *Epigoniad*, appropriately enough, owed its inception to Homer, or rather to the negligence of Homer. In Book IV of the *Iliad*, had not that honored bard alluded most intriguingly to the fall of Thebes and then not satisfied the curiosity he had aroused? Statius, to be sure, tells the story of the first and unsuccessful siege of Thebes. But of the actual capitulation of that city nothing was known beyond the hints in the *Iliad*. Infuriated by Agamemnon's taunt that he lacked the courage of his forbears, Sthenelos replied with vigor (let it be through the verses of Pope):

> What needs, O Monarch, this invidious praise,
> Ourselves to lessen, while our sires you raise?
> Dare to be just, Atrides! and confess
> Our valour equal, tho' our fury less.
> With fewer troops we storm'd the Theban wall,
> And, happier, saw the sev'nfold city fall.
> In impious acts the guilty fathers died;
> The sons subdued, for Heav'n was on their side.
> Far more than heirs of all our parents' fame,
> Our glories darken their diminish'd name.

Here was fodder for the poetical imagination! And acting on these suggestions, the daring Wilkie composed an entire epic: "The following poem is called the *Epigoniad*, because the heroes, whose actions it celebrates, have got the name of *The Epigones* (or *descendants*) being the sons of those who attempted the conquest of Thebes in a former expedition." [4] This work, in nine books of heroic couplets totaling 5,782 lines, was published anonymously at Edinburgh in May, 1757.

The endeavor to continue Homer in the mid-eighteenth century required a heroism almost unsurpassed in the annals of literature.

[4] *Epigoniad*, Preface, p. xli.

But Wilkie knew no fear—or was it that heroes rush in where wise men fear to tread? In a long critical Preface to his poem he displayed no inconsiderable acumen in discussing the difficulties besetting the modern epic writer but had the hardihood to attack both Milton and Pope, the one for breaking the rules of the epic, the other for his poetic diction. "The quaintness of Mr. Pope's expression, in his translation of the Iliad and Odyssey," pontificated Wilkie, "is not at all suitable, either to the antiquity or majestic gravity of his author, and contributes more to make his fable appear vain and absurd, than any circumstance that seems of so little moment, could easily be supposed to do." [5] This recklessness of Wilkie's invited retaliation, as he was soon to find out.

An anonymous Scot hastened to print *A Critical Essay on the Epigoniad; Wherein the Author's Horrid Abuse of Milton Is Examined.* "As I have received," this piece opens, "the highest pleasure in reading Milton, I cannot but think myself bound, in gratitude, to defend him for once, when he is openly misrepresented and vilified." And defend him he did by sufficiently horrid abuse of the *Epigoniad.* The Scottish critic also took upon himself the defense of Pope: "Very well! Pope makes Homer appear vain and absurd. This author hits exactly in with the taste and genius of the gentlemen of the Dunciad; nay, one would almost think he had stole it from one of them, who is recorded to have written, that Pope had burlesqu'd Homer." [6] The critical atmosphere was becoming thick. Who had continued whom, and who had burlesqued whom?

The English critics made short shift of the *Epigoniad.* They knew it was burlesque. The *Critical Review* for June, 1757, neglected no opportunity for ridicule:

The piece before us . . . resembles an epic poem in very little else but the outward form, and extent of it, dragging its slow length along through nine tedious books. . . . If the poem had merit sufficient to entitle it to a serious *critique,* we would gladly have taken the pains to collect the subject matter of every book, and given our observations on the conduct of the whole in regard to the fable, sentiment, diction, and machinery. . . .

[5] *Ibid.,* p. xl.   [6] *Critical Essay on the Epigoniad,* pp. 1, 8.

This our author calls an imitation of Homer; but if Homer himself had wrote this, would not Horace have cried out,

Quodcunque ostendis mihi sic, incredulus odi.

Does not this gentleman then, in regard to his imitation of Homer, put us in mind of Alexander's courtiers, who, because their sovereign had a wry neck, always carried their heads on one side out of complaisance to him? If the author of the Epigoniad has made thus free with Homer, so has he, if we are not mistaken, with his translator also, from whom he seems to have borrowed many lines and expressions. . . .

We had forgot to observe, in justice to our author, that, in his short preface to this poem, there are many just and sensible remarks on the beauties and defects of epic poetry, and that he had pointed out the right path, tho' he hath not himself trod in it; which brings to our mind the remark of one of our most eminent poets on the critics of his age, where he says,

> Rules for *good verse* they first with pains indite,
> Then shew us what is *bad* by what *they* write.

This was but faint damnation, however, in comparison with that meted out in the July *Monthly Review* by Oliver Goldsmith and Ralph Griffiths. Goldsmith set the tone: "The Epigoniad seems to be one of these *new old* performances; a work that would no more have pleased a peripatetic of the academic grove, than it will captivate the unlettered subscriber to one of our circulating libraries." But Griffiths, editor of the *Monthly*, soon took up the cudgels himself, going Goldsmith much better:

If bad rhimes are to be deemed, as some think they are, a capital defect, our Author will be capitally convicted on many an indictment in the court of criticism. For instance, p. 242, we have the following strange couplet

> *Graceful* the goddess turn'd, and with a *voice*,
> Bold, and superior to the vulgar *noise*,
> O'er all the field commands.——

The badness of the rhyme in the two first lines is, however, their smallest imperfection: Minerva, sure, will never pardon the *ungraceful* mention he has made of her goddessship's vociferation; which according to the idea here raised, would even silence the loudest water-nymph in the neighbourhood of Thames-street.

And in a huff over the prefatory attack on Pope, Griffiths caustically concluded his account of the critic-poet: "Had he published that discourse without the Epigoniad, and committed the latter to the flames, his reputation would have sustained no loss on that account."

II

Even before the publication of the *Epigoniad* David Hume was broadcasting its praises. On May 25, 1757, he had informed William Strahan: "I have wrote to Mr Millar of a new Epic Poem that is to be published this Week in Edinburgh: It is calld the Epigoniad, & is wrote by one Mr Wilkie, a Minister. It is a Production of great Genius. I recommend it to you to read when it comes to London. If you like it you will naturally speak of it among your acquaintance." Two days later the epic appeared and received immediate notice in the *Diary* of the Rev. George Ridpath: "*Friday, May 27th.* James Allan staid till after dinner. Read, along with him three books of Wilkie's poem, and all the rest of it after he had gone. It seems to be a very extraordinary work." [7]

On July 2, as already observed, Hume wrote to Gilbert Elliot, then in London:

I suppose that, by this time, you have undoubtedly read & admir'd the wonderful Production of the Epigoniad, and that you have so much Love for Arts, & for your native Country, as to be very industrious in propagating the Fame of it. It is certainly a most singular Production, full of Sublimity & Genius, adorn'd by a noble, harmonious, forcible, & even correct versification. We generally think the Story deficient & uninteresting; but perhaps the new Fancy of crossing the Invention of all modern Romance Writers may make some Atonement, and even bestow an Air of Novelty on the Imitation of Homer. As I cannot but hope that this Work will soon become a Subject of Conversation in London, I shall take this Opportunity of supplying you with some Anecdotes with regard to the Author, besides such as you already know, of his being a very worthy & a very entertaining man, adorn'd with all that Simplicity of Manners, so common to great Men, & even with some of that Rusticity & Negligence which serve to abate that Envy to which they are so much expos'd.

[7] Ridpath, *Diary*, p. 140.

And on July 21 Hume sought to learn the fate of the *Epigoniad* in London, writing Millar: "I shoud be glad to hear what the Connoisseurs with you say of that singular Piece the Epigoniad."

The verdict was soon forthcoming, and evidently the connoisseurs of London were unable to duplicate Ridpath's feat of endurance. For on August 9 Hume reluctantly admitted to Elliot: "I find the Public, with you, have rejected the Epigoniad, for the present. They may do so if they please: But it has a great deal of Merit, much more than any one of them is capable of throwing into a Work." By the beginning of September, Hume was convinced that the unfavorable reception of the poem was due principally to national prejudice but remained undeterred in his purpose of bringing it to the attention of the English public. The nature of this new effort is revealed in another letter to Millar: "Nothing surprizes me more than the Ill Usage which the Epigoniad has receiv'd. Every body here likes it extremely. The Plan & Story is not so much admired; as the Poetry & Versification: But your Critics seem willing to allow it no Merit at all. I fancy it has not been enough dispers'd; and that your engaging in it, wou'd extremely forward its Success. The whole Edition is out: There were 550 disposd of here: 200 sent to London. As the Author is my very good Friend & Acquaintance, I shoud be much pleasd to bring you to an understanding together; If the bad success on the first Edition has not discouragd you, I wou'd engage him to make you Proposals for that Purpose. He will correct all the Blemishes remark'd."

The "Conspiracy of the Booksellers," as he elsewhere phrased it, was no new complaint of Hume's. Already he had amassed considerable evidence on his own account that London publishers failed to coöperate in pushing the sale of books from provincial presses. This thesis was applied to Wilkie in a letter of September 29 to Colonel Edmonstoune in Dublin: "Tell me about the Epigoniad: Was there ever so much fine Versification bestow'd on so indifferent a Story? Has it had any Success in Ireland? I fancy not: For the Criticklings in Dublin depend on the Criticklings in London, who depend on the Booksellers, who depend on their Interest, which depends on their printing a Book themselves. This is the Cause,

why Wilkie's Book is at present neglected, or damn'd as they call
it: But I am much mistaken, if it end so. Pray, what says the Primate
of it? I hear he has the Generosity to support damnd Books, till
their Resurrection; and that he is one of the Saints who pray them
out of Purgatory. I hope he is an honest Fellow, and one of us." [8]
Archbishop Stone had assuredly gone out of his way to praise Hume's
History of the Stuarts on its first appearance; but whether he was
at one with the Scots concerning the *Epigoniad* is unknown.

Despite the poor sales and the poor reviews of that epic, neither
Hume nor Wilkie was dismayed. By 1759 the poet had corrected
"all the Blemishes remark'd," canceled the strictures on Pope in
the introductory essay, and added at the end of the volume a short
Spenserian poem. Brought out by Millar in London through the
good offices of Hume, this second edition was dignified with the
name of the author on the title page: *The Epigoniad; a Poem. In
Nine Books. By William Wilkie, V.D.M. The Second Edition, Carefully Corrected and Improved. To Which Is Added, a Dream. In
the Manner of Spenser.*

In order to attract the attention of the reading public, Hume,
in London at the moment, resorted to puffing. Coyly he wrote to
Adam Smith on April 12: "The *Epigoniad*, I hope, will do; but
it is somewhat up-hill work. As I doubt not but you consult the
Reviews sometimes at present, you will see in *The Critical Review*
a letter upon that poem; and I desire you to employ your conjectures in finding the author. Let me see a sample of your skill in
knowing hands by your guessing at the person." With William
Robertson, however, Hume gave up the air of mystery: "Our friend
Smith is very successful here, and Gerard is very well received.
The *Epigoniad* I cannot so much promise for, tho I have done all
in my power to forward it, particularly by writing a letter to the
Critical Review, which you may peruse. I find, however, some good
judges profess a great esteem for it, but *habent et sua fata libelli*:
however, if you want a little flattery to the author, (which I own
is very refreshing to an author) you may tell him that Lord Chesterfield said to me he was a great poet. I imagine that Wilkie will

[8] Hume, MS letter, National Library of Scotland, MS 1005. The version
in Hume, *Letters*, is incomplete and inaccurate.

be very much elevated by praise from an English earl, and a Knight of the Garter, and an Ambassador, and a Secretary of State, and a man of so great reputation. For I observe that the greatest rustics are commonly most affected with such circumstances."

III

The letter that David Hume sent to the *Critical Review* appeared in April, 1759, as official notice of the second edition of the *Epigoniad*. Though printed unsigned, it was prefaced with an editorial comment indicative of the prestige of the writer: "By perusing the following article, the reader will perceive, that how subject soever we, the Reviewers, may be to oversights and errors, we are not so hardened in critical pride, and insolence, but that, upon conviction, we can retract our censures, and provided we be candidly rebuked, kiss the rod of correction with great humility." This editorial recantation doubtless came from the pen of Smollett, possibly to mollify his Caledonian conscience for having so carelessly permitted unsympathetic accounts of both the Scottish Shakespeare and the Scottish Homer to appear in his periodical in 1757.

After calling attention to the proper uses of literary journals and to certain excusable abuses through the necessity of haste, Hume's letter proceeds:

The public has done so much justice to the gentlemen engaged in the Critical Review, as to acknowledge that no literary journal was ever carried on in this country with equal spirit and impartiality: yet I must confess that an article published in your Review of 1757, gave me great surprize, and not a little uneasiness. It regarded a book called the Epigoniad, a poem of the Epic kind, which was at that time published with great applause at Edinburgh, and of which a few copies had been sent up to London. The author of that article had surely been lying under strong prepossessions, when he spoke so negligently of a work which abounds in such sublime beauties, and could endeavour to discredit a poem, consisting of near six thousand lines, on account of a few mistakes in expression and prosody, proceeding entirely from the author's being a Scotchman, who had never been out of his own country. As there is a new edition published of this poem, wherein all or most of these trivial mistakes are corrected, I flatter myself that you will gladly lay hold of this opportunity of retracting your oversight, and doing justice to a performance, which may, perhaps, be regarded as one of the ornaments of our language. I appeal from your sentence, as an old woman did from a sentence pronounced by Philip of Macedon: I appeal from Philip, ill-counselled and in a hurry, to Philip, well-advised, and judging with deliberation. The authority which you possess with the public makes your censure fall with weight; and I question not but you will be the more ready, on that account to redress any injury, into which either negligence, prejudice, or mistake, may have betrayed you. As I profess myself to be an admirer of this performance, it will afford me pleasure to give you a short analysis of it, and to collect a few specimens of those great beauties in which it abounds. . . .

There remained a tradition among the Greeks, that Homer had taken this second siege of Thebes for the subject of a poem, which is lost; and our author seems to have pleased himself with the thoughts of reviving the work, as well as of treading in the footsteps of his favourite author. . . . The whole turn of this new poem would almost lead us to imagine, that the Scottish bard had found the lost manuscript of that father of poetry, and had made a faithful translation of it into English.

Outlining the plot of the *Epigoniad,* Hume candidly admits:

The reader may perhaps conjecture (what I am not very anxious to conceal) that the execution of the Epigoniad is better than the design, the poetry superior to the fable, and the colouring of the particular parts more excellent than the general plan of the whole. Of all the great Epic poems which have been the admiration of mankind, the Jerusalem of Tasso alone would make a tolerable novel, if reduced to prose, and related without that splendour of versification and imagery by which it is supported: yet in the opinion of many great judges, the Jerusalem is the least perfect of all these productions; chiefly, because it has least nature and simplicity in the sentiments, and is most liable to the objection of affectation and conceit. The story of a poem, whatever may be imagined, is the least essential part of it: the force of the versification, the vivacity of the images, the justness of the descriptions, the natural play of the passions, are the chief circumstances which distinguish the great poet from the prosaic novelist, and give him so high a rank among the heroes in literature: and I will venture to affirm, that all these advantages, especially the three former, are to be found in an eminent degree in the Epigoniad. The author, inspired with the true genius of Greece, and smit with the most profound veneration for Homer, disdains all frivolous ornaments; and relying entirely on his sublime imagination, and his nervous and harmonious expression, has ventured to present to his reader the naked beauties of nature, and challenges for his partizans all the admirers of genuine antiquity.

The "Letter to the *Critical Review*" concludes with mention of the Spenserian poem, which "is indeed," explains Hume, "a species of apology for the Epigoniad, wrote in a very lively and elegant manner: it may be compared," he adds, "to a well-polished gem, of the purest water, and cut into the most beautiful form." This gem expresses Wilkie's modest desire for fame as an imitator and lover of Homer. It is that "father of poetry" himself who renders the decision:

> He smil'd; and from his wreath, which well could spare
> Such boon, the wreath with which his locks were clad,
> Pluck'd a few leaves to hide my temples bare;
> The present I receiv'd with heart full glad.
> Henceforth, quoth I, I never will be sad;
> For now I shall obtain my share of fame:
> Nor will licentious wit, or envy bad,
> With bitter taunts, my verses dare to blame:
> This garland shall protect them, and exalt my name.[9]

I V

Hume's "Letter to the *Critical Review*" did not appreciably alter the verdict already handed down on the *Epigoniad*; and Wilkie, despite the indulgence of both Homer and Hume, was not granted his modicum of fame.[10] In order to specify five persons in London who deemed Wilkie "a great poet," *le bon David* was constrained to advance Lord Chesterfield as an eighteenth-century Pooh-bah. The English poet William Shenstone was unwittingly speaking for his nation when in October, 1759, he wrote Thomas Percy: "As for the Epigoniad, if you will excuse me, I will wholly decline the reading of it. My head will bear but a limited application; & it must be Books from which I have greater expectations, to which to the future I allott a part of mine. Rhime," he added significantly, "seems *actually* to have lost much ground in all Poems, of this Nature; &

[9] "A Dream," *Epigoniad*, 2d ed., p. 227.　　　[10] See Note E, below.

were Pope's Homer to make its first appearance now, he would be *greatly* blam'd for making use of it." [11]

The *Epigoniad* soon found its destined place in the limbo of rejected English epics, joining there *Prince Arthur, Gideon,* and *Leonidas.* Yet loyal Scots were loath to give up the Homer of the Lowlands. Henry Mackenzie professed to believe that Wilkie's imitation was "so successful that a person, ignorant of Greek, will, I believe, better conceive what Homer is in the original by perusing the Epigoniad, than by reading even the excellent translation of Pope." [12] Robert Fergusson, pupil of Wilkie's and predecessor of Burns, dedicated a Scottish eclogue to the memory of the fabulous Scottish Homer:

> Whose sangs will ay in Scotland be rever'd,
> While slow-gaun owsen turn the flowery swaird,
> While bonnie lammies lick the dews of spring,
> While gaudsmen whistle, or while birdies sing.[13]

Professor Carlo Denina, the Italian admirer of Scottish literature, had a kind word even for the *Epigoniad,* which, he averred, "would have been a most admirable poem, had it been wrote 2000 years ago. But as Homer is so well known in England, we cannot be surprised that Mr Wilkie has not a greater number of readers. We Italians at present neglect the *Avarchide di Luigi Alamanni,* which like the *Epigoniad,* is too close an imitation of the *Iliad.*" [14] But perhaps the last word on the *Epigoniad* was inadvertently said by Charles Lamb in a letter to Thomas Manning, describing a visit from George Dyer and Dr. James Anderson:

The Doctor, in the course of the conversation, mentioned a poem called "Epigoniad" by one Wilkie, an epic poem, in which there is not one tolerable good line all through, but every incident and speech borrowed from Homer. George had been sitting inattentive seemingly to what was going on—hatching of negative quantities—when, suddenly, the name of his old friend Homer stung his pericranicks, and, jumping up, he begged to know where he could meet with Wilkie's work. "It was a curious fact that there should be such an epic poem and he not know of it; and he

---

[11] Shenstone, *Letters*, p. 371.   [12] *Life of Home,* p. 16.
[13] "An Eclogue, to the Memory of Dr William Wilkie."
[14] Quoted in *Scots Magazine,* XXVI (1764), 467.

must get a copy of it, as he was going to touch pretty deeply upon the sub-ject of the Epic—and he was sure there must be some things good in a poem of 1400 lines!" I was pleased with this transient return of his reason and recurrence to his old ways of thinking.[15]

Sad end of an epic to become a test of sanity!

V

Wilkie's literary career was not over with the second edition of the *Epigoniad*. In 1759 he became Professor of Natural Philosophy in St. Andrews University, where he was venerated as a perfect specimen of the absent-minded professor. Meeting a student on the street one day, Professor Wilkie inquired:

"I am sorry to hear, my dear boy, that you have had the fever in your family. Was it you or your brother who died of it?"

"It was I, Sir," replied the young wag.

"Ah, dear me, I thought so. Very sorry for it." [16]

The academic routine did not dampen Wilkie's poetical ardor; and in 1768 a volume of *Fables* met with the same inglorious reception as the late lamented epic. The concluding poem, "A Dialogue. The Author and a Friend," is an ingenuous confession of literary faith:

> Be't so; I claim by precedent and rule
> A free-born Briton's right, to play the fool:
> My resolution's fix'd, my course I'll hold,
> In spite of all your arguments when told:
> Whether I'm well and up, or keep my bed,
> Am warm and full, or neither cloath'd nor fed,
> Whether my fortune's kind, or in a pet
> Am banish'd by the laws, or fled for debt;
> Whether in Newgate, Bedlam, or the Mint,
> I'll write as long as publishers will print.[17]

Speaking modestly through his friend in the same poem, Pro-fessor Wilkie linked his fate with that of the second Scottish Homer,

[15] Lamb, *Letters*, I, 213.
[16] Thompson, *A Scottish Man of Feeling*, pp. 46-47.
[17] *Fables*, pp. 138-39.

who had in the meantime made a startling advent into the literary
realm:

> You take me wrong: I only meant to say,
> That ev'ry book that's new will have its day;
> The best no more: for books are seldom read;
> The world's grown dull, and publishing a trade.
> Were this not so, cou'd OSSIAN's deathless strains,
> Of high heroic times the sole remains,
> Strains which display perfections to our view,
> Which polish'd Greece and Italy ne'er knew,
> With modern Epics share one common lot,
> This day applauded and the next forgot? [18]

The appearance of James Macpherson in 1760 had removed any
remote possibility that William Wilkie might be remembered as
the Scottish Homer. Though David Hume had been unable to persuade many non-Scots to read the *Epigoniad*, there was no necessity
for persuasion so far as Ossian was concerned. Therein lay Hume's
ultimate embarrassment, for that genial skeptic was never completely
taken in by Macpherson's guile. The honor of Scotland was at stake;
and, as national literary spokesman, that was Hume's express concern.

THE HOMER OF THE HIGHLANDS

The role of David Hume as guardian of Scottish literary integrity is apparent throughout the Ossian affair. Possibly the none too
happy efforts in behalf of Thomas Blacklock, John Home, and
William Wilkie had left the philosopher vigilant of this portentous
new literary meteor. Yet the case of Macpherson differed fundamentally from theirs. With the Scottish Pindar, the Scottish Shakespeare,
and the first Scottish Homer, the problem was primarily one of
criticism—though beclouded, to be sure, by benevolence, friendship,
and nationalism. With Macpherson, however, prior to all criticism,
was the problem of authenticity, for his claims were advanced solely
as translator. From the outset, therefore, Hume's nationalistic pride
over the second Scottish Homer was tempered by his philosophy of
skepticism, of suspending belief until there is evidence for believing.

[18] *Ibid.*, p. 126.

I

The Homer of the Highlands was first discovered in 1759 when he was taking the cure at Moffat together with John Home, the Scottish Shakespeare. James Macpherson, born in 1736 at Ruthven, Inverness-shire, received his early education at Inverness. Proceeding to the universities of Aberdeen and of Edinburgh, he returned in 1756 to become schoolmaster in his home town. Two years later he made his literary debut, publishing at Edinburgh a six-canto poem entitled *The Highlander*. Wholly unsuccessful in this venture, the young poet momentarily hesitated between a career of preaching and teaching, finally to accept a position as private tutor.

It was eminently fitting that John Home, having derived his own tragedy of *Douglas* from an ancient ballad, should be the discoverer of James Macpherson, who exploited other ancient ballads for two complete epics. Ever since William Collins had presented him with "An Ode on the Popular Superstitions of the Highlands of Scotland, Considered as the Subject of Poetry," John had been on the lookout for folk motifs. Not unnaturally, when he met Macpherson that subject arose. The incident has been recounted by David Hume: "These two gentlemen were drinking the waters together at Moffat last autumn, when their conversation fell upon Highland poetry, which Mr Macpherson extolled very highly. Our friend, who knew him to be a good scholar, and a man of taste, found his curiosity excited, and asked whether he had ever translated any of them. Mr Macpherson replied, that he never had attempted any such thing; and doubted whether it was possible to transfuse such beauties into our language; but, for Mr Home's satisfaction, and in order to give him a general notion of the strain of that wild poetry, he would endeavour to turn one of them into English. He accordingly brought him one next day, which our friend was so much pleased with, that he never ceased soliciting Mr Macpherson, till he insensibly produced that small volume which has been published."

That small volume was the famous *Fragments of Ancient Poetry, Collected in the Highlands of Scotland, and Translated from the Galic or Erse Language,* published anonymously at Edinburgh early in 1760. An anonymous Preface by the Rev. Hugh Blair, popular lecturer on literature, reassuringly promised that, "The Public may depend on the following Fragments as genuine Remains of ancient Scottish Poetry." The unpretentious collection was favorably received both north and south of the Tweed. Though some doubts were expressed of the fragments' actually representing the work of a Caledonian bard of the third century, there was no doubt that they were distinctive.

The first of the fifteen fragments which confronted the readers of 1760 was the sentimental and pathetic "Shilric, Vinvela":

VINVELA: My Love is a Son of the Hill. He pursues the flying Deer. His grey Dogs are panting around him; his Bow-string sounds in the Wind. Whether by the Fount of the Rock, or by the Stream of the Mountain thou liest; when the Rushes are nodding with the Wind, and the Mist is flying over thee, let me approach my Love unperceived, and see him from the Rock. Lovely I saw thee first by the aged Oak of *Branno;* thou wert returning tall from the Chace; the fairest among thy Friends.

SHILRIC: What Voice is that I hear? That Voice like the Summer-wind.—I sit not by the nodding Rushes; I hear not the Fount of the Rock. Afar, *Vinvela,* afar I go to the Wars of *Fingal.* My Dogs attend me no more. No more I tread the Hill. No more from on high I see thee, fair-moving by the Stream of the Plain; bright as the Bow of Heaven; as the Moon on the western Wave.

VINVELA: Then thou art gone, O *Shilric!* and I am alone on the Hill. The Deer are seen on the Brow; void of Fear they graze along. No more they dread the Wind; no more the rustling Tree. The Hunter is far removed; he is in the Field of Graves. Strangers! Sons of the Waves! spare my lovely *Shilric.*

SHILRIC: If fall I must in the Field, raise high my Grave, *Vinvela.* Grey Stones, and heaped-up Earth, shall mark me to future Times. When the Hunter shall sit by the Mound, and produce his Food at Noon, "Some Warrior rests here," he will say; and my Fame shall live in his Praise. Remember me, *Vinvela,* when low on Earth I lie!

VINVELA: Yes!—I will remember thee—indeed my *Shilric* will fall. What shall I do, my Love! when thou art gone for ever! Through these

Hills I will go at Noon: I will go through the silent Heath. There I will see the Place of thy Rest, returning from the Chace. Indeed, my *Shilric* will fall; but I will remember him.

Mr. David Hume had some critical qualms about this rhythmical prose and inquired whether the fastidious Mr. Thomas Gray did not detect many actual verses in it, "and all of them in the same measure with Mr Shenstone's famous ballad":

> Ye shepherds so careless and free,
> Whose flocks never carelessly roam, &c.,

and whether Gray deemed such verses a blemish. Mr. William Shenstone, for his part, professed delight with the *Fragments*, found the moment favorable for experimentation with the cadences of prose, but intimated that the translator might conceivably have had "a finer ear." [19]

Critics were particularly intrigued with the announcement in the Preface that several of the present poems were but fragments of "one Work of considerable Length, and which deserves to be styled an heroic Poem." "Every body in Edinburgh," continued Hume in the above letter of August, 1760, was so convinced that the poems "had become in a manner national works" that:

> we have endeavoured to put Mr Macpherson on a way of procuring us more of these wild flowers. He is a modest, sensible young man, not settled in any living, but employed as a private tutor in Mr Grahame of Balgowan's family, a way of life which he is not fond of. We have, therefore, set about a subscription of a guinea or two guineas apiece, in order to enable him to quit that family, and undertake a mission into the Highlands, where he hopes to recover more of these fragments. There is, in particular, a country surgeon somewhere in Lochaber, who, he says, can recite a great number of them, but never committed them to writing; as indeed the orthography of the Highland language is not fixed, and the natives have always employed more the sword than the pen. This surgeon has by heart the epic poem mentioned by Mr Macpherson in his preface; and as he is somewhat old, and is the only person living that has it entire, we are in the more haste to recover a monument, which will certainly be regarded as a curiosity in the Republic of Letters.

[19] Shenstone, *Letters*, pp. 423, 428.

The first fruit of this subsidized Highland expedition appeared late in 1761 [20] as *Fingal; an Ancient Epic Poem, in Six Books: Together with Several Other Poems, Composed by Ossian, the Son of Fingal. Translated from the Galic Language, by James Macpherson.* A second expedition produced in 1763 *Temora; an Ancient Epic Poem, in Eight Books: Together with Several Other Poems, Composed by Ossian, the Son of Fingal. Translated from the Galic Language, by James Macpherson.* Like Homer, Ossian now had his two epics; and the parallel could be used either to praise or to damn. Political as well as literary criticism was involved since it was well known that Lord Bute had supplied the financial backing for the publications.

Smollett's *Critical Review* enthusiastically hailed Ossian. But the conservative *Monthly Review* [21] had suggestively remarked of the *Fragments*, "Did we put no confidence in the assertion of the anonymous Editor, we should think, notwithstanding such evident marks of authenticity, that they *might be* the production of a later age," and now was frankly hostile to *Fingal:* "As the production of an antient Scottish or Irish bard, this work is undoubtedly an object of great curiosity, and worthy of admiration; but, considered in the light of an Epic Poem, and set in comparison with those of Homer and Virgil, it looks like the statue of a dwarf beside the Colossal Apollo of Rhodes." The account of *Temora* states fully the controversial issues as they appeared in 1763:

Indeed, notwithstanding all the pains Mr. M'Pherson hath taken to convince the public of the regularity of tradition among the Highland Songsters, we cannot help thinking, that both Fingal and Temora are (as he confesses of the latter) "in some measure become his own." Not that we mention this to derogate from the merit of the work, or of the Editor; or that we doubt of the authenticity of these poems, farther than what relates to their general form and composition. There is, indeed, very little room for any farther doubt; for we may say, of these poems, as a celebrated French Writer expressed himself, on a different occasion, that they abound with strokes *si grands, si frappans, si parfaitement inimitables, que l'Inven-*

[20] Dated 1762 on the title page.
[21] *Monthly Review*, XXIII (1760), 204-11; XXVI (1762), 41-57, 130-41; XXVIII (1763), 274-81.

teur en seroit plus etonnant que le Heros. In like manner, it hath been often observed on this occasion, that to have written thus in the character of Ossian, Mr. M'Pherson must have had much greater talents than Ossian himself. We must own, nevertheless, that we should have been pleased to have found our Editor still more explicit on this head; as it was what the public expected, and, perhaps, had a right to expect, after the very favourable reception and encouragement it afforded his design. It is true, he hath here published a part of the original of Temora: but this bears too small a proportion to the whole to be very satisfactory. There is also something singular in his manner of excusing himself from publicly giving any farther proofs of the authenticity, which he confesses to be pretty generally called in question. . . . "To me . . . ['these suspicions'] give no concern, as I have it always in my power to remove them."

A few lines of verse quoted in the same article—

> A Scot's a genius, if he write and read;
> And all's sublime that comes across the Tweed;
> But from the Highlands, 'tis a matchless prize;
> 'Tis dropt from heaven; 'twas written in the skies!—

are good-natured raillery and very different from the productions of the Scotch-baiting Wilkes and Churchill. In *The Poetry Professors* Wilkes offered advice and hinted at politics:

> Better be native in thy verse,—
> What is *Fingal* but genuine Erse?
> Which all sublime sonorous flows,
> Like Hervey's Thoughts in drunken Prose.
>
> . . .
>
> Macpherson leads the flaming Van,
> Laird of the *new* Fingalian Clan;
> While Jacky Home brings up the rear,
> With new-got pension, neat and clear,
> Three hundred *English* pounds a year.

In the *Prophecy of Famine* Churchill acknowledged England's indebtedness to Scotland:

> Thence issued forth, at great Macpherson's call,
> That old, new epic pastoral, Fingal;

and in *The Ghost* he belabored the literary critics:

> By truth inspired, our critics go
> To track *Fingal* in Highland snow,
> To form their own and others' creed
> From manuscripts they cannot read.

No doubt the English were also aroused by the effusive praise of the Highland epic poet that continued to flow from the pen of Hugh Blair, now become Professor of Rhetoric and Belles-Lettres at the University of Edinburgh. His *Critical Dissertation on the Poems of Ossian, the Son of Fingal* of 1763 assumed as axiomatic that Ossian was a poet of the same caliber as Homer and Virgil, Dante, Tasso, and Milton. Proceeding to apply "the Rules of Criticism to Fingal, as an Epic Poem," Blair demonstrated its artistic unity and extolled its sublimities as "The Poetry of the Heart." Nothing short of Homeric perfection sufficed. "Aristotle," argued Professor Blair with somewhat less than Aristotelian logic, "studied nature in Homer. Homer and Ossian both wrote from nature. No wonder that among all the three, there should be such agreement and conformity." [22]

II

It was at this most logical juncture that David Hume intervened to direct the controversy toward ascertainable matters of fact. Making the distinction between "authenticity" and "great antiquity," Hume had early expressed the conviction, on the basis of reports that the fragments "are in every body's mouth in the Highlands," that they were, in some sense, authentic translations from the Gaelic. But as to their great antiquity, he was not completely satisfied; "and if a regular epic poem, or even anything of that kind, nearly regular, should also come from that rough climate or uncivilized people, it would appear to me a phenomenon altogether unaccountable." Hume was also perfectly aware of the influence of "national prepossessions," which, he granted, were "a little strong." Nevertheless, on February 9, 1761, he had provided James Macpherson, en route to London to arrange for the publication of *Fingal*, with a glowing letter to

---

[22] *Critical Dissertation*, Advertisement, and pp. 21, 24.

William Strahan, introducing him as the translator of the *Fragments* and as "a sensible, modest young Fellow, a very good Scholar, and of unexceptionable Morals."

By 1762, however, Hume was becoming more and more distressed over the turn of events. Macpherson was no longer the "sensible, modest young Fellow" who with seeming reluctance had let himself be persuaded to publish the *Fragments*, and Blair's impending *Dissertation* might do more harm than good by overmuch praise. On November 4 Hume discussed the whole situation with his young friend, James Boswell. "*Fingal*," he pointed out, "is not much heard of at present. The English were exceedingly fond of it at first but hearing that it was Scotch, they became jealous and silent. Doctor Blair's *Dissertation* will awaken attention to it. It is a fine piece of criticism; but it were to be wished that he had kept it a little lower than Homer. For it might be a very excellent Poem and yet fall short of *the Iliad*. Macpherson, the Translator, is a most curious fellow. He is full of highland Prejudices. He hates a Republic and he does not like Kings. He would have all the Nation divided into Clans, and these clans to be allways fighting. He has got a dislike to study and cannot settle to read a quarter of an hour. Lord Bute does not know what to do with him. . . . As he is a Scotchman, Lord Bute does not chuse to put him upon the list of Pensioners, and therefore generously gives him two hundred a year out of his own pocket." [23]

The publication by 1763 of Macpherson's two epics and of Blair's misguided *Dissertation* precipitated such violent hostility as finally to impel Hume to see what might be done to settle the fundamental issue of authenticity. So, on September 19, 1763, he forwarded to Hugh Blair from London the outlines of a sweeping factual investigation:

DEAR SIR,

I live in a place where I have the pleasure of frequently hearing justice done to your Dissertation; but never heard it mentioned in a company where some one person or other did not express his doubts with regard to the authenticity of the Poems, which are its subject; and I often hear them totally rejected with disdain and indignation, as a palpable and most impu-

[23] Boswell, *Private Papers*, I, 127-28.

dent forgery. This opinion has indeed become very prevalent among the men of letters in London, and I can foresee, that in a few years the poems, if they continue to stand on their present footing, will be thrown aside, and will fall into final oblivion. It is in vain to say, that their beauty will support them, independent of their authenticity: No; that beauty is not so much to the general taste as to ensure you of this event; and if people be once disgusted with the idea of a forgery, they are thence apt to entertain a more disadvantageous notion of the excellency of the production itself. The absurd pride and caprice of Macpherson himself, who scorns, as he pretends, to satisfy any body, that doubts his veracity, has tended much to confirm this general scepticism: and I must own, for my own part, that, though I have had many particular reasons to believe these poems genuine, more than it is possible for any Englishman of letters to have, yet I am not entirely without my scruples on that head. You think that the internal proofs in favour of the poems are very convincing; so they are; but there are also internal reasons against them, particularly from the manners, notwithstanding all the art, with which you have endeavoured to throw a varnish on that circumstance: and the preservation of such long, and such connected poems by oral tradition alone, during a course of fourteen centuries, is so much out of the ordinary course of human affairs, that it requires the strongest reasons to make us believe it. My present purpose therefore is, to apply to you in the name of all the men of letters of this, and I may say of all other centuries, to establish this capital point, and to give us proof that these poems are, I do not say so ancient as the age of Severus, but that they were not forged within these five years by James Macpherson. These proofs must not be arguments, but testimonies. People's ears are fortified against the former; the latter may yet find their way, before the poems are consigned to total oblivion. Now the testimonies may, in my opinion, be of two kinds. Macpherson pretends that there is an ancient manuscript of part of Fingal in the family, I think, of Clanronald. Get that fact ascertained by more than one person of credit; let these persons be acquainted with the Galic; let them compare the original and the translation; and let them testify the fidelity of the latter.

But the chief point in which it will be necessary for you to exert yourself, will be to get positive testimony from many different hands, that such poems are vulgarly recited in the Highlands, and have there been long the entertainment of the people. This testimony must be as particular as it is positive: it will not be sufficient, that a Highland gentleman or clergyman say or write to you that he has heard such poems: nobody questions, that there are traditional poems in that part of the country where the names of

Ossian and Fingal, and Oscar and Gaul, are mentioned in every stanza. The only doubt is whether these poems have any farther resemblance to the poems published by Macpherson. I was told by Burke, a very ingenious Irish gentleman, the author of a tract on the Sublime and Beautiful, that on the first publication of Macpherson's book, all the Irish cried out, *we know all these poems, we have always heard them from our infancy*. But when he asked more particular questions, he could never learn, that any one had ever heard, or could repeat the original of any one paragraph of the pretended translation. This generality then, must be carefully guarded against, as being of no authority.

Acceding to Hume's warning that "the child is, in a manner, become yours by adoption, as Macpherson has totally abandoned all care of it," Blair determined to make good his own lack of Gaelic by following the instructions specified. And Hume wrote again at the beginning of October: "I am very glad you have undertaken the task which I used the freedom to recommend to you. Nothing less than what you propose will serve the purpose. You need expect no assistance from Macpherson, who flew into a passion when I told him of the letter I had wrote to you. But you must not mind so strange and heteroclite a mortal, than whom I have scarce ever known a man more perverse and unamiable. He will probably depart for Florida with Governor Johnstone, and I would advise him to travel among the Chickisaws or Cherokees, in order to tame him and civilize him." Yet, despite the best and the most honorable intentions, it becomes all too apparent in the event that Blair never really understood the full import of Hume's insistence that the testimony be "as particular as it is positive." Succeeding only in playing Watson to Hume's Sherlock, the gentle, fussy, little Edinburgh Professor of Rhetoric and Belles-Lettres was never able to solve the mysterious case of Macpherson and the purloined manuscripts.

Though always exceedingly polite to his good friend, Hume continued in his private opinion of the Ossianic poems, "that, tho' great Beauties, they are greater Curiosities, and that they are a little tedious by reason of their Uniformity." "I cannot but allow," he wrote on another occasion, "that the whole is strange, passing strange." Even after Blair's testimonial Appendix of 1765 had expressly certified that, "Ossian has been always reputed the Homer

of the Highlands," [24] Hume explained that, "My Scepticism extends
no farther, nor ever did, than with regard to the extreme Antiquity
of those Poems; and it is no more than Scepticism." The following
year he bantered the professor, "No body ever heard you express
any Remorse for having put Ossian on the same footing with
Homer."

I I I

The furor over Ossian, though temporarily augmented in 1765
with the presentation of Blair's new evidence, had pretty generally
subsided by 1770. Upon Macpherson's return from his Chickisaws
and Cherokees, he appeared, indeed, to have abandoned fine letters
for politics in becoming journalistic hack to Lord Bute. But his
Introduction to the History of Great Britain and Ireland of 1771, a
highhanded attempt to substantiate his earlier thesis that Ireland
had been settled through Scotland rather than the reverse as was
customarily believed, was also an answer to those Irish scholars and
patriots who maintained that Ossian was Hibernian and not Caledonian. The astonishing scholarship of the new historian prompted
Hume's comment to Adam Smith that, "of all men of Parts," Macpherson "has the most anti-historical Head in the Universe." There
will be few to disagree with that expert judgment.

In 1773, presumably at the instigation of Hugh Blair, Adam
Ferguson, and William Robertson, Macpherson turned his hand
directly to Homer with a translation of the *Iliad*. This English prose
version, he blandly assured his readers, was not "MERE PROSE"; but
he added quixotically, "He has the vanity to think, that, with the
expence of a little more time, than he has employed, in his present
version, he might have been able to have presented the Iliad to the
Public, in English blank verse." [25] Yet no Homeric translation was
ever blanker or ever fell flatter. Critics and public alike were scan-
dalized that the man who had Homerized Ossian should now Ossian-
ize Homer. Robertson, however, was not to be gainsaid his praise
of Macpherson: "It is the only translation in which Homer appears
like an ancient poet in his own simple magnificence." [26] But Hume

[24] Appendix to *Crit. Diss.*, in *Works of Ossian*, II, 450.
[25] Preface to *Iliad*, pp. xviii, xix.
[26] Quoted by Saunders, *Life and Letters of Macpherson*, p. 222.

queried of Adam Smith: "Have you seen Macpherson's Homer? It is hard to tell whether the Attempt or the Execution be worse." Again, Hume's judgment is unimpeachable.

The main Ossianic controversy, however, was really only quiescent. In 1773 it flared up to new heights when Dr. Johnson took the tour of Scotland with Boswell. Ten years previous on a visit to London, Hugh Blair had "found the Giant in his den," as he facetiously remarked to Boswell.[27] The subject of Ossian inevitably came up, and Blair ventured to ask Dr. Johnson whether he thought any man of a modern age could have written such poems. Unaware of Blair's recently published *Dissertation*, Johnson replied with deliberation, "Yes, Sir, many men, many women, and many children."

Despite this rebuff, the buoyant Blair in 1764 had boasted to Hume, then in Paris, that "I have converted even that Barbarian Sam. Johnston . . . who as L. Elibank tells me owns himself now convinced. Will you still have any Scruples? I assure you, & you may assure all France, that they are genuine antient Highland Poems; though the precise Æra of their antiquity I never attempted to fix." [28] Blair, however, had either been misinformed or gulled concerning the conversion of the great English "Barbarian"; for in 1768 Johnson clinched an argument with Boswell over the future life of brutes by urging that if Blair's soul was allowed to be immortal, why not a dog's? [29] And now in 1773 much local inquiry in the Highlands only confirmed Johnson's original skepticism. By the end of 1774 it was generally rumored in literary circles that his forthcoming *Journey to the Western Islands of Scotland* would publicly attack James Macpherson.

Growing apprehensive of the impending blow at his reputation, that worthy politely sought to have the literary dictator retract his "injurious expressions" before publication. But Johnson had made up his mind that Macpherson was "the father of Ossian," and that was that. Ill-advisedly, the irate parent now resorted to threats, and may actually have gone so far as to challenge the aged man of letters to

[27] *Life of Johnson*, I, 396.
[28] Blair, MS letter, Royal Society of Edinburgh, Hume MSS, III, 53.
[29] Boswell, *Private Papers*, VII, 176.

a duel. So justly indignant was Johnson at this barbarity, that he bought a stout cudgel to defend his person and wrote Macpherson one of the most famous letters [30] in the English language:

MR JAMES MACPHERSON—I received your foolish and impudent note. Whatever insult is offered me I will do my best to repel, and what I cannot do for myself the law will do for me. I will not desist from detecting what I think a cheat, from any fear of the menaces of a Ruffian.

You want me to retract. What shall I retract? I thought your book an imposture from the beginning, I think it upon yet surer reasons an imposture still. For this opinion I give the publick my reasons which I here dare you to refute.

But however I may despise you, I reverence truth and if you can prove the genuineness of the work I will confess it. Your rage I defy, your abilities, since your Homer are not so formidable, and what I have heard of your morals disposes me to pay regard not to what you shall say, but to what you can prove.

You may print this if you will.

Jan. 20. 1775   SAM: JOHNSON

The great Doctor had spoken, and Macpherson forcibly subsided into impotent silence.

However indisputably right Johnson was in his published exposure of Macpherson's fabrications, he was certainly less than generous in his attitude toward those Scots who had been innocently duped. Equally skeptical of the great antiquity of the alleged Ossianic translations, David Hume was provoked by Johnson's tone of superiority and shocked by his unseemly abuse of Scotland. This was not casual conversation or private correspondence, in both of which exaggeration may be condoned, but the published work of a highly respected literary critic and moralist. Was such a man in earnest when he wrote that, "The Scots have something to plead for their easy reception of an improbable fiction: they are seduced by their fondness for their supposed ancestors. *A Scotchman must be a very sturdy moralist, who does not love* Scotland *better than truth: he will always love it better than inquiry; and if falsehood flatters his vanity, will not*

---

[30] *R. B. Adam Library,* I, 58, with photographic reproduction of the original.

be very diligent to detect it"? [31] And if he was not in earnest, why did he so irresponsibly affront an entire nation?

Dr. Johnson had clearly not reckoned with David Hume and his lifelong dedication to the pursuit of truth. Here, indeed, *was* a very sturdy moralist. Faced with clearing the national character of Scotland while granting the imposture of one Scotsman, with maintaining the good faith of Hugh Blair, Adam Ferguson, John Home, William Wilkie, and the other believers in the Homer of the Highlands while exposing the bad faith of James Macpherson, Hume the Inquirer composed a brief tract, *Of the Authenticity of Ossian's Poems*.[32] This penetrating eighteenth-century critique on that much disputed subject opens with a smashing indictment of Macpherson:

I think the fate of this production the most curious effect of prejudice, where superstition had no share, that ever was in the world. A tiresome, insipid performance; which, if it had been presented in its real form, as the work of a contemporary, an obscure Highlander, no man could ever have had the patience to have once perused, has, by passing for the poetry of a royal bard, who flourished fifteen centuries ago, been universally read, has been pretty generally admired, and has been translated, in prose and verse, into several languages of Europe. Even the style of the supposed English translation has been admired, though harsh and absurd in the highest degree; jumping perpetually from verse to prose, and from prose to verse; and running, most of it, in the light cadence and measure of Molly Mog. Such is the Erse epic, which has been puffed with a zeal and enthusiasm that has drawn a ridicule on my countrymen.

But, to cut off at once the whole source of its reputation, I shall collect a few very obvious arguments against the notion of its great antiquity, with which so many people have been intoxicated, and which alone made it worthy of any attention.

Hume then proceeds with ten ingenious arguments from the external evidences, the internal evidences, and the character of the author. The two important related problems of Blair's *Dissertation* and of the national character of Scotland are handled with extreme delicacy:

[31] *Boswell and Johnson Tour*, p. 108. My italics.
[32] *Phil. Works*, IV, 415-24. The "Molly Mog" of the first paragraph is the ballad by John Gay.

But it may reasonably be expected [continues Hume] that I should mention the external positive evidence, which is brought by Dr. Blair to support the authenticity of these poems. I own, that this evidence, considered in itself, is very respectable, and sufficient to support any fact, that both lies within the bounds of credibility, and has not become a matter of party. But will any man pretend to bring human testimony to prove, that above twenty thousand verses have been transmitted, by tradition and memory, during more than fifteen hundred years; that is, above fifty generations, according to the ordinary course of nature? verses, too, which have not, in their subject, any thing alluring or inviting to the people, no miracle, no wonders, no superstitions, no useful instruction; a people, too, who, during twelve centuries, at least, of that period, had no writing, no alphabet; and who, even in the other three centuries, made very little use of that imperfect alphabet for any purpose; a people who, from the miserable disadvantages of their soil and climate, were perpetually struggling with the greatest necessities of nature; who, from the imperfections of government, lived in a continual state of internal hostility; ever harassed with the incursions of neighbouring tribes, or meditating revenge and retaliation on their neighbours. Have such a people leisure to think of any poetry, except, perhaps, a miserable song or ballad, in praise of their own chieftain, or to the disparagement of his rivals?

I should be sorry to be suspected of saying any thing against the manners of the present Highlanders. I really believe that, besides their signal bravery, there is not any people in Europe, not even excepting the Swiss, who have more plain honesty and fidelity, are more capable of gratitude and attachment, than that race of men. Yet it was, no doubt, a great surprise to them to hear that, over and above their known good qualities, they were also possessed of an excellence which they never dreamt of, an elegant taste in poetry, and inherited from the most remote antiquity the finest compositions of that kind, far surpassing the popular traditional poems of any other language; no wonder they crowded to give testimony in favour of their authenticity. Most of them, no doubt, were sincere in the delusion; the same names that were to be found in their popular ballads were carefully preserved in the new publication; some incidents, too, were perhaps transferred from the one to the other; some sentiments also might be copied; and, on the whole, they were willing to believe, and still more willing to persuade others, that the whole was genuine. On such occasions, the greatest cloud of witnesses makes no manner of evidence. . . .

The only real wonder in the whole affair is, that a person of so fine a taste as Dr. Blair, should be so great an admirer of these productions; and one of so clear and cool a judgment collect evidence of their authenticity.

Hume's critique was directly inspired by Johnson's *Journey to the Western Islands of Scotland,* which had appeared about the middle of January, 1775. According to Boswell, who visited him on March 6, Hume was full of resentment over the book and pointed out wherein his own rejection of Ossian differed from Johnson's. To Johnson it was purely a question of evidence (*Where are the manuscripts?*); while to Hume it was a question of the whole nature of the thing, as in the similar philosophical argument of his *Essay on Miracles.* The conversation with Boswell [33] affords an informal version of the major points of the critique, which presumably had recently been completed or was even then being written. Almost certainly it was completed before the middle of June, for by that time Hume had become acquainted with Macpherson's newly published *History of Great Britain, from the Restoration, to the Accession of the House of Hannover*—"the worst style he had ever read," he told Boswell.[34] Neither this work nor its two companion volumes of *Original Papers* is mentioned by Hume in that section of his critique examining the character of Macpherson as evidenced through a catalogue of "all his publications." *Of the Authenticity of Ossian's Poems* had already been set aside and was never revised. Also it was never published by Hume.

In exploding Macpherson as an impudent impostor, Johnson had incidentally libeled the national character of Scotland. Hume's critique was designed to defend the honor of his native country by demonstrating, first, that at least one Scottish Inquirer was even more thoroughly skeptical of Ossian than the Englishman; and, second, that the Scottish "will to believe" in a national heroic poem was a perfectly natural psychological phenomenon and in no wise immoral. If Hume had published his critique in 1775 or 1776, it would indubitably have aroused widespread interest as the authentic reply of enlightened Scotland, openly repudiating the fraudulence of Macpherson and tacitly—for it names no names—rebuking the intemperance of Johnson. Why then, it may well be asked, did he not publish?

It was certainly not because of any fear of Macpherson. It was just as certainly not because of any fear of Johnson. The reason that Hume did not publish was respect for his friends. The case is illus-

[33] See Chapter 7, sec. II, below.   [34] Boswell, *Letters,* I, 231.

trative of the perennial conflict between the two aspects of Hume's character, the Inquirer after truth and *le bon David*. Hume the Inquirer was constantly arriving at conclusions that made it difficult for *le bon David* to remain on companionable terms with the less philosophical. "Scotland," he had confided to the broad-minded Adam Smith in 1759, "suits my Fortune best, & is the Seat of my principal Friendships; but it is too narrow a Place for me, and it mortifies me that I sometimes hurt my Friends." Nothing in 1775 would more have hurt his friends than the publication of the Ossianic critique; nothing, therefore, would more have mortified *le bon David*.

"Zeal for Ossian, and for the Island in which I was born," Lord Kames had written Mrs. Montagu in 1771, "made me seriously think of setting about a vindication of that poet as a true historian; and after making many collections from various authors, I have been successful beyond my hope." [35] This intransigent attitude on the part of distinguished literary Scots acted upon Hume as a deterrent from publishing. Such friends as Hugh Blair and John Home were even more intimately associated with Macpherson than Lord Kames. Hume's letter [36] of June 9, 1775, to John Home, discoverer, defender, and imitator of Ossian, clarifies his personal problem: "You are so much mistaken Dear John, in your Conjecture, that Macpherson's Name was never so much as mention'd in Company yesterday. But really, I know not for what reason I may not declare every where my Sentiments of him and all his Productions, except where you are present, since it disobliges you: For I am not likely to meet with any body else, that will care a farthing about the matter. . . . However, as Macpherson and his History begin to be very little spoke of, and soon will never be spoke of at all, it is not likely I shall ever have occasion to mention them again; and for a very small Inducement cou'd promise you never to mention them. Tho' it is unlikely that you shou'd make your Peace of Mind depend upon the Opinion of the World with regard to Macpherson." Again on February 8, 1776, he wrote to the martial poet, his "Dear Tyrtæus," of "the Effrontery" and "the Absurdity by which that learned Gen-

[35] Tytler, *Life of Kames*, II, 90.
[36] Hume, MS letter, National Library of Scotland, MS 1034, No. 100.

tleman's Writings are so eminently distinguished," but then inquired apologetically, "Are you angry with me for what I have said of Macpherson?" [37]

Ossian, *le bon David* must ultimately have become convinced, was insufficient cause for straining such fine friendships as those with Hugh Blair, John Home, and William Robertson. For life is not solely a matter of the intellect, and compromise on nonessentials may make for increased happiness. Besides, Hume was in no mood to stir up unpleasantness of any variety. "In spring 1775," he placidly noted in *My Own Life*, "I was struck with a Disorder in my Bowels, which at first gave me no Alarm, but has since, as I apprehend it, become mortal and incurable." The Inquirer had done his task and the critique was written. *Le bon David* would leave the manuscript among his papers and let his literary executor, Adam Smith, decide about publication. Smith apparently elected to let well enough alone; and the tract did not see the light until 1846, more than seventy years after it had first been called into being by Dr. Johnson's warranted attack on Macpherson and unwarranted attack on the Scottish national character.[38]

IV

The Ossianic debate was not closed by Johnson's outburst, though it might conceivably have been by Hume's critique had he seen fit to publish. In the meanwhile, Ossian was accepted as a reliable source for ancient history by so diligent an antiquarian as Dr. Robert Henry. Henry's partiality for Ossian was but added proof of Hume's analysis of national wishful thinking. This blunder, however, did not deter *le bon David* in 1773 from writing a friendly review of the second volume of Henry's *History of Great Britain* when asked to do so by the much persecuted author.[39]

Edward Gibbon, more critical historian than Henry, manifested

[37] Hume, MS letter, Edinburgh University Library, MSS Laing, II, 173. The version in Hume, *Letters*, is incomplete.

[38] See Note F, below.

[39] E. C. Mossner, "Hume as Literary Patron; a Suppressed Review of Robert Henry's *History of Great Britain*, 1773," *Modern Philology*, XXXIX (1942), 361-82.

cavalier doubts of "the pleasing supposition, that Fingal lived, and that Ossian sung." When the first volume of the *Decline and Fall* was published in 1776, "a letter from Mr Hume," the author candidly admitted, "overpaid the labour of ten years." [40] Expressing high regard for Gibbon's work as well as feigning polite surprise that a contemporary Englishman could write so well, Hume referred to Ossian: "I see you entertain a great Doubt with regard to the Authenticity of the Poems of Ossian. You are certainly right in so doing. It is, indeed, strange, that any men of Sense coud have imagin'd it possible, that above twenty thousand Verses, along with numberless historical Facts, could have been preservd by oral Tradition during fifty Generations, by the rudest, perhaps, of all European Nations; the most necessitous, the most turbulent, and the most unsettled. Where a Supposition is so contrary to common Sense, any positive Evidence of it ought never to be regarded. Men run with great Avidity to give their Evidence in favour of what flatters their Passions, and their national Prejudices. You are, therefore, over and above indulgent to us in speaking of the Matter with Hesitation."

The final attitude of two eminent Scots, both of whom at first were believers in Ossian, is indicative that the force of "national Prejudices" was spending itself. Henry Mackenzie, who as titular Scottish Man of Feeling welcomed all Noble Savages, published in 1805 the results of the first public investigation into Ossian. The *Report of the Committee of the Highland Society of Scotland, Appointed to Inquire into the Nature and the Authenticity of the Poems of Ossian* concluded that, while there was an undoubted body of genuine Ossianic poetry, there was no positive evidence that Macpherson had actually translated from ancient manuscripts. Although Hume's *Of the Authenticity of Ossian's Poems* was unknown to Mackenzie and his committee, they were proud to open their *Report* with the full quotation of his letters of 1763 to Blair. "It is flattering to the Committee," wrote Hume's former literary page, "that the line of conduct here chalked out for the Doctor by his illustrious friend, is not dissimilar to that which, without the advantages of

---

[40] Gibbon, *Decline and Fall*, chap. vi; *Memoirs*, p. 167.

knowing Mr Hume's advice to Dr Blair, the Committee followed, when it published and circulated the set of queries." [41]

The second Scottish man of letters to repudiate Ossian was Walter Scott, whose love of Scotland has never been impugned. As a boy, Scott had received Ossian from the hands of Dr. Blacklock and through those writings had developed a deep love for the ancient national traditions. As a mature critic, however, Scott changed his mind concerning their authenticity. Reviewing Mackenzie's *Report* in 1806, Scott stated his conviction that Macpherson's translations hold much the same relationship to the genuine Ossianic canon as John Home's *Douglas* to the ballad of "Gil Morrice." "But," continued Scott, "while we are compelled to renounce the pleasing idea, that 'Fingal lived, and that Ossian sung,' our national vanity may be equally flattered by the fact, that a remote and almost a barbarous corner of Scotland, produced, in the 18th century, a bard, capable not only of making an enthusiastic impression on every mind susceptible of poetical beauty, but of giving a new tone to poetry throughout all Europe." [42]

Despite the unprecedented European influence of Macpherson, Scott's ultimate rejection is high evidence that Ossian never had a firm hold upon the British imagination. It never really enchanted because its sublimity was sham, its language was tumid. In the English-speaking nations today, Ossian is almost unread and almost unreadable. Most lovers of English literature will readily agree with Dr. Johnson that it is "a mere unconnected rhapsody, a tiresome repetition of the same images," and with the particularized disgruntlement of Horace Walpole that, "It tires me to death to read how many ways a warrior is like the moon, or the sun, or a rock, or a lion, or the ocean." [43] Few will dispute the concise criticism of David Hume that Ossian is "a tiresome, insipid performance."

V

Both the Scottish Homers, it will readily be granted, were failures. The mistake of the Homer of the Lowlands was slavish imitation of original sources. At best, Wilkie could never have produced

[41] *Report*, p. 11. [42] *Edinburgh Review*, VI (1806), 462.
[43] *Life of Johnson*, II, 126; Walpole, *Letters*, V, 150.

more than occasional good verses. The mistake of the Homer of the Highlands was reckless improvisation upon original sources, while defiantly pretending to be translating literally. At worst, Macpherson was a clever impostor; at best, an original genius. In point of fact, he was a bit of both—with a considerable infusion of mediocrity.

The Attic program for Scottish poetry so guilelessly sponsored by Hume and his circle did not achieve conspicuous success. The inspiration of Thomas Blacklock and William Wilkie was too patently borrowed, that of John Home too patently rhetorical. James Macpherson achieved distinction (and notoriety) in using (and misusing) traditional Scottish themes. And although Hume himself repudiated Macpherson, his own poetical friends and protégés—all of them to a man—Blacklock, Home, and Wilkie, maintained implicit faith in the authenticity of Ossian and accepted his extraordinary talents. Thus ended Hume's personal campaign among the Scottish poets.

Though that campaign was largely sterile in terms of poetry, it was by no means a total failure and some of its by-products hold distinguished places in eighteenth-century literary history. Hume's Dedication of 1757 is the Scottish Declaration of Literary Independence. Hume's "Letter to the *Critical Review*" of 1759 is the Scottish Bill of Literary Rights, asserting the indefeasible national privilege of composing epics as bad as the contemporary English. Hume's *Of the Authenticity of Ossian's Poems* of 1775 is the verdict of Scotland's Supreme Court of criticism and, as such, holds in retrospect a triple significance: First, as the answer of David Hume to Samuel Johnson; second, as a vindication of the Edinburgh critics; and, third, as a bulwark of Scottish national integrity. The campaign that produced those monuments of friendship, of nationalism, and of criticism was not entirely fruitless.

PART III

THE
CONTROVERSIALISTS

Not being very irascible in my Temper, I have easily kept myself clear of all literary Squabbles.—HUME, *My Own Life*

Ever since I was acquainted with your works, your talents as a writer have, notwithstanding some differences in abstract principles, extorted from me the highest veneration. But I could scarce have thought that, in spite of differences of a more interesting nature, even such as regard morals and religion, you could ever force me to love and honour you as a man. Yet no religious prejudices (as you would probably term them,) can hinder me from doing justice to that goodness and candour, which appear in every line of your letter.—THE REV. GEORGE CAMPBELL TO HUME, JUNE 25, 1762

CHAPTER 5

HUME AND WALLACE

THE FRIENDLY rivalry between David Hume and the
Rev. Robert Wallace was not unknown even before Rousseau ensured it world fame in his *Confessions*. Rousseau himself had
got the story from Earl Marischal Keith of Scotland who could
always be counted on to embroider a good anecdote. But, in this
case, the actual facts are still more interesting. Although Rousseau's
garbled version of how Hume had revised the manuscript of Wallace's *Dissertation on the Numbers of Mankind*, a work maintaining
the viewpoint diametrically opposite to his own in *Of the Populousness of Antient Nations*, has frequently been corrected in details,
all the facts have not hitherto been available. The population controversy was actually but a small part of the friendship between the
Great Infidel and the liberal clergyman, the complete story of
which may now be told for the first time. It provides the framework
for the career of a strangely neglected intellect of the Scottish Enlightenment, and it affords further evidence of the urbanity, generosity, and humanity of *le bon David*. As controversy it stands at
the opposite pole from the Rousseau affair: that was to be lamented
by all the world, while this was to become the stock example of
how wise men may disagree without quarreling.

I

In 1751 at the time of their first meeting, Robert Wallace was
fifty-four, Hume's senior by fourteen years, and at the peak of an
eventful and successful career. His mind was of a boldness that might
well command the respect of an original Inquirer after truth. Minister in the Church of Scotland, Wallace had in 1737 defied the
national government over the Porteous Riots and in 1739, the Edin-

burgh city council over his translation to the New North Church. In ecclesiastical polity he was a Moderate and one of the leaders of the group including Hugh Blair, Alexander Carlyle, and Adam Ferguson, which kept William Robertson at the helm of the Edinburgh General Assembly from 1762 to 1780. The Moderatist philosophy was succinctly expressed by Wallace in the title of an early sermon: *Ignorance and Superstition a Source of Violence and Cruelty.*

Queen Caroline the Illustrious had been among the first to recognize Wallace's capabilities, and his distinguished ecclesiastical career perfectly justified that early faith. In 1742 he was instrumental in organizing the Ministers' Widows' and Children's Fund; in 1743, was named Moderator of the General Assembly; and in the following year, became one of the Royal Chaplains-in-Ordinary. From 1742 to 1746 during the interregnum following the collapse of the Walpole ministry, he was in full charge of royal church patronage in Scotland. Finally in 1746 his merit was signalized by the award of the degree of D.D. by Edinburgh University.

Even for an age in Scotland notable for clergymen of high intellectual caliber, Wallace's learning was remarkable. He was a capable mathematician and a writer of liberal views on politics, ethics, and religion. "Dr. Wallace," declares Henry Mackenzie, "with the most perfect correctness of clerical character, was a man of the world in that better sense of the term, which implies a knowledge of whatever human science or learning has done to enlighten mankind." His interests extended to fine letters, Virgil and Seneca among the ancients, and Shaftesbury among the moderns, being his favorite authors. Mackenzie further records that, "in a sermon, comparing modern morals, manners, and attainments, with those of the ancients," Wallace introduced "a high encomium on 'Gray's Elegy in a Country Church Yard,' which had been published a short while before, which he said he would venture to compare with the most celebrated specimens of ancient classic poetry." [1] He is also reputed to have been one of the principal contributors in 1737-38 to *The Reveur*, a short-lived Edinburgh periodical. In fine, Wallace's intel-

[1] *Life of Home*, p. 17.

lectual verve was such that among his brother clerics he was known simply as "the philosopher." [2]

What the clerics would have thought of their philosopher had they been able to peruse the numerous manuscripts that, with abiding discretion, he refrained from publishing must remain conjecture. These unpublished writings,[3] in addition to two on Hume, include such seemingly unclerical subjects as an "Essay on the Principles and Art of Dancing" and "Of Venery; or, The Naturall Commerce of the 2 Sexes & Proposalls to Prevent Debauchery & Render Marriage More Happy." The latter is an early excursion into the theory of the trial marriage. On the outside cover of the manuscript the author has written: "There are many good hints here but so contrary to our present notions & manners, That it will be needless & by no means proper to publish them att least att present." Whatever his contemporaries might have thought, full publication would certainly have guaranteed Wallace recognition today as a much more potent intellectual force than is customarily realized.

Convinced of the usefulness of learned societies, Wallace was one of the founders about 1717 of the Rankenian Club, a group of liberal spirits that Bishop Berkeley was pleased to correspond with, and that yet had the Caledonian hardheadedness to reject his offer of permitting them to partake in the chimerical project of establishing a college in Bermuda for the education of the clergy and the Christianization of the American Indians. Wallace was also among the founders about 1739 of the Philosophical Society of Edinburgh. Upon its reorganization and expansion in 1751, David Hume entered as one of two secretaries; and it was through the Philosophical Society that Hume and Wallace became acquainted.

II

Even before 1751, however, Hume's writings were not unknown to Wallace; for he had certainly read the essay *Of National Characters* which appeared in the late autumn of 1748 in *Essays Moral*

[2] Somerville, *My Own Life and Times*, p. 59.
[3] Wallace MSS in Edinburgh University Library. The two unpublished tracts relating to Hume and summarized below are in MSS Laing, II, 97.

and Political. What particularly held his attention there was a long digressive footnote on the character of clergymen, an excoriating analysis purporting to show how their peculiar vices are caused by the very nature of their profession. Wallace was deeply shocked because he honored his profession—certainly, at least, his brother Moderates. When after a year or so no public refutation was forthcoming, he decided to write one himself.

This unpublished refutation took the form of "A Letter from a Moderate Freethinker to David Hume Esquire concerning the Profession of the Clergy. In Which It Is Shewed That Their Vices Whatever They Are Are Owing to Their Disposition and Not to the Bad Influence of Their Profession." After an ironical opening concerning the detachment and candor of the freethinking brotherhood, Wallace proceeds with a not entirely unfair epitome of Hume's position:

In this manner you have stated the Case and set the Clergy in a very bad light, the whole seeming to amount to this, that the Clergy acquire an uniform character which is entirely their own & not the most amiable, that excepting open drunkenness & lewdness which they must guard against out of Decency, the greater part of them are & must be hypocriticall, cunning, promoters of superstition, affecters of grimace, often void of Candour & ingenuity, proud & conceited, Disposed to overrate their Devotion & to think it attones for every violation of morality, that they must be ambitious and promoters of ignorance & pious frauds to satisfy their ambition, that they must be lastly united against their antagonists, furious when contradicted, more implacable in their rancour than other men, disturbers of the world, & when they are of a Society, must for ever be actuated by ambition, pride, & a persecuting spirit. In fine, according to your reasonings, the Clergy are a faction & must for ever combine into faction against which all wise Governments ought to be for ever on their Guard.

Yet Wallace is willing to make generous concessions:

Had you confined your satire to certain times & circumstances, it had been more excusable. There have been times when the Clergy in Generall have been dangerous to the interests of Religion, Learning, virtue, society, & mankind. There have been times when their profession it self, by means of a Corrupted Religion, has been dangerous to their virtue & honesty & exposed them to peculiar & very strong temptations. Neither will I enter into any Dispute whether they have not in some ages or in some nations been Generally corrupted both in their principles & practise.

He insists, however, upon the beneficial influences of the modern enlightened clergy:

Have not we seen a great number of the Protestants take a great deal of trouble to promote knowledge and an impartiall examination of all Doctrines & opinions, even the most sacred, and to banish implicit faith and pious frauds? In truth, we who are freethinkers have been generally obliged to them. 'Tis pity that we should not be more gratefull. Who were the Persons who had the cheif hand in raising an extraordinary spirit for inquiring into naturall Philosophy as well as into the foundations of Divinity & Morality, towards the end of Oliver Cromwell's life & immediately after the Restoration of Charles IId? Were they not the Latitudinarian Divines, as they were called att that time? Who have been cherishing this spirit ever since, and called loudly upon mankind to search and examine all Doctrines and opinions of whatsoever nature & whatsoever importance, to prove all things, to hold fast on to that which is good, not to believe every spirit, but to prove the spirit? Have they not been the Protestant Clergy? Have they not been taking every thing to pieces in Religion & morality, & calling upon the Laity to admitt nothing but what was either self evident or could be deduced from self evident propositions by a clear inference? Have they not consented, nay, have they not been earnestly exhorting mankind to examine all doctrines & approve or condemn according to reason as what was necessary in order to the [establishing] most genuine & most generose piety? Has not the examining spirit taken its use or derived its cheif Credit from the Protestant Clergy themselves & been in a manner forced upon the people, who were not calling in Question the Principles of Religion & morality & had no doubts about their truth? That the spirit of inquiring might be encouraged & promoted, have not the Clergy found out a multitude of Objections to their own Doctrines, which had never entered into any heads but their own? . . . It is certain that ever since the Restoration there is a high spirit in Brittain for inquiring into all Doctrines & opinions whatsoever, & that this spirit has been much promoted by the Clergy. Sceptics have been much obliged to them. Without their assistance the freethinkers had never been able to do the mighty feats they have done, and were the Clergy intirely to.abandone our Interests, we would perhaps find it

Difficult to preserve our Conquests & might be in a fair way to be totally routed. When I consider this I cannot att all justify your severity against the Clergy in this article.

The "Letter from a Moderate Freethinker" concludes in good spirits, making several palpable hits against Hume:

Thus I have made some remarks on your Performance and cannot help thinking that on this occasion you have come short of your usual accuracy. I cannot Discover such a depth of Genius as I have often admired in you, even in cases in which I imagined you was mistaken. I cannot but observe that there are few Subjects in which One would less choose to be Dogmaticall. Never the less you appear to be more of a Dogmatist & less inclined to Scepticism than usual. The truth is that every Condition & profession is attended with peculiar temptations. Which of them is exposed to the strongest and most numerous is such a Difficult Calculation that a Freethinker might well excuse himself from being positive about the matter. But to pretend that the Profession of a Clergyman as instructor in Religion & moralls, which hitherto most men have thought exposed to fewer temptations than many others are, to have such a peculiar & extraordinary tendency to corruptness of morals and temper is a sort of paradox scarce suitable to be maintained by an impartiall searcher after the truth of characters.

I dare say that there are very few of our fraternity who are much disposed to quarrel with the Clergy of Great Brittain. We generally live in good Correspondence with them and have not the least intention to pull down the Order. I would not therefore wish that such an unfavourable opinion concerning the nature & tendency of the Profession should generally pass as approved by us, in which view I have used the freedom to rectify your mistakes & appear in Defence of the Clergy. I could heartily wish that none of us should betray any [insuperable] aversion to them, but that we would treat them with Decency as an order of men who are not only of late years become entirely innocent & harmless, but are in severall respects usefull in Society and contribute to maintain the peace and order of the world. . . .

How unaccountable is it that wise and good men who are well acquainted with [life] & have seen the world should for often go out of their way to fall upon the [inoffensive] Clergy, a body of men who have appeared in all nations in all ages and in all Religions. Especially since it is impossible to get rid of them. . . . I protest such a Conduct would allmost look like bigottry in any other sett of Gentlemen than freethinkers: But

I hope that our order will Correct their mistakes, and I dare say no man will be more ready than your self to give them a good example.

Hume had attacked the clerical character by confining himself to the fanatics. Wallace defended the clerical character by confining himself to the Moderates. How right both were, each in his way, will be observable in the later attempts of the fanatics to excommunicate Hume and in Wallace's reactions to those attempts. Yet, on the basis of their own opinions, there was no reason why Hume and Wallace should not be friends. And, indeed, they took an immediate fancy to one another. Doubtless it was this affinity that induced Wallace not to publish the "Letter from a Moderate Freethinker," which had apparently been completed shortly before he met Hume in the summer of 1751.

Not until 1760 was the clerical character publicly exonerated in a sermon on *The Influence of the Pastoral Office on the Character Examined; with a View, Especially, to Mr. Hume's Representation of the Spirit of That Office,* by Professor Alexander Gerard, one of that group of ministers at Aberdeen called by Hume, "my friendly adversaries." This sermon, preached before the Synod of Aberdeen, failed to make any appreciable stir; and the then ancient controversy died without further ado. Several years afterward while looking over some old manuscripts, Wallace picked up his "Letter from a Moderate Freethinker," read it through, and then penned on the envelope:

I can read the pamphlet easily enough. It is a good pamphlet & in a manner is quite finished.

It was written soon after Mr Hume's piece was published, att least before I had seen any Sermon or refutation of Mr Hume's observations.

I have never compared it with Mr Gerard's Sermon on the same Subject; & do not think it needfull to publish it.

This is written, Wednesday, September 5. 1764.

Long since a good friend of Hume's, Wallace regarded the incident as permanently closed.

III

At a meeting of the Philosophical Society of Edinburgh previous to Hume's secretaryship, Wallace had read a paper on population in which he maintained that the ancient world was considerably more peopled than the modern. The same thesis was then subscribed to by a host of thinkers, of whom Montesquieu was but the most distinguished. Wallace's original contribution was the ingenious argument that population varies directly with the food supply and that the presumed superior agriculture of the ancients afforded sufficient proof of their superior numbers. This paper he revised and expanded into *A Dissertation on the Numbers of Mankind in Antient and Modern Times* and, upon being introduced to Hume, immediately solicited his opinion. Returning the compliment, Hume permitted Wallace to read his own manuscript *Of the Populousness of Antient Nations,* upon which he had been working since early in 1750. There, for the first time in the long history of the question, Hume maintained the superior populousness of the modern world.[4]

Having thus learned to respect one another's opinions, Hume and Wallace were prepared for enduring friendship. Their mutual civility, setting in the words of Hume, "a new Example of Politeness," may seem at times excessive, yet it was deliberate. Hume was scrupulous of injuring the good name of a clergyman by associating it with that of an infidel; Wallace was struggling desperately to live up to the tenets of liberalism; and both were supremely conscious that in treating one another with toleration and courtesy they were achieving the highest standards set by the Age of Enlightenment.

On September 22, 1751, Hume wrote Wallace,[5] informing him of his decision to publish a group of twelve papers under the general title of *Political Discourses.* "Before that on the Populousness of antient Nations," he explained, "I intend to prefix a Note to the following Purpose":

An eminent Clergyman in Edinburgh having wrote, some Years ago, a Discourse on the same Question with this of the Populousness of antient Nations, was pleasd lately to communicate it to the Author. It maintain'd the opposite Side of the Argument to what is here insisted on, & contain'd much Erudition & good Reasoning. The Author acknowledges to have borrow'd, with some Variations, from that Discourse two Com-

---

[4] See Note G, below.
[5] Hume, eight MS letters, Edinburgh University Library, MSS Laing, II, 96.

putations *viz* that with regard to the Number of Inhabitants in *Epirus,* and that with regard to those in *Belgium.* If this learned Gentleman be prevail'd on to publish his Dissertation, it will serve to give great Light into the present Question, the most curious & important of all Questions of Erudition.

"This Note," Hume forewarned his reverend friend, "however unexceptionable it may seem to me, I woud not venture to print without your Consent; as not knowing how far you might relish it. I hope it will give Offence to no Body, that you & I have a Correspondence together on literary Subjects." That such delicacy on Hume's part was not affectation will be observed later when a clergyman, by merely being seen in the company of a known infidel, became fit subject for debate before the General Assembly of the Scottish Church. In the letter, Hume also promised to send Wallace a copy of his forthcoming *Enquiry concerning the Principles of Morals.* "I hope," he piously added, "you will not find my Ethics liable to much Exception, on the Side of Orthodoxy, whatever they may be on the Side of Argument & Philosophy."

Unintimidated by possible notoriety, Wallace entered with great zest into the literary correspondence with Hume:

SIR

What you write from Glanderston of your resolution to print your twelve Political Discourses gives me a great deal of pleasure. The sight you was pleased to allow me of one of them makes me long for the rest and I am perswaded they will be very ingenious & full of fine observation.

I thank you for the present you have ordered me of a Copy of your "Inquiry concerning the Principles of Moralls." Whether Orthodox or Heterodox I cannot answer but I dare say it will be curious and give me a usefull instruction: and I can be finely entertained with an ingenious vain of Thinking tho very different from my own & much out of the common road (the more uncommon perhaps the greater the entertainment, if one is not a bigott & can make proper allowances to a philosophicall genius). If ever I publish any thing I shall make you some small requitall, for I cannot hope to repay you in full value.

As for your intended Note relating to my Discourse on the numbers of mankind I have very great reason to be much pleased with it. If ever my little work shall be published such an encomium cannot fail to be an usefull introduction to it & create a mighty prepossession in my favour. It is more to be sure than I deserve & I could never have had the assurance to have proposed it but it might be interpreted rather whim & conceit than real modesty should I refuse such a handsome recommendation & a favourable testimony from such a fair & ingenious antagonist. I wish only it be not too favourable, & when the Discourse appear, it may answer expectation & you may not be thought rather to have been partial than just & to have been misled by an excess of generosity.

I will only add that I am not afraid our Correspondence will give any offence, nor do I believe that any with whom I have any great Connexion have such narrow souls. But if they have it would be too great a sacrifice to refuse what is so agreeable, the compliment of such an ingenious & learned Gentleman as Mr Hume & I hope I shall allways have the boldness to do justice to Gentlemen of your Character.

Edinburgh, 26th of September, 1751

P.S. I shall be glad to know by the shortest note when your Discourses will be published.

This "very obliging Letter," Hume answered three days later with the information that it would probably be two or three months before the publication of the *Political Discourses*. Much pleased with the respectful attitude of Wallace, Hume queried, "Why cannot all the World entertain different Opinions about any Subject, as amiably as we do?"

The cordial relationship already established prompted Wallace to accept Hume's invitation to print the *Dissertation on the Numbers of Mankind* and to submit the proof sheets to him for further criticism. Hume willingly undertook the task, one that he was not unaccustomed to do for friends. Emendations and additions were freely suggested. A corroborative passage from "Matchiavel" about the grain of Flanders was presented with the remark: "I very fairly lend it you. You know I am in your Debt." The fact was retailed on the authority of a Captain Rutherford, "that in New York, they seldom raise black Children in their Cities (which deserve only the Names of Villages). They give them away for nothing to the People in the Country, who raise them." And when it came to correcting Wallace's newly composed "Appendix Containing Additional Observations concerning the Numbers of Mankind in Antient and Modern

Ages; with Some Remarks on Mr. *Hume's* Political Discourse, Intituled, *Of the Populousness of Antient Nations*," a work as long again as the original *Dissertation*, Hume playfully pushed civility to extremes: "You almost frighten me for my Argument; you collect so much Learning & Reasoning."

One small request Hume did make. "Yesterday," he informed Wallace, "there was read in the Society an Advertisement which Lord Morton desird you shoud insert. If it be not printed off, I shoud be pleas'd that in mentioning my Name, you woud call me Secretary to the Society." Wallace sent proofs to Lord Morton, President of the Philosophical Society, and to Hume. The latter replied, "I find nothing to alter either in the Sheet or Advertisement." The Advertisement itself proclaims:

The Author of this Dissertation on the *Numbers of Mankind*, is desired by the *Philosophical Society* at *Edinburgh*, to acquaint the Public, that it was composed several Years ago, and was read before them.

For his own part, as he has the Honour to be a Member of this *Society*, he had no Thoughts of publishing it, till it should have had a Place among their Works. However, as they had not determined when they were to publish their Transactions, he was advised to embrace an Opportunity of publishing his *Dissertation* at a Time, when he might hope for the Attention of the Learned, which had been already directed towards the Subject, by the Publication of Mr. *Hume's* Political Discourse, *Of the Populousness of antient Nations*. He has therefore published it in its original Form; only some inconsiderable Additions have been made to it, since it was presented to the *Philosophical Society*.

The *Dissertation* is followed by an *Appendix* on the same Subject, which was not read before the *Philosophical Society*. The Author thought he should not have done Justice to his Argument, if he had omitted to subjoin those Observations, with which he was furnished by a Review of the Subject, and by a careful Perusal of Mr. *Hume's Political Discourse*.

Curiously, this Advertisement, approved of by Hume, does not comply with his request that he be called "Secretary to the Society"!

The introductory section of the Appendix reveals Wallace's tone; and it is to be observed that, unlike Hume, he was not successful in maintaining complete dispassion:

Since the preceeding *Dissertation* was composed, a Discourse, *Of the Populousness of antient Nations,* has been published by Mr. *Hume,* in which the learned Author depreciates antiquity, exalts modern times, and endeavours to prove, by all the arguments a lively and acute genius could suggest, that the superior populousness of the antient to that of the modern world, is not so certain, as is believed by the passionate admirers of antiquity.

The author of the dissertation, though much pleased with that Gentleman's uncommon ingenuity, and struck with the brilliancy of his arguments, continued still to be of opinion, that what seemed to be confirmed by so many concurring testimonies, and to be supported by the uniform evidence of all antient history, could not well be false. He suspected therefore, that Mr. *Hume's* arguments were ill-founded, and resolved to review a subject so curious, so important, and so fertile in consequences; and to try if he could discover the latent fallacy of those pompous arguments, which puzzled, but did not convince. Thus, after having considered more accurately the force of his arguments, inspected more carefully some of the authors of antiquity, and reflected more attentively on the state of the antient world, he now offers to the publick the result of his observations, in which he endeavours to illustrate more fully some things that were only hinted at in the dissertation; and at the same time to obviate the objections arising from what Mr. *Hume* has advanced in his discourse.

Hume's chief value to Wallace had been in making stylistic emendations: "I have endeavour'd to correct a few Expressions with regard to the Language." He was, of course, finical about Scotticisms, that bugaboo of the Edinburgh men of letters of the Enlightenment. "The word (expiscate) which you use Page 170," he warned, "is Scotch; and I suspect (Prestalious) which is us'd in Page 176." A typical variation in the proof sheets shows the alteration in Hume's hand from the awkward, "for tho' they did not neglect trade, yet among them it was more confined to agriculture, being their chief employment," to the more refined, "among them fewer hands were employed in Trade; Trade was more confined; agriculture was more encouraged, & was indeed their principall occupation." Yet in point of number, Hume did not make a great many changes, evidently not enough for the zealous author. At any rate, Hume gallantly explained, "It is not for Want of Care & Attention in me that you do not see more Alterations on your Margin; but from your own Care & Attention."

After the appearance of the *Dissertation on the Numbers of Mankind* early in 1753, Wallace dispatched a copy to Hume. In returning thanks for "the agreeable Present," Hume paid compliment by indirection: "When my Political Discourses were publish'd, I ordered the Bookseller to send you a Copy, which he neglected. Permit me at present to execute my Intention. You have a Copy in which I had bound some Sheets of Paper, with a View of writing any Alterations I shoud make for a new Edition; and on the Margin I had already made a few. Your Work has convinc'd me, that I must make a great many Alterations, and I find I shall have great Use for these Sheets. I must therefore use the Liberty to beg of you, that you woud send."

In actuality, however, Hume did not make many alterations in his own dissertation, apparently in the conviction that a few miscellaneous factual errors in a long and complex study could little influence the general tenor of the argument. But in 1756 he did substitute a new note on Wallace, clarifying the skeptical method:

An ingenious writer has honoured this discourse with an answer, full of politeness, erudition, and good sense. So learned a refutation would have made the author suspect, that his reasonings were entirely overthrown, had he not used the precaution, from the beginning, to keep himself on the sceptical side; and having taken this advantage of the ground, he was enabled, tho' with much inferior forces, to preserve himself from a total defeat. That Reverend gentleman will always find, where his antagonist is so entrenched, that it will be difficult to force him. VARRO, in such a situation, could defend himself against HANNIBAL, PHARNACES against CÆSAR. The author, however, very willingly acknowledges, that his antagonist has detected many mistakes both in his authorities and reasonings; and it was owing entirely to that gentleman's indulgence, that many more errors were not remarked. In this edition, advantage has been taken of his learned animadversions, and the Essay has been rendered less imperfect than formerly.[6]

[6] *Phil. Works*, III, 58. The note was dropped after 1768.

I V

In the spring of 1756 the Presbytery of Edinburgh, roused by the "drum ecclesiastic" beat by the choleric George Anderson, considered an overture directed against Hume:

The general assembly, judging it their duty, to do all in their power to check the growth and progress of infidelity; and considering, that as infidel writings have begun of late years to be published in this nation, against which they have hitherto only testified in general, so there is one person, styling himself *David Hume, Esq;* who hath arrived at such a degree of boldness as publicly to avow himself the author of books containing the most rude and open attacks upon the glorious gospel of Christ, and principles evidently subversive even of natural religion, and the foundations of morality, if not establishing direct Atheism: therefore the assembly appoint the following persons . . . as a committee to inquire into the writings of this author, to call him before them, and prepare the matter for the next general assembly.[7]

Anderson was out for infidel blood of all varieties. Having previously failed in attempts against Lord Kames, Hume himself, and the printers of the posthumous works of Lord Bolingbroke, he now redoubled his efforts against Hume. After a warm debate lasting two days, the Moderates emerged victorious. Led by the fiery young elder, Alexander Wedderburn, later Lord Chancellor of England, and by the vigorous but cautious William Robertson, they succeeded in quashing the overture while still in committee by the decisive vote of 50-17.

Robert Wallace and Hugh Blair were known to have been among the Moderates opposing Anderson—Hume's "Anderson, the godly, spiteful, pious, splenetic, charitable, unrelenting, meek, persecuting, Christian, inhuman, peace-making, furious Anderson." Blair was also known to have been the author of a tract the year before in extenuation of Lord Kames and Hume. But what apparently no one knew was that Wallace had been so perturbed by the fanaticism of the Anderson clique as to compose a treatise explaining those principles of Moderatism by which Hume had been excul-

[7] *Scots Magazine,* XVIII (1756), 281.

pated. With customary prudence, however, he ultimately decided
not to publish.

When Wallace first came to an Edinburgh church in 1733, he
had been called on the carpet by "the old clergy," who, as Ramsay
of Ochtertyre so neatly put it, were "very dexterous at spying heresy
where none was meant." [8] Although his explanations were duly
accepted, Wallace never forgot this initial taste of the extreme
narrowness of the high Calvinists. His secret sympathy for David
Hume was followed in 1757 by secret sympathy for the Rev. John
Home, the Scottish Shakespeare, when he was persecuted by the
Highflyers for his tragedy of *Douglas*. And when the Rev. Alexander Carlyle, charged with having merely attended that play, put
up a vigorous defense, Wallace secretly applauded. In admiration,
he sent Carlyle several anonymous letters which, admitted Carlyle,
"supported me in my resolution, and gave me the soundest advice
with respect to the management of my cause." [9] The action was
typical of Wallace, high-spirited and liberal, but discreet.

What especially piqued Wallace in the Hume affair of 1756 was
the holier-than-thou attitude on the part of the rigidly righteous
that a Christian minister must never so much as be seen in the company of unbelievers. Wallace was also thoroughly aroused by the
biased account of the church debates that had appeared in the June,
1756, issue of the *Scots Magazine*. The title of his manuscript em-
phasizes these two points: "The Necessity or Expediency of the
Churches Inquiring into the Writings of David Hume Esquire and
Calling the Author to Answer before the Spiritual Courts. Considered with Some Reflections on Christians Being Occasionally in Company with Scepticall or Infidell Writers. In Which There Are Some
Animadversions on the Account in the Scotch Magazine for June,
1756 of the Debates in the Committee of Overtures of the Generall
Assembly 1756 concerning These Subjects. Printed Edinburgh
1756." The last phrase indicates how close the tract came to publication.

The cover is endorsed in Wallace's hand: "This pamphlet was
intended to have been published in the year 1756 but it was not

[8] *Scotland and Scotsmen*, I, 242.
[9] Carlyle, *Autobiography*, p. 333. See also Note H, below.

done. There is no occasion for it now: but if ever any debate arise about such subjects it will be of great use & contains many good materials. It is a good pamphlet & well written & either finished or all most finished & might be soon fitted for being published: tho it has many blots and passages scored out, yet the references are clear and I can read it very easily & it is not difficult to read it. However, if I have leisure I will perhaps read it over & make it more legible. This is written on Monday September 3. 1764."

The Advertisement is a model of forthright statement in controversy:

Tho perhaps it had been better that no publick notice had been taken of the debates in the committee of overtures of the Late Generall Assembly concerning the inquiry which was proposed to be made into the writings of David Hume, Yet since an imperfect account of these debates has been published in the Scotch Magazine for June last, it is proper for the honour of the Church to give the publick a more Distinct view of this matter: the subject too is of some importance & in some part connected with the peace of the Country.

Tho I was present att these Debates, I do not pretend to give a compleat account of them. It is not easy to recollect the Different Speeches that are made and the different turns that are given to an argument in such Debates; neither perhaps would they set the subject in the clearest light; but I will give a short and different view of this matter as it struck me upon hearing these Debates in the Committee of Overtures & in the order I think most proper for illustrating the question.

I do not accuse the Author of the account in the magazine for being unfair. I shall allow that the Gentleman has given the best account he could; but as it is visible that he leans to that opinion that the church ought to inquire into the writings of Mr Hume, so he has much mistaken some of the arguments on the other side. I propose to correct his mistakes & set the arguments against such an inquiry in a more just light, for I will confess I was clearly of opinion that those who contended against the churches meddling in this matter had by far the better in the Debate.

"The debate" itself, Wallace testifies, "was managed cheifly by the ministers. I can only remember one or two of the Ruling Elders who spoke upon it (I think few were present). And of the ministers, not only a great majority opposed the overture but ministers of all sorts & complexions, young and old ministers, ministers who scarce agreed in any other Vote during the whole Assembly and such as think very differently in many other matters of Ecclesiasticall Polity." A striking testimonial to the personal popularity of *le bon David!* But lest he give the wrong impression, Wallace makes clear that, "Att the same time it was evident to all that were present that not one of the members of the committee justified any of Mr Humes errors, not one of them asserted the innocence of error, or that errors as well as vices were not the proper object of church Censure. The whole debate turned on the necessity or expediency of inquiring into the writings of Mr Hume or calling the Author before the church Courts."

Two major arguments employed by the Moderates are summarized by Wallace. First, the express Scriptural commands of Christ to exercise discipline against such as teach false or pernicious doctrines, quoted endlessly by the Highflyers, were for the purpose of edification only and not for punishment. And second, David Hume in particular is not susceptible of being edified on the subject of religion. He is too subtle a philosopher to change his mind merely because of a public censure; and it would be exceedingly difficult to determine his exact opinions, because "this Gentleman, having so much of the sceptick in him, rarely admitts any thing on any one side of a Question but he finds out something to plead for the other." Furthermore, he has in effect by his public utterances already ejected himself from the church, which has thereby lost its prerogative of questioning him.

"Are there not," demands Wallace, "many criminalls in higher & lower life, vitious, immoral, and abandoned in their lives, Drunkards, revellers, whoremongers, adulterers, contemnors of Christian Worship, despisers of Christian Piety, open supporters of impious, lewd, and immoral Principles in companies? . . . Why will [the supporters of the overture] not therefore exercise Discipline impartially against all who in the abstract deserve high Censures according to the Christian law, or will they stop short att David Hume and a few calm, contemplative, wronghead writers?" The case against Hume is in reality the case against all who differ in any way from the local Presbyterian body, and if prosecuted against the one, ought to be prosecuted against all. But from such obvious absurdity, even the most fanatic will flinch and see that discipline must vary with historical circumstances.

"Let us," Wallace urges, "exercise this Discipline as far as it is practicable in our times, which must be confessed to be greatly corrupted. But let us not exercise a Discipline that will do more harm than good. Let us not lay down rules either for censuring errors or vices, as absolutely necessary, that are absolutely impracticable, & which if followed out in all their consequences would give occasion to dangerous convulsions. Let us allwayes remember that if the Doctrine & worship & essentiall parts of the Government of a church are kept pure, Discipline may be greatly relaxed att the same time that the Church may continue a happy instrument in the hands of Providence of comforting & confirming the pious, reclaiming the wicked, & may serve as a mighty bulwark against vice, errors, & impiety."

Wallace's composure was no little ruffled by the "impotent & ridiculous" insinuation against the good character of certain clergymen, "that they had been seen accidentally standing in the streets with Mr Hume or had been known to have been in companies where he was present, especially as this Gentleman with all his errors is confessed to be a very honest and benevolent man in common life & entertaining in Conversation." Some people are blind enough, avers Wallace, not to be able to distinguish between the immorality of a profligate and the mistaken arguments of a serious thinker. Yet it will not do to inveigh too strongly against the "unco guid," for toleration must work in both directions:

I will not impute the maxims of such as carry the rules of avoiding the company of hereticks too far to pride, ill nature, affectation of popularity, or any corrupt or worldly design whatsoever. I abhor all unhandsom insinuations of every kind and leave them to those whose cause stands in need of such support. No doubt there have been ill designing men who have endeavoured to raise their reputation & promote their worldly Designs by establishing rules of this kind. Such sort of men were the Pharisees in antient times. Thus they reproached our Saviour for eating & conversing with Publicans & sinners. But as there is in nature and holy writ a foundation for rules to avoid bad company, good men must not be pronounced hypocrites because thro mistake they carry them too far. Such

Gentlemen as converse more freely may sometimes go too great a length & stand in need of charitable constructions as well as others. In truth, mankind ought not to be severe upon one another, all of them are liable to mistakes.

Moreover, first appearances are often deceptive. The clergyman who converses with the philosopher, skeptical or otherwise, is reckoned by the educated as ingenious; the clergyman who refuses to consort with the philosopher is reckoned by the multitude as pious. "But the world often judge wrong in both cases, and a man will be often misled who believes a man either to be or not to be more ingenious or more pious upon the verdict of the one or the other."

V

During Hume's keepership of the Advocates' Library from 1752 to 1757, he made it free of access to his friends, presumably including Wallace. From 1754 both Hume and Wallace were members of the local Select Society and came together frequently at the fortnightly meetings. They were also associated, as has been seen, in the *Douglas* controversy, fighting shoulder to shoulder, as it were, for Scottish literature and humanity and against Scottish bigotry.

In 1757 appeared the Rev. John Brown's *Estimate of the Manners and Principles of the Times*, a narrow-minded Jeremiad that aroused Wallace's optimism into publishing the next year *Characteristics of the Present Political State of Great Britain*. In the course of this work Wallace made frequent reference to Hume's *Political Discourses* and *History of England*, sometimes in disapproval, but always with a respect that contrasts strongly with Brown's invidious abuse. About Hume's *History of England*, for instance, Wallace commented: "It is extremely difficult to be wholly impartial. Mr. Hume has not been able to hinder himself from shewing a visible bias in favour of King Charles I. and of the party who supported him; and against the zealous defenders of civil and religious liberty. It is very possible that I am biassed on the other side." [10] Privately, Wallace termed Hume "a candid Tory."

In 1761 Wallace followed up his remonstrance against Brown with a more mature philosophical disquisition, *Various Prospects of*

[10] *Characteristics*, pp. 39-40.

Mankind, Nature, and Providence, directed against the freethinkers. Doubtless Hume was the chief contemporary in the mind of the writer. The Advertisement is the essence of liberalism and toleration: "This regard for the benefit of the Freethinkers, whom he would rather convert than irritate; an aversion to the bitterness of controversy, which he contracted at an early time in life; a sense of the difficulty of finding out the truth by the pure dint of criticism and philosophy; a remembrance of his own errors, and compassion for those of others; are the causes why he reasons so coolly, and appears less severe against the persons, or less to contemn the genius of his antagonists, than some others who have had the same good intention, but have used greater sharpness of stile. . . . Charity and generosity to the characters of our antagonists shines with a peculiar grace and beauty." [11] And in the concluding "Advices to Certain Freethinkers" Wallace pleads with his friend—though without actually naming him—not to reduce ethics to utility, not to attack the doctrine of immortality, and not to deny the being of a Divinity. Wallace customarily speaks with the voice of Moderatism. He occasionally speaks with the voice of pride, going out of his way to mention that the population controversy, stimulated by the contributions of Hume and himself, had produced a dissertation at Cambridge University in which the ancient or Wallace side was upheld.

From 1763 to 1766 while Hume was an important public figure as Secretary to the British Embassy in Paris, but one letter from Wallace survives. In it, under the date of April 3, 1764, the clergyman makes compliments, requests favors, and offers friendly criticism. He rejoices in the respect shown Hume in France, a respect which will increase on further acquaintance. He asks for information about the Genevan ministry and professors. He recommends Colonel Alexander Leslie of Edinburgh to the favor of Hume. And he severely criticizes Professor Thomas Reid's recent *Inquiry into the Human Mind on the Principles of Common Sense,* a work directed against Hume. Reid, so Wallace contends, though well versed in mathematics and in optics, is bewildered when dealing with metaphysics.[12]

[11] *Various Prospects,* pp. iv-v.
[12] *Calendar of Hume MSS,* VII, 93; Burton, II, 193.

Hume's reply to this letter is not extant, which is particularly unfortunate in connection with the recommendation of Colonel Leslie: "I dare say you will introduce him to the good company where you are, and will be ready to put him on the best methods of enjoying and improving himself at Paris." A similar request from Hugh Blair, a more intimate friend than Wallace, provoked the unusually blunt retort from *le bon David:*

Before I was favour'd with Yours, I had seen Coll Lesly, who waited on me, as is usual with the British, who come to Paris. I returnd his Visit, and introduc'd him to the Ambassador, who askd him to dinner, among seven or eight of his Countrymen. You will be surpriz'd, perhaps, when I tell you, that this is the utmost of the Civilities, which it will ever be possible for me to show Mr Lesly; for as to the ridiculous Idea of Foreigners, that I might introduce him to the good Company of Paris, nothing can be more impracticable: I know not one Family to which I coud present such a man, silent, grave, awkward, speaking ill the Language, not distinguishd by any Exploit or Science or Art: Were the French Houses open to such People as these, they woud be very little agreeable, considering the immense Concourse of Strangers to this Place. But it is quite otherwise: No people are more scrupulous of receiving Persons unknown; and I shoud soon lose all Credit with them, were I to prostitute my Recommendations of this Nature. Your Recommendations have great Weight with me; but if I be not mistaken, I have often seen Coll. Lesly's Face in Edinburgh: It is a little late, he has bethought himself of being *ambitious,* as you say, of being introducd to my Acquaintance: The only Favour I can do him is, to advise him, as soon as he has seen Paris, to go to a Provincial Town, where People are less shy of admitting new Acquaintance, and are less delicate Judges of Behaviour.

When Hume returned to London in 1766 with Rousseau, he was Britain's most influential man of letters. An ironical aspect of this period was the role he played in steering Scottish church patronage into the proper channels, that is to say, to the Moderates. Many of his friends in that group asked for favors. Among these was Wallace who, in the summer of 1766, was seeking the vacant office of Dean of the Order of the Thistle; another was Hugh Blair, seeking the office of Dean of the Chapel Royal.

Both cases are covered in the reply to Blair. "I did not apply,

in your Favour," wrote Hume, "to any Minister of State, because
any small Interest I may be suppos'd to possess was already bespoke
for Mr Drysdale, who wants it much more than you, and whom
you yourself seem'd not willing to enter into Competition with. I
shou'd willingly have seconded Dr Wallace's Application for the
Thistle; but as the Dr had, of himself, appeald to me for a Character, which I coud with Pleasure have given him in the amplest
Manner, I expected every day that Mr Conway wou'd have spoke
to me of the Matter, which he never did: The Secretary told me
yesterday that for these two small Offices more Applications had
been made to him by able and learned Divines than if Canterbury
& Durham had been both vacant: a Proof what poor Prizes you in
Scotland have to contend for." When Hume became Undersecretary
of State in 1767 his concern with Scottish church patronage was more
direct, and he soon learned to be less diffident in asking for favors
from those in power. There is no record, however, that Wallace ever
approached him again regarding ecclesiastical preferment.

The next act of friendship that Hume was able to do for Wallace
was the criticism of yet another manuscript; but it can hardly be
said that, at the moment, the writer benefited. The incident is not
a little amusing. Wallace had sent Hume a long, tedious, and almost
illegible letter covering five and a half foolscap pages, the general
purport of which was to ask the great man what he thought of the
enclosed scheme of a proposed book, "Advice to All True Patriots,
or Proposals to Promote the Grandeur and Prosperity of Great
Britain," in six more foolscap pages equally illegible. After considerable delay Hume returned the manuscript with the only conceiv-
able decorous comment: "Certainly it is impossible for any body to
object to this Scheme of a Book; and he must be very captious indeed
who woud pretend to find fault with it. I return it with many
Thanks for your Goodness in allowing me to peruse it. I shoud
have returnd it sooner; but really it is wrote in so small a hand,
that it was with Difficulty I coud read it, and it was some time
before I cou'd fully decypher it."

Even with the death of Wallace in 1771, Hume's kindly services
did not end immediately. The clergyman had left behind many
papers, including a "Treatise on Taste" that his son wished to have

published. George Wallace, an Edinburgh advocate of distinction, was on good terms with Hume and sought his advice. The sanguine Hume felt that £500 would be a reasonable offer and was accordingly authorized to settle for that amount. On April 2, 1774, he broached the subject to his London publisher, William Strahan: "There is a Subject which I was desird to mention to you, but which I delay'd, till your Application to Parliament were finish'd, that you might know on what footing your literary Property was to stand: It is with regard to Dr Wallace's manuscript, which was certainly finishd for the Press and which I think a very good Book: I told his Son about four or five months ago, before the Decision of the House of Peers, that he ought not to expect above 500 pounds for it; and he has return'd so far to my Sentiments, as to leave the Matter entirely to me; I shoud wish to know, therefore, what you think you cou'd afford. . . . I ask 500 pounds for it; as you desire that a positive Demand shoud always be made, which is indeed but reasonable. It is about half the Size of Lord Kaims's Sketches; and is better writ."

Hume's terms were peremptorily rejected by Strahan as much too high for an author whose works had never sold well even while he was alive. Boswell, who had read part of the manuscript, condemned it as unoriginal and tedious,[13] a judgment that is to be compared with Hume's. Strahan did, however, offer to bring the book out at his own expense and to share with George Wallace half the net profits; but the latter ultimately decided to let the whole matter drop. This frustrated effort of Hume on behalf of Robert Wallace's "Treatise on Taste" brings a long and cordial relationship to a close.[14]

VI

The friendship-in-controversy between Hume and Wallace—though restricted to the few facts hitherto available concerning the population dispute—did not fail to win the admiration of many liberals both before and after Rousseau. Especially was this true among the *philosophes*, of whom in this regard, Montesquieu, Mirabeau the elder, and Chastellux were the most prominent. Montesquieu, two chapters of whose *Spirit of the Laws* Hume had helped

[13] *Private Papers*, IX, 185.   [14] See Note I, below.

get translated into English and put through the Edinburgh press in 1750, later had the opportunity of returning the courtesy. For the Earl of Morton, President of the Philosophical Society of Edinburgh, wrote him on May 25, 1753:

I have taken the liberty to send you some treatises lately published by . . . the members. . . .

1. *A Dissertation on the Numbers of Mankind in ancient and modern Times.* The author has not put his name to it; but they call him Mr. Wallace: he is one of the ministers of the city of Edinburgh, a man of learning and a good mathematician, but his style of writing, not very elegant.

2. *Political Discourses,* by David Hume, esq. This gentleman is now one of the secretaries of our Society and keeper of the Advocates' library. The tenth *Discourse* treats of the same subject with Mr. Wallace's *Dissertation,* in which the writer takes the different side of the question.[15]

Though himself committed to the side of antiquity in the population aspect of the ancient-modern controversy, Montesquieu found a French translator for both books and on July 13, 1753, wrote Hume: "The public, which will admire the two works, will equally admire the two friends who have so nobly relinquished the petty interests of the intellect for those of friendship; as for myself, I shall be most pleased if I can hope for some place in that friendship." And on September 13, 1754, he replied to an inquiry from the Abbé Le Blanc, translator of Hume's *Political Discourses:* "It is true, Sir, that I have received two letters, one from Mr. Wallace and one from Mr. Hume, in which those two illustrious men who think so differently on the same question both speak in such a noble, disinterested manner and so modestly concerning themselves that I could scarcely admire their candor sufficiently and was inclined to have their letters printed, had they consented, and had certain complimentary passages concerning me permitted it. They did not write me in order to settle their dispute, as you were informed; I am not capable of that and, if I were arbiter, I should decide just as he did who judged the contest between the two shepherds in Virgil."[16]

Unable to gain the reading of the Hume and Wallace letters

[15] Montesquieu, *Correspondance,* II, 460-61.
[16] *Ibid.,* II, 480, 537-38. See Virgil, Eclogue III, the close.

from Montesquieu, the undaunted Abbé wrote to Hume, asking for copies to publish. Hume responded: "I cannot recollect the Contents of my Letters to the President Montesquieu; but I can trust to his Judgement with regard to the Propriety of publishing them. Any Expressions of my Esteem for the President, I must certainly desire to have known; because they wou'd do honor to my Understanding all over the World." Thus unavailable to Le Blanc, the letters were not printed.

With Hume and Wallace accessible in translation to the French public, so great was the interest in the population debate that Victor, Marquis de Mirabeau, in 1756 published *The Friend of Humanity; or, Treatise on Population*. In this diffuse and tedious study, Mirabeau attempted to maintain the general principles of Wallace against those of "Mr. David Hume, the English writer, one of the most distinguished political scientists known to us." The gift copy that Mirabeau forwarded to Hume was never received; and Hume expended considerable effort to procure the reading of his polite adversary, "for," as he informed the Abbé Le Blanc, "I am far from being positive in any of my Opinions." He did not, however, write an answer to Mirabeau as suggested by Le Blanc and, indeed, had not even read the work when he later met the author in Paris. Mirabeau was greatly offended and, on hearing of the Rousseau-Hume quarrel in 1766, at once wrote to Jean-Jacques consoling him and offering him hospitality in France.[17]

Yet not all the *philosophes* favored Wallace over Hume. François Jean, Marquis de Chastellux, who, Hume was informed, had "learned the English language on purpose to read your works in the Original" and who had later become his good friend, published in 1772 *An Essay on Public Happiness, Investigating the State of Human Nature, under Each of Its Particular Appearances, through the Several Periods of History to the Present Times.* Summarizing the Hume-Wallace dispute, this work awards the final verdict to Hume. Chastellux's account provides a keen contemporary appreciation of Hume's skeptical method:

[17] Mirabeau, *L'Ami des hommes*, I, 25; and Rousseau, *Correspondance générale*, XVI, 233-44. For Le Blanc, see Monod-Cassidy, *Un Voyageur-Philosophe*, pp. 407, 417.

The great writer and amiable philosopher Mr. Hume, who blends the elegance of discussion, with all the allurements of erudition, and who possessing in a most distinguished degree the art of making others decide, whilst he remains himself in doubt, knows continually how, under the appearance of an enlightened scepticism, to bring others over to that opinion, whereto he is secretly inclined; Mr. Hume hath *conjectured,* and *persuaded* us, that the antient nations were not more populous, than are the modern nations. On his part, he hath spared no enquiries, in order to enable the reader to determine this point. He was informed of the dissertation, written by Mr. Wallace, and maintaining an opinion directly opposite to his own. He invited the author to publish his performance. Mr. Wallace did publish it, and added an answer to Mr. Hume; but in this answer, erudition and argument, not being entirely exempted from prejudice, sophistry, and even harshness, sometimes betray the *Caledonian* in the friend of the Greeks.[18]

In Germany, Hume found an ardent backer in the person of the Rev. Johann Peter Süssmilch, most important Continental writer of the eighteenth century on the theory of population. Although never fulfilling his intention of writing at large on the Hume-Wallace controversy, Süssmilch had much to say on that subject in the 1761 edition of his *Divine Order in the Changes of the Human Race Shown by Its Birth, Death, and Propagation.* And while his primary purpose—as the title suggests—was theological, he was perfectly delighted to acknowledge, "*Der Herr Ritter Hume* is completely on my side."[19] Knighted so cavalierly, Sir David and the doughty Süssmilch ride to triumph over all opponents. Another German, the famed theologian Hermann Samuel Reimarus, in *The Principal Truths of Natural Religion Defended and Illustrated,* followed Süssmilch in favoring Hume over Wallace, but then suggested a compromise: "Possibly a comparison of these two writers, each of whom is only intent on peopling the world in his own way, may bring an enquirer nearer to the truth."[20]

Fittingly, the contributions to demography of Hume and Wallace were reconciled two years before the close of the eighteenth century in what is certainly the most renowned study of that sub-

[18] *Essay on Public Happiness,* II, 205-8.
[19] Quoted by Bonar, *Theories of Population,* p. 168.
[20] *Principal Truths,* p. 30*n.*

ject ever made. In his *Essay on the Principles of Population, as It Affects the Future Improvement of Society,* the Rev. Thomas Malthus acknowledged indebtedness to his predecessors. And so the friendly union of Hume and Wallace during their lifetime was fused for posterity into the Malthusian synthesis. In that happy hunting ground of distinguished demographers, Hume and Wallace may be permitted to rest tranquil. "It was agreed on all sides," wrote Ramsay of Ochtertyre, "that the controversy was conducted with great ability and good temper." [21] Indeed, it was the amicable controversy with Wallace in the early 1750's that established Hume's reputation throughout Europe as *le bon David.*

[21] Ramsay, *op. cit.,* I, 242-43.

CHAPTER 6

HUME AND ROUSSEAU

PERHAPS the strangest sequel to the strange quarrel between Rousseau and Hume was its omission from both their autobiographies. *My Own Life,* classically concise and restricted to "little more than the History of my Writings," spans a career of sixty-five years in some ten pages. The *Confessions,* romantically extravagant with the profession to tell all, covers in two sizable volumes but fifty-three years of a career of sixty-six. The reticence of Hume was studied, for he had vowed to write no more about Rousseau. The reticence, however, of Rousseau, who had variously vowed to write more and no more about Hume, was complex. Although Rousseau lived until 1778, the *Confessions* significantly stops short with 1765, the very moment before he put himself under the protection of Hume. Therein lies an inscrutable mystery.

High scandal that it was, the Rousseau-Hume quarrel is ever intriguing. Yet it endures, not because it was scandal, but rather because it offers a rare study in the psychology of genius. Frequently told in connection with Rousseau, its purpose here is to display the character of Hume during the most public and most publicized episode of his career. To misunderstand his motives and his conduct in the relationship with Rousseau is to insinuate that in "the most critical Affair, which, during the Course of my whole Life, I have been engaged in," Hume was not *le bon David.* Such misunderstanding has been possible because the entire sequence of events has not been known and because some parts have been falsified or distorted beyond recognition. More amazing than any of the fictions emanating from it, the true story does not traduce the sincerity of either Hume or Rousseau. Its foundations lie deeper than is customarily believed and were laid earlier. What happened after the arrival of patron and "pupil" in England is of less psychological consequence than what happened before. And the affair is nothing if not psychological.

I

Almost of an age, both Hume and Rousseau became well established as men of letters in the 1750's: Hume by the *Political Discourses* and the *History of England*; Rousseau by the *Discourse on Learning and Art* and the *Discourse on Inequality*. In 1761-62 Rousseau's brilliant sequence of the *New Heloise*, the *Social Contract*, and the *Emile* achieved wide renown but aroused the wrath of the bigots. On June 11, 1762, a copy of *Emile*, condemned because of the alleged impiety of the "Savoyard Vicar's Profession of Faith," was ripped asunder and burned by the public executioner at the foot of the grand staircase in the Palace of Justice in Paris; and its author fled the country.

Three days later the first overtures on behalf of Rousseau were made to Hume. Like most important events in the colorful career of Jean-Jacques, these overtures came from a woman. Long the friend of Rousseau, the Comtesse de Boufflers had opened a secret correspondence with Hume three months earlier, because he was, so she said, "a perfect philosopher, a statesman, an historian of genius, an enlightened political scientist, a true patriot." What more natural than that she should attempt to bring the two great men together, especially since Rousseau needed sanctuary? Would Hume become his protector in England? "M. Rousseau," the Comtesse hastened to make clear:

passes with most people in this country for a singular man. That epithet, in its true meaning, is justly applied to him because he differs widely from accepted ways of behavior and of thought. He is sincere, noble-minded, and disinterested. He dreads every form of dependence and, consequently, has preferred being in France earning his living by copying music to receiving favors from his best friends who are eager to mend his ill fortune. This delicacy may seem excessive but is not blamable, and it attests high ideals. He shuns contact with the world and is happy only in solitude. This predilection for retirement has made him enemies; the pride of those who sought him out has been wounded by his rebuffs. But despite his apparent misanthropy, I do not believe that the man exists who is more gentle, more humane, more compassionate of the afflictions of others and more patient in his own. In a word, his virtue is so pure, so constant, so uniform, that those who hate him have been able to find only in their own hearts reasons for suspecting him. As for me, I would rather be deceived by these favorable appearances than doubt his sincerity.[1]

"I assure your Ladyship," replied Hume promptly from Edinburgh, "there is no man in Europe of whom I have entertained a higher idea, and whom I would be prouder to serve; and as I find his reputation very high in England, I hope every one will endeavour to make him sensible of it by civilities, and by services, as far as he will accept of them. I revere his greatness of mind, which makes him fly obligations and dependance; and I have the vanity to think, that through the course of my life I have endeavoured to resemble him in those maxims. . . . We are happy at present in a king, who has a taste for literature; and I hope M. Rousseau will find the advantage of it, and that he will not disdain to receive benefits from a great monarch, who is sensible of his merit." The following day Hume extended his good services to Rousseau in getting established in London or in seeking a haven in Edinburgh. He also requested several friends in London to assist the exile in all possible ways. Misdirected to London, Hume's letter did not reach Rousseau until February, 1763.

Meanwhile, the campaign to bring the two men of letters together proceeded apace. The Comtesse de Boufflers forwarded to Rousseau a copy of Hume's reply and elicited a startlingly frank analysis of the differences, intellectual and temperamental, between Hume and himself. "Mr. Hume," acknowledged Rousseau, "is the truest philosopher that I know and the only historian that has ever written with impartiality. He has not loved truth more than I have, I venture to believe; but I have sometimes put passion into my researches, and he has put into his only wisdom and genius. Pride has often led me astray by my aversion for what was evil or what seemed so to me. I have hated despotism in the republican and intolerance in the theist. Mr. Hume has said: here is what makes intolerance, and here is what makes despotism. He has seen from all points of view what passion has let me see only from one. He

[1] Hume, *Letters*, II, 367-68.

has measured and calculated the errors of men while remaining above their weaknesses." [2]

Rousseau's confession of his own weakness in comparison with the strength of Hume receives indirect confirmation from that philosopher himself. Asked by the Comtesse de Boufflers for an opinion of Rousseau, Hume replied: "All the writings of that author appear to me admirable, particularly on the head of eloquence; and if I be not much mistaken, he gives to the French tongue an energy, which it scarce seems to have reached in any other hands. But as his enemies have objected, that with this domineering force of genius there is always intermingled some degree of extravagance, it is impossible for his friends altogether to deny the charge; and were it not for his frequent and earnest protestations to the contrary, one would be apt to suspect, that he chooses his topics less from persuasion, than from the pleasure of showing his invention, and surprizing the reader by his paradoxes." Through their respective writings and long before meeting, Rousseau and Hume, like the men of genius they were, had appraised one another with no inconsiderable astuteness.

Rousseau, meantime, had found asylum at Môtiers-Travers in Neuchâtel, an independent principality in the Jura under the protection of the King of Prussia. Here he had the advantage of being neither in France nor in Switzerland, from both of which he was now proscribed. Here also he had the good fortune to find a kind friend in the person of the genial governor, George Keith, Hereditary Earl Marischal of Scotland. Keith fully understood the tribulations of an exile as he himself had been attainted as a rebel after the Jacobite rising of 1715 and had only recently bought his peace with the Hanoverian dynasty. Lord Marischal was also a friend of David Hume's and was at once struck with the same thought as Mme de Boufflers. Affectionately he gave his new friend, the "honest savage," an engraving of *le bon David*. Ceaselessly he praised his virtues, instancing the amicable controversy with Wallace and the attempt of the clergy to excommunicate "this Antichrist (for such he is in Scotland just as you are in Switzerland)." Embellishing an already good story, Keith went on: "David sat down among the lamas and listened with an admirable *sang-froid* to all the abuse

[2] Rousseau, *Correspondance générale*, VIII, 71. Cited hereafter as *Corr. gén.*

directed against him, taking his snuff and keeping his silence. His *sang-froid* disconcerted the lamas; they left without excommunicating him." [3] It was the Marischal's standing joke to address the Great Infidel as "Defender of the Faith."

Admittedly building "castles in Spain," Keith suggested that all three (Jean-Jacques, David, and himself) live together in Keith Hall, near Aberdeen. "I shall give you," he urged Rousseau, "a couple of rooms in my house, and as many to *le bon David*. Neither of you will enter the rooms of the other; there will be a parlor for the exchange of visits. We shall have *placidam sub libertate quietam*, which is my motto. Each of us will contribute to the upkeep of the little republic according to his income, and each will tax himself. Food will be no great item, inasmuch as trout, salmon, seafood, and vegetables cost me nothing. David will pay for the roastbeef because he eats it. We shall need two carriages when we feel the urge for a drive. There will be no necessity for other rules or laws in our republic; each will make his own spiritual and temporal regulations. Such is my castle; the foundations are already laid." [4]

More practically, the kindhearted Marischal urged Frederick the Great to provide Rousseau with a hermitage and a pension. The tender conscience of Jean-Jacques, however, would not accept such munificence: "I have thought and spoken too ill of the King of Prussia ever to accept his gifts; but I shall love him all my life." [5] The Comtesse de Boufflers, the Marquise de Verdelin, and the other ladies, George Keith, David Hume, and the other men, all outwardly applauded this determined independence but inwardly wondered what was eventually to be done with the necessitous Philosopher of Geneva.

In February, 1763, Hume's long delayed letter finally reached Neuchâtel. Responding with gallantry, Rousseau expatiated on the inestimable joys of living in Scotland with Lord Marischal and David Hume; but ill health will not permit his making so extended a journey. On his side, Hume was still eager to coöperate. "I even ventured to mention to Lord Marischal," he informed Mme de Boufflers in July, "that I had an appartment in my house, which was not occupied, and which I would think myself happy, if so illus-

---

[3] *Ibid.*, VIII, 97.　　　　[4] *Ibid.*, VIII, 170.　　　　[5] *Ibid.*, VIII, 175.

trious a fugitive would be pleased to accept of. I dared not to proceed any farther with a person of his turn; especially as the situation of my house in the midst of a city, joined to the circumstances
of our climate, which is not favourable, made me doubtful how far
such an offer, even if accepted, might in the issue prove agreeable
to him."

The castle in Spain, however, took on momentary realism later
in the summer when Keith, resigning as governor of Neuchâtel,
returned to Scotland after an absence of forty-eight years. He would
look over the situation in person and report back. But almost at the
moment of his arrival, David Hume, heartbroken at upsetting
Keith's plans, departed for London and later for Paris as secretary
to the English ambassador, Lord Hertford. A second disappointment
to Keith was Scotland itself. Bigotry was rife, "Milord" informed
Rousseau: "I see that our *bon David* is regarded by many people
as a monster. I imagine that's what determined him to go to
France." [6] Finally, the climate was even more insufferable than he
had remembered. The Scottish philosophical retreat *à trois* seemed
irrevocably doomed to remain a castle in Spain.

I I

Reaching Paris before the end of October, *le bon David* instantly
became the rage. The mistresses of the *salons* vied with one another
to entice his presence. Not to know Hume was to be nobody. The
friends of Rousseau looked on with unfeigned astonishment. "I don't
know how he stands it all," exclaimed Mme de Verdelin. "This
rage, even if it lasts beyond the moment, can never satisfy the
heart." [7] No follower of the great exemplar of individualism could
long endure literary society. The *salons*, moreover, were habituated
chiefly by the *philosophes*, personal enemies all of Rousseau. A
friend of theirs could scarcely be a friend of his.

That, clearly, was the interpretation of Rousseau. "When I took
refuge in this country," he replied to Mme de Verdelin, Hume
"wrote me a fine letter to offer me his friends and his friendship,
should I wish to retire into England; I scarcely foresaw then that
one day he would be *à la mode* in Paris. But henceforth it doesn't

[6] *Ibid.*, X, 126.   [7] *Ibid.*, XI, 106.

matter. I lose a true friend for whom I shall grieve all my life and whom I shall never replace." [8] Pleased with having kept her Jean-Jacques away from England, a country and a people she intensely disliked, Mme de Verdelin later clarified her own position: "Mr. Hume is a great favorite with all the pretty women here; that is probably why he is not a favorite with me." [9] Whatever did she mean by that, one wonders?

Brushing aside all thoughts of Hume and of England, Rousseau soon found himself in trouble with the authorities, ecclesiastical and civil. In 1763 upon his resignation of the once proudly held citizenship of Geneva, he became a man without a country—or rather, a Citizen of the World. The following year a defense of that step in the *Letters from the Mountain* began to stir up the bigots in Neuchâtel. When Mme de Verdelin visited him on September 1, 1765, she found him unhappy and restive. Bethinking herself of the renounced Hume, she suggested that Jean-Jacques take advantage of his good offices. The philosopher equivocated; but Mme de Verdelin, her mind made up, wrung from him a reluctant consent.

On her return to Paris, a mere hint to Hume brought renewed assurances of friendship. She did not have to resort to pleading and, indeed, was surprised at his ardor. For Hume, long attracted to Jean-Jacques through the "character" of him drawn by Mme de Boufflers and Lord Marischal, was now completely won to his side. The previous year Colonel Edmonstoune, writing from Geneva, had suggested bluntly: "I wish you could do something for Rousseau without his knowing it. Print his works in England for his benefit." [10] And Lord Marischal, expatiating on his persistent refusal to accept presents, had concluded: "Jean-Jacques is too virtuous a man for this world, which seeks to turn his scrupulousness into ridicule." [11] All this inside information and persuasion began to bear fruit early in 1765 when Alexis-Claude Clairaut, the distinguished mathematician, gave Hume to read a pathetic letter from Rousseau, describing his poverty and distress.

Immediately conceiving a benevolent scheme to assist him without wounding his pride, Hume borrowed the letter from Clairaut

[8] *Ibid.*, XI, 150.
[10] Burton, II, 187.
[9] *Ibid.*, XIII, 231.
[11] *Eminent Persons*, pp. 60-61.

to show to Jean-Jacques's friends in Paris and to solicit funds from them.[12] The scheme was to employ the influence of Clairaut to engage the publisher bringing out Rousseau's *Dictionary of Music* to pay more than the stipulated copy money, Hume and the others secretly to make up the difference. The sudden death of Clairaut on May 17, however, brought the project to an end. Now in October at the express desire of Mme de Verdelin, Hume subordinated everything to procuring a retreat for the exile in England.

His first thought was to obtain permission, through the influence of Horace Walpole, for Rousseau to live in Richmond New Park. But recollecting certain political difficulties, Hume dropped this plan and decided to conduct further investigations. These were handled by John Stewart in London, who was later joined by Gilbert Elliot, bringing over Hume's newest instructions. The idea was to engage for Rousseau and his mistress good board and room in the country at £50-60 a year, of which Rousseau was to pay £20-25 and Hume to make up the difference—secretly, of course. A place was found with a respectable French family at Fulham, which might prove satisfactory; but the house, Stewart warned Hume, "is as dirty as a Frenchman's in France." [13]

On October 22 Hume wrote to assure Rousseau: "I flatter myself, that in England you woud find an absolute Security against all Persecution, not only from the tolerating Spirit of our Laws, but from the Respect, which every one there bears to your Character." The letter tactfully concluded with the useful information that, "As the English Booksellers can afford higher Prices to Authors than those of Paris, you will have no Difficulty to live frugally in that Country, on the Fruits of your own Industry. I mention this Circumstance, because I am well acquainted with your Resolution, of laying Mankind under Obligations to you, without allowing them to make you any return." The envelope was addressed in the hand of Mme de Verdelin *à Monsieur Rousseau à l'Ile Saint Pierre au Canton de Berne en Suisse.*

For in the interim Rousseau had been expelled from Neuchâtel. In turn, he was expelled from l'Ile Saint-Pierre where he sought temporary shelter. Barred from France and from Switzerland, he

---

[12] *Concise Account*, pp. 7-10.   [13] Burton, II, 311*n.*

would go to Berlin and accept the hospitality of the King of Prussia and possibly later on proceed to England. In Strasbourg, however, where he paused for several weeks on the trip, Hume's letter caught up with him. With a rapid shift of plans, Rousseau put himself on December 4 under the protection of David Hume, "the most illustrious of my contemporaries, a man whose goodness surpasses his fame." [14] Safeguarded by a special royal passport procured by Mme de Verdelin, he arrived in Paris on December 16, 1765, and was magnificently established in an apartment of the Prince de Conti in the Temple.

Jean-Jacques Rousseau, who detested Paris, instantly outshone all Paris. Substantial bribes were offered Hume to parade his "pupil" at set times so that nobility and populace alike might see him. "I am sensible," wrote David to Hugh Blair on December 28, "that my Connexions with him, add to my Importance at present. Even his Maid, La Vasseur, who is very homely and very awkward, is more talkd of than the Princess of Monaco or the Countess of Egmont, on account of her Fidelity and Attachment towards him. His very Dog, who is no better than a Coly, has a Name and Reputation in the World." Actually, Rousseau was traveling only with his dog; Thérèse Le Vasseur was still in Switzerland and did not reach Paris until after the departure of the two philosophers.

Hero worship of Rousseau swept the city, and a young Scotsman, protégé of Hume, became seriously infected. Robert Liston described the symptoms in a charmingly guileless letter to his sister:

You perhaps know that the celebrated Monsieur Rousseau, has been obliged to quit Geneva for the religious part of his Emilius, that he has been flying about Switzerland for some time to avoid persecution and assassination, and that he could find no asylum to secure him from the zeal of these *overmuch righteous* pastors; you perhaps know likeways, that, in consequence of an invitation from David Hume, he came here, and is now on his way to England, and that he is to be boarded in a house at Fulham, a village a little way up the river from London. But you surely don't know what I am going to tell you.

You know I am a great admirer of Rousseau, and no man has a more irresistible Curiosity to see great men than I. But as all M. Rous-

[14] Hume, *Letters*, II, 383.

seau's former acquaintances crowded to see him, and I had been always told he was the shyest and most misanthropical creature in the world, I did not chuse to ask Mr. Hume to make me acquainted with him. However, for fear he should die before I returned to London, I resolved to see him once before he went away, and with this view went to the Street where he lodged the morning he set off, in order to stare at him as he and David were going into their post-chaise.

After waiting an hour or two in a Coffee-house opposite, I saw Mr. Hume come out and go toward the chair. Now, thought I, now is the time. I run out and got as near as possible. But behold! no Rousseau appeared. David observed me, and expressed some surprise at seeing me there.

"I am just come to have a peep at Jean Jacques," says I; "I beg you'll not take any notice of me, but let me stare in full liberty."

"No, no, you shall go in and I'll present you to him."

"I'd rather not, I've nothing to say to him, and he's so shy."

"Well, but we'll perhaps be long before we're ready; you shall at least go in, and sit in an antichamber where you'll see him at your ease." Saying this he pulled me in by the arm.

I waited in a parlour and when said famous personage came through carrying out a bundle to his chaise, I made him a low bow which he returned. Mr. Hume in the inner room, while Rousseau was absent, had told the Countess of Boufflers (a very famous woman and a great protectress of men of learning) that I was in the anti chamber, and my motives for coming. She came out immediately, commended my curiosity, made me some compliments, and insisted upon introducing me to Jean Jacques. So when he came back she and Mr. Hume together presented me to him. I can't enter into the particulars of our Conversation,—but upon the whole he received me very well. I was about an hour there, saw him dine, and had the Honour to help him into the Chaise. He said he would be glad to crack with me when I came to England, &c.

His person is very thin & delicate looking, his face, and especially his sharp black Eyes promise every thing he has shown himself possessed of. His manners simple and affable. If I had more paper I would say more. Adieu my Dear—

R. LISTON [15]

Yet not all Paris worshiped so innocently at the shrine of Rousseau. The *philosophes*, to be sure, did not; and neither did a cer-

[15] E. C. Mossner, "Rousseau Hero-Worship; an Unpublished Intimate Record of 1766," *Modern Language Notes*, LV (1940), 450-51.

tain English gentleman. It was not for love of the *philosophes,* however, that the Hon. Horace Walpole refrained. That dilettante of dilettantes affected to despise all men of letters in general and foreigners in particular. Walpole had been no little amused, and perhaps just a bit piqued, by the enthusiasm of the *salons* over Hume, a mere writer. "Madame du Deffand," he wrote back to England in December, "says I have *le feu moqueur,* and I have not hurt myself a little by laughing at whisk and Richardson, though I have steered clear of the chapter of Mr. Hume; the only Trinity now in fashion here." [16] Walpole became sardonic over the sudden switch from Hume to Rousseau. Biding his time, he would indulge his mocking spirit.

Walpole's *jeu d'esprit* was a feigned letter to Rousseau from the King of Prussia. The irony was mordant:

MY DEAR JEAN-JACQUES,

You have renounced Geneva, your native soil. You have been driven from Switzerland, a country of which you have made such boast in your writings. In France you are outlawed: come then to me. I admire your talents, and amuse myself with your reveries; on which however, by the way, you bestow too much time and attention. It is high time to grow prudent and happy; you have made yourself sufficiently talked of for singularities little becoming a truly great man: show your enemies that you have sometimes common sense: this will vex them without hurting you. My dominions afford you a peaceful retreat: I am desirous to do you good, and will do it, if you can but think it such. But if you are determined to refuse my assistance, you may expect that I shall say not a word about it to any one. If you persist in perplexing your brains to find out new misfortunes, chuse such as you like best; I am a king and can make you as miserable as you can wish; at the same time, I will engage to do that which your enemies never will, I will cease to persecute you, when you are no longer vain of persecution.

Your sincere friend,
FREDERIC [17]

Having written his squib, Walpole had the good grace to keep it pretty well under cover while Hume and Rousseau were in Paris.

[16] Walpole, *Letters,* VI, 370.
[17] *Concise Account,* pp. 20-21.   See also Note J, below.

He refrained from calling on Jean-Jacques when nearly everyone else did, "thinking it wrong to go and make a cordial visit to a man, with a letter in my pocket to laugh at him." Nor did he, though living in the same hotel with Hume, ever show it to him, out of courtesy to the patron of Rousseau. The letter was not widely circulated in *salon* society until after the departure of the two for England and did not get into print until after they reached London. Then as the acknowledged author, Walpole became the new literary lion in place of Jean-Jacques, the butt of his mockery. He basked in his glory and continued his witticisms.

Hume first saw the letter in London, recognizing it at once as the extension of a dinner-table jest that Walpole had made within his hearing at the Paris residence of Lord Ossory. In reality, however, it seems to have first occurred to Walpole one evening at Mme Geoffrin's, and the French had been touched up later by Helvétius and the Duc de Nivernais. Much distressed, Hume wrote to Mme de Boufflers early in February: "I suppose, that by this time you have learned it was Horace Walpole who wrote the Prussian letter you mentioned to me. It is a strange inclination we have to be wits, preferably to every thing else. He is a very worthy man; he esteems and even admires Rousseau; yet he could not forbear, for the sake of a very indifferent joke, the turning him into ridicule, and saying harsh things against him. I am a little angry with him; and I hear you are a great deal: but the matter ought to be treated only as a piece of levity." So *le bon David*, compassionate of all concerned, tried to smooth things over.

The *philosophes* of Paris, with whom Hume was on the best of terms, regarded Rousseau as a deserter from their ranks and, moreover, a quarrelsome one. They, therefore, warned Hume against his suspicious mind and his persecution mania. Hume listened placidly and, at the first opportunity, sought out Mme de Verdelin. "I do not want," he told that lady, "to serve a man merely because he is celebrated. If he is virtuous and persecuted, I would devote myself to him. Are these stories true?" Reassured of Jean-Jacques's uprightness, he expressed complete satisfaction.[18]

When about to leave Paris, Hume went to say farewell to Baron

[18] *Corr. gén.*, XV, 185, letter of Mme de Verdelin to Rousseau.

d'Holbach, full of enthusiastic plans to settle Rousseau permanently in England and to make him happy forever. The Baron was not greatly impressed. "You don't know your man," he insisted. "I tell you plainly, you're warming a viper in your bosom." *Le bon David* was impervious to all such insinuations: he and Rousseau were good friends and would never quarrel. But Holbach reiterated, "You don't know your man, David, you don't know your man." Hume smiled tolerantly.[19]

I I I

Did Hume really know his Rousseau? He obviously thought he did and actually possessed considerable information about him. Hume knew that Rousseau was a genius but overinclined to sensibility, that he was idealistic but overconscientious, that he was independent but overindependent. Hume had been instructed by both friends and enemies of Rousseau that he was sensitive, whimsical, and fond of the solitary life. He had been warned by Rousseau's enemies that he was suspicious and quarrelsome, by Rousseau's friends that he could be helped only clandestinely. Hume had met Rousseau personally and found him affectionate and sociable. He was convinced that he could handle the situation and preserve the delicate balance. After all, he was a professional diplomat, was he not? He felt secure in the knowledge that his own intentions were the best in the world; and he was confident that "this nice little man," as he fondly spoke of Jean-Jacques, would respond in kind.

Did Rousseau know his Hume? He was not quite so positive; there was something enigmatical about the man. Their common friends kept repeating endlessly that Hume was *le bon David*, and so he must be. Rousseau knew that Hume was a genius but felt that he was overintellectual; he knew that Hume was sociable but felt that he was lacking in personal warmth. Rousseau was just a little uncomfortable about their whole relationship because he had never really liked the English and was now accepting refuge in England chiefly under friendly pressure. Rousseau had not forgotten how he had once given up Hume merely on learning that he was *à la mode*

[19] Morellet, *Mémoires*, I, 109; Marmontel, *Mémoires*, II, 257. See also Note K, below.

in Paris. Rousseau was aware that Hume was still *à la mode* in Paris; he was also aware that Hume was on good terms with the *philosophes*. It was well everyone was so perfectly sure that Hume was *le bon David*, otherwise. . . .

Such was the information that Hume and Rousseau had of one another as they prepared to leave Paris. They had the facts but not the means of interpreting them. Yet, in retrospect, the interpretation is simple. They would be friends until Rousseau suspected that Hume was not *le bon David*, and that he would never be able to do on the basis of facts. They would, therefore, always be friends provided that Rousseau was perfectly sane. But if Rousseau *was* paranoiac, if he *did* have a persecution mania, if Holbach *was* right, then it is clear that the friendship would sometime end in violent rupture.

For Rousseau was already possessed of sufficient information about Hume to believe him an enemy whenever he felt so inclined. Whatever might happen in England, therefore, was nonessential, the circumstance rather than the cause. Hume had only to render sufficient services to assume great importance in the mind of Rousseau, and Rousseau had then only to brood about Hume. The test of Rousseau's possible monomania would inevitably occur because Hume was *le bon David*, a man whose essential characteristic was benevolence. The services would be rendered and Rousseau would be given the opportunity to brood. The future was entirely up to Rousseau.

IV

But to return to Paris. After ten days as cynosure, Rousseau became frantic. "I do not know how much longer I can endure this public scene," he complained. "Could you, for charity's sake, hasten our departure a little?" [20] The plea was directed to M. de Luze of Neuchâtel, who was to accompany them to London. Preparations were accordingly hastened, doubtless also prompted by an official order from the Duc de Choiseul for Rousseau to move on. Publicly announcing their departure for January 2, 1766, they did not actually leave until two days later. The traveling arrangements were

[20] *Corr. gén.*, XIV, 351.

simple. "You will take your post-chaise," Rousseau had instructed De Luze; "Mr. Hume will take his; and we shall change from time to time." Presumably Sultan, the collie, always remained with its master. The two carriages kept close together to avoid mishaps.

In an inn at Roye, one of the stages on the journey, the three gentlemen were compelled to share the same room in three different beds. The two philosophers were overexcited and restless. In the middle of the night, Rousseau thought he heard Hume muttering to himself, "Je tiens Jean-Jacques Rousseau, Je tiens Jean-Jacques Rousseau," over and over again. At the moment, this "I have Jean-Jacques Rousseau" made no distinct impression on his mind, although he broke out into a cold sweat. The incident was, however, not to be forgotten.[21]

The party finally reached Calais after a leisurely trip. Detained there by contrary winds, Hume took the occasion to broach a delicate subject, one that had been in the back of his mind since 1762. Would Jean-Jacques consider accepting a pension from the King of England? How could he without seeming ungrateful toward the King of Prussia, whose pension he had refused? The two cases are entirely different, Hume explained, since a pension from the King of England would in no wise endanger his independence. Well, if the offer was actually made him, Rousseau would consult Lord Marischal. Knowing full well what Keith's answer would be, Hume took this as tacit acceptance. The future welfare of his "pupil" seemed assured, and he felt vastly relieved.

Hume was also pleased that he had encouraged Jean-Jacques in a new literary enterprise. "I exhorted him on the road," he confided in Mme de Boufflers, "to write his Memoirs. He told me, that he had already done it with an intention of publishing them. At present, says he, it may be affirmed, that nobody knows me perfectly any more than himself; but I shall describe myself in such plain colours, that henceforth every one may boast that he knows himself, and Jean-Jacques Rousseau. I believe," added Hume critically, "that he intends seriously to draw his own picture in its true colours: but I believe at the same time that nobody knows himself less."

[21] *Ibid.*, XV, 156; Hume, *Letters*, II, 399-400.

The evening of January 9, the three travelers finally embarked. The Channel was rough, and the crossing took twelve hours. Rousseau was sick but remained on deck in the icy blasts. Hume was sicker and sought refuge in his cabin. Everyone was happy to reach Dover. A free man at last, Rousseau silently embraced *le bon David*, his deliverer from persecution and his patron in the land of liberty, covering his face with kisses and bathing it in tears.[22]

V

London, where they arrived January 13, proved a second Paris. Rousseau, therefore, wished to leave immediately for the country. A trip to the Fulham farmhouse justified Stewart's description. Numerous other situations were offered, each of which had to be investigated in turn. All that took time. Most appealing to Rousseau was an ancient monastery in the Welsh mountains, which had been converted into a dwelling: "If in that distant and most savage country I can pass the last days of my life in peace, forgotten by mankind, that interval of repose will soon make me forget my miseries, and I shall be indebted to Mr. Hume for all the happiness to which I can still aspire." [23] But Hume deemed Wales too far away for a foreigner who knew no English and never wished to learn it.

After two weeks Rousseau could no longer endure the metropolis while awaiting a permanent settlement; and Hume was compelled to hustle him off to Chiswick to board with a grocer. For nearly two months Hume looked into various prospects in the Isle of Wight, Cornwall, and Plymouth. A visit to the Surrey hills seeming to please Rousseau, Hume made an unsuccessful attempt to purchase the house and grounds where he had stayed.[24] From Edinburgh, Mrs. Alison Cockburn wrote, urging Hume to bring Rousseau to Scotland: "Sweet old man, he shall sit beneath an oak and hear the Druid's songs. The winds shall bring soft sounds to his ear, and our nymphs with the songs of Selma shall remember him of joys that are past. O bring him with you; the English are not worthy of him; I will have him!" [25] James Boswell had also entertained the thought of Jean-Jacques in the land of Ossian. But Hume

[22] Hume, *Letters*, II, 386.
[24] *Concise Account*, pp. 11-12.
[23] *Corr. gén.*, XV, 21.
[25] *Eminent Persons*, p. 125.

knew that the climate was unsuitable. Finally Derbyshire was decided on, where a wealthy gentleman was eager to lend his country estate at Wooton [26] to the distinguished refugee, mistress, and dog.

Like all cities, London was a great trial to Rousseau. "It is incredible the Enthusiasm for him in Paris and the Curiosity in London," Hume observed to his brother. This nice distinction between "enthusiasm" and "curiosity" was well drawn. "I prevaild on him," continued Hume, "to go to the Play-house, in order to see Garrick, who placd him in a Box opposite the King and Queen. I observd their Majestys to look at him, more than at the Players. I shoud desire no better Fortune than to have the Privilege of showing him to all I please. The hereditary Prince payd him a Visit a few days ago; and I imagine the Duke of York calld on him one Evening when he was abroad. I love him much and shall separate from him with much Regreat."

One special reason for English curiosity, in addition to the notorious career of the much persecuted philosopher, was his extraordinary costume, a caftan. This Armenian dress he had assumed, he told Hume, because "he has had an Infirmity from his Infancy, which makes Breeches inconvenient for him." In his long purple robe, trimmed and lined with dark fur, and his fur cap, Rousseau was a sight to engage the stares of the London populace. As a special favor to Hume, he obligingly sat to a portrait in oils by Allan Ramsay. Hearing of this, the King requested to see it and suggested that engravings be made. They were, and Hume distributed copies among Rousseau's friends and patrons in Paris. The painting itself was presented to Hume by the artist, his very good friend. Ramsay also, at about the same time, painted the portrait of *le bon David*.[27]

Though becoming more and more aware of Jean-Jacques's whimsicalities, Hume still believed that he was "a very agreeable, amiable Man," even boasting to Hugh Blair on February 11 that "the Philosophers of Paris fortold to me, that I coud not conduct him to Calais without a Quarrel; but I think I cou'd live with him all my

[26] Wooton is actually just over the line into Staffordshire, but the postal address in the eighteenth century was Derbyshire.
[27] For the Hume portrait, see the Frontispiece.

JEAN-JACQUES ROUSSEAU, HUME'S "PUPIL," IN 1766
FROM THE PAINTING BY ALLAN RAMSAY IN THE
NATIONAL GALLERY OF SCOTLAND, EDINBURGH

This terrible portrait! The face of a frightful Cyclops!
—ROUSSEAU, JUDGE OF JEAN-JACQUES

Life, in mutual Friendship and Esteem." All, however, was not idyllic. Hume had discovered by accident that Rousseau was not quite so indigent as he made out to be, that he actually had accepted presents. But, as Hume informed Mme de Boufflers, "It is only matter of mere curiosity. For, even if the fact should prove against him, which is very improbable, I should only regard it as one weakness more, and do not make my good opinion of him to depend on a single incident."

Yet as early as January 16 William Rouet had written to Scotland, "David Hume is busy to gett Rousseau disposed of. Till then he is a kind of prisoner." And on January 25 Rouet continued: "Our friend David is made the shower of the Lion. He is confoundedly weary of his pupil, as he calls him; he is full of oddities and even absurdities. . . . He looks upon Tronchin's being here as a spy set by Geneva upon him; and his being accidentally lodged where Hume always used to lodge, (and where he is to come as soon as Rousseau is fixed in the country,) confirms him in this foolish conceit."[28] John Home, the Scottish Shakespeare, also noticed David's increasing difficulties with the philosopher who allowed himself to be ruled equally by his dog and his mistress.

Thérèse Le Vasseur arrived in London on February 13 in the company of James Boswell, her escort from Paris. Boswell had indeed exceeded the usual capacity of an escort, but as the two solemnly vowed never to reveal their *affaire*—at least while Rousseau was alive—no one was a whit the wiser for that.[29] Though always hypersensitive of injuries to his honor, Rousseau apparently never suspected this very real injury. Reunited with Jean-Jacques, Thérèse at once reassumed her customary domination. "She governs him as absolutely as a nurse does a child," De Luze had informed Hume. Nothing could be decided without consulting her; and her likes and dislikes were unpredictable. Though her influence was always paramount, it is yet undefinable since she almost never put anything into writing or confided in any correspondent. She did not because she had never really mastered reading and could write only with exceeding difficulty. Jean-Jacques, himself, admitted her

[28] *Caldwell Papers*, Part II, pp. 61, 63-64.
[29] See Chapter 7, sec. II, below.

stupidity. Everyone else thought her not only stupid but malevolent.

In the absence of Thérèse, Rousseau's dog had temporarily acquired the ascendant. Twice Sultan caused a furor in London. Once it strayed away and got lost. Hume inserted advertisements in the papers and was happily able to restore it to the distracted Jean-Jacques. On the occasion of going to the Drury Lane Theatre, Sultan again interfered. Rousseau was unwilling to leave the dog behind for fear that it would run off and get lost a second time. When it was locked in his room on Hume's advice, he could not bear to hear it howl. With difficulty David retained his wonted equanimity. "I caught him in my arms," he wrote the Marquise de Barbentane, "and told him, that Mrs Garrick had dismissed another company in order to make room for him; that the King and Queen were expecting to see him; and without a better reason than Sultan's impatience, it would be ridiculous to disappoint them. Partly by these reasons and partly by force, I engaged him to proceed." It was especially necessary that the King be not disappointed since he had already consented to a pension of a hundred pounds a year, "a mighty accession to our friend's slender revenue," thought Hume. Final negotiations were still proceeding.

March 18, the eve of departing for Derbyshire, Rousseau and Thérèse came in from Chiswick and spent the night with Hume in his chambers at Lisle Street, Leicester Fields. All arrangements for Wooton were completed. Having a country house which he seldom used, Richard Davenport had kindly offered it to Rousseau, together with a complement of servants. Knowing full well that Jean-Jacques would never accept such generosity, Hume suggested the payment of thirty pounds a year in board. Davenport laughed heartily at the sum mentioned, but good-humoredly assented. Wishing, however, to do something special for Rousseau, he hit upon the scheme of paying for a chaise to Wooton out of his own pocket while pretending that it was a *retour* chaise which would cost but a trifle. In order to deceive his future guest the better, Davenport had an advertisement to that effect inserted in the newspapers; and Hume wrote to Chiswick acquainting him with the stroke of luck.

Though he had originally accepted the offer, Rousseau's suspicions were soon aroused by such an extraordinary coincidence as a *retour* chaise to a distant part of the country on the very day of his departure. He now complained that he was being treated like a child and accused Hume of perpetrating the cheat. Hume answered that he knew no more about it than what Davenport had told him. The incident, he related to Hugh Blair a week later:

Never tell me that, reply'd he [Rousseau], *if this be really a Contrivance of Davenports, you are acquainted with it, and consenting to it; and you cou'd not possibly have done me a greater Displeasure.* Upon which he sate down very sullen and silent; and all my Attempts were in vain to revive the Conversation and to turn it on other Subjects: He still answerd me very dryly & coldly. At last, after passing near an Hour in this ill-humour, he rose up and took a Turn about the Room: But Judge of my Surprize, when he sat down suddenly on my Knee, threw his hands about my Neck, kiss'd me with the greatest Warmth, and bedewing all my Face with Tears, exclaim'd, *Is it possible you can ever forgive me, my Dear Friend: After all the Testimonies of Affection I have receivd from you, I reward you at last with this Folly & ill Behaviour: But I have notwithstanding a Heart worthy of your Friendship: I love you, I esteem you; and not an Instance of your Kindness is thrown away upon me.* I hope you have not so bad an Opinion of me [continued Hume to Blair] as to think I was not melted on this Occasion: I assure you I kissd him and embrac'd him twenty times, with a plentiful Effusion of Tears. I think no Scene of my Life was ever more affecting.

To Mme de Boufflers, Hume repeated the story, asking her to tell it only to the ladies in her circle, because "I scarce know a male who would not think it childish."

With Rousseau off to the country apparently reconciled, Hume breathed a sigh of relief, confident that he had acted and was continuing to act for the welfare of his "pupil." He was, however, not without misgivings. "This Man, the most singular of all human Beings, has at last left me," he informed Blair; "and I have very little hopes of ever being able for the future to enjoy much of his Company; tho' he says, that, if I settle either in London or Edinburgh, he will take a Journey on foot every Year to visit me." After describing the situation at Wooton, the letter continued: "He was desperately resolv'd to rush into this Solitude, notwithstanding all my Remonstrances; and I forsee, that he will be unhappy in that Situation, as he has indeed been always, in all Situations. He will be entirely without Occupation, without Company, and almost without Amusement of any kind. He has read very little during the Course of his Life, and has now totally renounc'd all Reading: He has seen very little, and has no manner of Curiosity to see or remark: He has reflected, properly speaking, and study'd very little; and has not indeed much Knowledge: He has only felt, during the whole Course of his Life; and in this Respect, his Sensibility rises to a Pitch beyond what I have seen any Example of: But it still gives him a more acute Feeling of Pain than of Pleasure. He is like a Man who were stript not only of his Cloaths but of his Skin, and turn'd out in that Situation to combat with the rude and boisterous Elements, such as perpetually disturb this lower World."

VI

"The Peake of Derby, situated amidst Mountains and Rocks and Streams and Forrests"—to use Hume's description—was where Rousseau found the solitude he had been pining for. With difficulty he communicated his simplest desires to the servants. Deliberately he sat silent when visitors came to pay their compliments. Exultantly he boasted that he would employ the same tactics even when he knew sufficient English to be able to carry on a conversation; he could always, as a last resort, speak French until the visitors left.[30] The seclusion of Wooton was not wasted. Rousseau had a puzzle to solve, and he devoted the time to thinking, brooding, feeling. Within nine days he had pieced together most of the fragments. A week later the chance reading of a London newspaper supplied an important clue. It was not, however, until April 9 that all the details were worked out.

Writing to Mme de Verdelin on that date,[31] Rousseau dramatically announced the uncovering of a stupendous conspiracy to dishonor him. This David Hume was a villain! Rousseau had reached that startling conclusion on the basis of an accumulation of evidence. There were, for instance, the English newspapers. Their accounts of his travels through Switzerland and France and of his stay in London were inaccurate and inclined to give too much credit to the

[30] *Corr. gén.*, XV, 128.   [31] *Ibid.*, XV, 154-57.

influence and patronage of Hume. They had also printed, only the previous week, the fabricated letter from the King of Prussia with no indication that it was not genuine. Again, nobody really seemed to care for Mlle Le Vasseur. Furthermore, the friends of Hume were always trying to force money upon Rousseau. Above all, there was Hume himself.

That man was actually on good terms with many of Rousseau's enemies! He lived in the same house in London with the son of Tronchin, the desperate Swiss quack and Rousseau's mortal foe. Jean-Jacques's letters were opened before he received them—by whom else but David? Finally, two incidents definitely established his iniquity. One night on the road to Calais Hume had cried out in his sleep, "I have Jean-Jacques Rousseau," a remark, to be sure, which might be interpreted favorably—but not after the second incident. That was completely damning.

The day before leaving for Wooton, March 18, Rousseau was writing a letter to Mme de Chenonceaux at Hume's desk in his London quarters. Hume paced up and down the room, evidently anxious to know the contents; but Rousseau deliberately closed the letter without telling him. Immediately Hume asked for it, saying that he would have it posted. Rousseau felt constrained to give it to him, and he placed it on the table. Lord Nuneham dropped in to visit and, for a moment, David left the room. Rousseau seized the opportunity to pick up his letter again, murmuring that he would have time to post it himself. Lord Nuneham kindly offered to send it in the packet of the French Ambassador. Rousseau accepted. Lord Nuneham addressed the envelope and took out his seal. Returning at that instant, David insisted that his seal be used. A servant was called, and Lord Nuneham handed over the letter with instructions that it be instantly taken to the home of the Ambassador. Rousseau sensed that Hume would follow the servant out of the room—and he did. That letter, Mme de Verdelin need hardly be told, would never reach its destination, at least unopened!

But wait, the incident was not yet over. That same evening during and after supper, Hume kept looking at Rousseau, frightening him with stares of unnatural intensity. Rousseau, on his side, tried to return the look but became dizzy and had to lower his eyes. He was swept by a violent emotion, ending in complete remorse. Bursting into tears, he threw himself into the arms of *le bon David* and cried out: "No, David Hume is not a traitor; that is impossible. If he is not the best of men, he must be the blackest." Hume neither joined in the weeping nor got angry. Calmly he patted Rousseau on the back, saying over and over, "My dear Sir! What is the trouble, my dear Sir?" This aroused Rousseau all the more because Hume did not demand to know why he was accused of being a traitor.

"My mind is greatly agitated," Rousseau confided in Mme de Verdelin. For the next several weeks he repeated the story of Hume's baseness, in more or less detail, to his various correspondents. Yet Mme de Verdelin and Lord Marischal remained unconvinced.[32] Did not Rousseau see that Hume had no possible motive to injure him? Did not Rousseau know the character of *le bon David?* Did not Rousseau recognize that all his evidence could bear a favorable as well as an unfavorable interpretation? Above all, was it not the most curious way in the world to defame someone by procuring for him the signal honor of a pension of £100 a year from the King of England?

Having made up his mind, however, Rousseau was not to be deterred. Besides, once his supposition was accepted, corroborative evidence kept piling up in overwhelming proportions. The newspapers continued to attack him on intimate points that could have been supplied, he argued, only by Hume or his henchmen. Rousseau would handle his own defense in his own way. Without saying anything directly to Hume, he had already conceived and partially executed a series of what he called "slaps in the face" against his patron and betrayer.

Rousseau's campaign against Hume was trifold.[33] First, he broke off correspondence with him. Second, he sent a letter to the editor of the *St. James's Chronicle,* complaining of the publication of the fictitious letter from the King of Prussia, denouncing it as having been fabricated in Paris, "and, what rends and afflicts my heart, that the impostor has his accomplices in England." Third, upon receipt of a letter from Hume announcing the award of the royal

[32] *Ibid.,* XV, 184-88, 191-92.   [33] Hume, *Letters,* II, 394 ff.

pension, he replied, not to Hume, but to General Conway, the Secretary of State, declining the offer in terms of great ambiguity and hinting at a grievous calamity that had overtaken him.

VII

In London, meanwhile, Hume was continuing his efforts on behalf of his "pupil," blissfully unaware of what was going on at Wooton. Rousseau's campaign was far too subtle to perturb one who had already come to the conclusion that that man was "the most singular of all human Beings." Hume was not perturbed by the lack of letters from Rousseau because they had informally agreed not to burden one another in that respect. Besides, on March 22 immediately upon his arrival at Wooton, Jean-Jacques had sent an affectionate note of thanks and another one a week later, ending, "Good-by, my dear patron; I embrace you and love you with all my heart." [34] Hume was not perturbed even by Rousseau's insinuations in the *St. James's Chronicle* because it never occurred to him that they were directed against himself.

Hume's imperturbability, however, was shattered by Rousseau's letter to General Conway, not indeed because it was directed to the Secretary, but because it declined the pension that had previously been accepted. Even this refusal, embarrassing as it was to the King of England, General Conway, Lord Marischal, and Hume himself, did not immediately bring the rupture so assiduously provoked by Rousseau. Nevertheless, Hume was greatly vexed and on May 16 expressed his true sentiments to the Comtesse de Boufflers: "Was ever any thing in the world so unaccountable? For the purposes of life and conduct, and society, a little good sense is surely better than all this genius, and a little good humour than this extreme sensibility."

With Rousseau personally, however, *le bon David* made another trial of good will, beseeching him to accept the pension. When no reply was received within a month, he made yet another attempt. The only stipulation of George III had been that the pension be private. Both Lord Marischal and Hume had imagined that secrecy would be especially pleasing to Rousseau. Now, however, Hume

[34] *Corr. gén.,* XV, 129.

came to the conclusion that he was offended by it. Applying once more to General Conway, Hume suggested that the requirement of secrecy be lifted. The General agreed but insisted that Rousseau pledge his word in advance to accept a public pension if it should be offered him so "that His Majesty may not be exposed to a Second Refusal."

This information Hume forwarded on June 19 and earnestly desired Rousseau to comply with the request. Another letter and still no word from Wooton. Finally by June 23 Rousseau, finding his hand forced, came out into the open. In answer to Hume's barrage Rousseau now, in "the last letter you will receive from me," cryptically charged him with the lie direct: "You brought me to England, ostensibly to procure a haven for me, but actually to dishonor me." [35]

Utter bewilderment was Hume's first reaction to this preposterous accusation, made without the slightest substantiation and without any opportunity for denial. But bewilderment soon gave way to anger, anger mingled with fear. Hume was angry because he knew that the accusation was not only baseless but that he had actually been devoting himself for more than six months—not to mention the time in Paris—to ensure the well-being of his accuser. He was afraid because the very vagueness of the charge seemed an intimation of something sinister behind it, perhaps a deliberate attempt to ruin him in the eyes of the world. In virtuous indignation he related the whole strange narrative to his friends in London and penned an account of it to Baron d'Holbach in Paris and to Hugh Blair in Edinburgh.

Hume was especially anxious to make a clean breast of things to the Baron. Earlier, on March 6, he had ventured to exult that the dire prophecy about Rousseau had not been fulfilled. To this the Baron had good-naturedly replied: "I am very glad to hear that you have not occasion to repent of the kindness you have shown to M. Rousseau. . . . For my part, I wish heartily he may find, in your country, that repose his imagination and the sourness of his temper have deprived him of hitherto." [36] Now Hume, deeply mortified, admitted his tragic error: "You are quite right, Monsieur le Baron,

[35] Hume, *Letters*, II, 384-85.   [36] *Eminent Persons*, pp. 254-55.

Rousseau is a monster." [37] To Blair, Hume called Rousseau unequivocally, "the blackest and most atrocious Villain, beyond comparison, that now exists in the World; and I am heartily asham'd of any thing I ever wrote in his Favour."

"This is a deliberate and a cool plan to stab me," Hume protested to the Comtesse de Boufflers; "for here is the great distress which he mentioned to General Conway, and which neither you nor I could understand." In an attempt to forestall further action by Rousseau, Hume took two cautionary measures. First, he made a determined effort to elicit the facts. In a moderate and polite letter, dated June 26, charitably assuming that he had been aspersed by "some infamous Calumniator," Hume entreated Rousseau to name the specific charge in order to secure "the Privilege of proving my Innocence, and of refuting any scandalous Lye which may have been invented against me." This letter he sent to Davenport because, "You and you alone can aid me in the most critical Affair, which, during the Course of my whole Life, I have been engaged in." Would Davenport please read the letter, deliver it to Rousseau, and then discuss the issues with him? Hume himself had no faith that anything constructive would be accomplished.

The second step in self-defense was the determination to place the facts on record. Hume explained his position to Mme la Présidente de Meinières: "I had many Reasons for not concealing the Affair. I know Rousseau is writing very busily at present, and I have Grounds to think that he intends to fall equally on Voltaire & on me. He himself had told me, that he was composing his Memoirs, in which Justice wou'd be equally done to his own Character, to that of his Friends, and to that of his Enemies. As I had passed so wonderfully from the former Class to the latter, I must expect to make a fine Figure: And what, thought I, if these Memoirs be published after his Death or after mine? In the latter Case, there will be no-one to vindicate my Memory: In the former case, my Vindication will have much less Authenticity." Lord Hertford and General Conway urged immediate publication. Hume was uncertain. He hesitated over private publication with the distribution of a few

---

[37] Marmontel, *Mémoires*, II, 258. The letter is not extant, but several phrases are known.

copies to persons implicated. There was no possibility of total suppression. For all Europe was already ringing with news of the great scandal.

The Rev. Hugh Blair, who did not know Rousseau personally but who admired his writings greatly, expressed to Hume the same stupefied ignorance concerning the cause of the quarrel as did Mme de Boufflers to Rousseau:

Your Letter Astonishes me beyond measure [wrote Blair on July 10]. How or about what should Rousseau have had the Occasion to show malignity towards you, his Guide & his Benefactor? I have bewilder'd my self in Conjectures. It could surely be nothing about opinions; it could not I think be any thing relating to Mony; I can Conjecture nothing, unless he has told some lies concerning your political Conduct in France. Whatever the matter be, it must have been something extremely gross on his part, I am sure, that could overcome not only your natural Philanthropy, but your strong prepossessions in his favour. He must be a very sad fellow; and it gives me great pain that he should turn out so. But for Gods sake do not be in a haste in publishing any thing about him. Nothing but Necessity should oblige you to this. You know the ill natured pleasure the world enjoys in a Paper war between two persons of such fame & Eminence as you & him. Both parties often suffer in such personal Contests; & how clear soever the right may be on your Side, yet Envy to you will raise Partizans for him. You will see many reasons for deliberating very Cooly concerning this step; and perhaps too you may in part have been imposed upon by reports which may have aggravated some thing in his Conduct. As to your Letters to me I cannot think these need give you the least uneasiness. Though they were all published, they would only serve to show your attachment, & regard to him & would justify you the more to the World, if he has acted Unworthily to you.[38]

Mme de Boufflers, who had received a copy of Rousseau's "outrageous letter" from Hume, was deeply offended. She wrote Rousseau, July 27: "I have never seen anything like it. All your friends are in consternation and reduced to silence. . . . Mr. Hume a dastard! a traitor! Great God! . . . Madame la Maréchale de Luxembourg and I impatiently await your explanations of this incomprehensible conduct. I pray you, Sir, do not defer them, so that we

[38] Blair, MS letter, Royal Society of Edinburgh, Hume MSS, III, 59.

may at least know how to excuse you, if you cannot be completely vindicated. The silence into which we are forced blackens you more than anything else." [39]

Meanwhile on July 6 Davenport had described to Hume his interview with Rousseau. "I am really sorry for him," acknowledged that kindly gentleman, "he's uneasy, frets perpetually, & looks terribly—tis almost impossible to conceive the odness of his extreme Sensibility, so that I conclude when he's Guilty of an error, his nerves are more in fault, than his heart—things vex him, to the utmost extent of vexation which would not even move such a dull Soul as mine is. In short I perceive his disorder is Jealousy, he thinks you are fond of some Savant Hommes, who he unfortunately thinks his Enemys." As near as Davenport could make out, the affair of the pension was still bothering Rousseau; and he closed the letter in the hope that everything would soon be "set right again." [40] Hume was not so confident. "I see," he returned on the eighth, "that this whole affair is a complication of wickedness and madness; and you may believe I repent heartily, that I ever had any connexions with so pernicious and dangerous a man. He has evidently been all along courting, from ostentation, an opportunity of refusing a pension from the King, and at the same time, of picking a quarrel with me, in order to cancel at once all his past obligations to me." [41]

Despite the firsthand information from Davenport, Hume was but little prepared for the reply he finally received from Rousseau under the date of July 10. Opening, "I am sick, Sir, and little able to write," Rousseau's letter goes on in a very small and neat hand for eighteen folio pages.[42] "To day," July 15, Hume informed Blair:

I receiv'd a Letter from him, which is perfect Frenzy: It woud make a good eighteen-penny Pamphlet; and I fancy he intends to publish it. He there tells me, that D'Alembert, Horace Walpole and I had from the first enterd into a Combination to ruin him; and had ruin'd him: That the first Suspicion of my Treachery arose in him, while we lay together in the same Room of an Inn in France: I there spoke in my Sleep and

[39] *Corr. gén.*, XV, 350-51.   [40] Hume, *Letters*, II, 407-8.
[41] *Corr. gén.*, XV, 297. The letter does not appear in Hume, *Letters*.
[42] Hume, *Letters*, II, 385-401.

betray'd my Intention of ruining him: That young Troncin lodg'd in the same House with me at London; and Annie Elliot [the housekeeper] lookd very coldly at him as he went by her in the Passage: That I am also in a close Confederacy with Lord Lyttleton, who he hears is his mortal Enemy: That the English Nation were very fond of him on his first Arrival; but that Horace Walpole & I had totally alienated them from him. He owns, however, that his Belief of my Treachery went no higher than Suspicion while he was in London; but it rose to Certainty after he arrivd in the Country: For that there were several Publications in the Papers against him, which coud have proceeded from no body but me or my Confederate Horace Walpole. The rest is all of a like Strain, intermix'd with many Lyes and much Malice. I own, that I was very anxious about this Affair but this Letter has totally reliev'd me.

This "last mad letter" completely altered Hume's attitude toward Rousseau. His anger melted and his fears dissipated. A certain indignation remained that he had been exposed to such a harrowing experience, but that too gradually gave way before charity and forbearance. At the moment Hume was relieved to discover the meaning of Rousseau's dark hints. Why! They were no more than the devious offspring of extreme sensibility and solitary brooding, stimulated perhaps by the malignant whisperings of Thérèse Le Vasseur. The question "Was Rousseau a madman?" could not, however, so easily be settled. Davenport still found his "wild philosopher" entirely normal in other respects, just as Hume always had. But no longer did Hume attribute everything to malice; there was at least a mixture of causes. Rousseau himself, to be sure, complicated the issue by insisting on his own sincerity one way or the other: "I am the most unhappy of human beings if you are guilty; I am the vilest if you are innocent."

Writing to Davenport immediately after receiving the letter, Hume admitted, "I am really sorry for him; so that, tho' I intended to be very severe on him in my Answer, I have been very sparing; as you may see. . . . If I may venture to give my Advice, it is, that you wou'd continue the charitable Work you have begun, till he be shut up altogether in Bedlam, or till he quarrel with you and run away from you." Hume's last letter to Rousseau in answer to the defiance: "If you are innocent, deign to justify yourself," confined

itself to straightening out the facts of the much disputed "Conversation between us the Evening before your Departure." Rousseau's
"long Letter," after relating how he had tried to outstare Hume
but was overcome with an inexplicable giddiness and was forced to
lower his eyes, had proceeded: "The external features and the de-
meanor of *le bon David* denote a good man; but where, Great God,
did this good man get those eyes with which he transfixes his
friends?" Hume was content merely to remind him that most studious men are subject to "Reveries or Fits of Absence, without being
exposed to such Suspicions."

VIII

Still undecided about publication, Hume continued to piece together an account of his relationship with Jean-Jacques. The situation was not basically altered by the knowledge of Rousseau's partial
or complete insanity, for insane or not, he wielded the most eloquent
pen in Europe. Anyone reading the letter of July 10 without knowing all the facts would certainly be swayed by his art. The with-
holding of the "I have Jean-Jacques Rousseau" dream until near
the close builds up to a final and pathetic series of "Yes, Mr. Hume,
you have me" that keeps the reader spellbound—a magnificent piece
of rhetoric. Rousseau was now writing furiously at Wooton, presumably on the *Confessions*. Letters to his partisans in Paris began
to be circulated, some of them getting into print. Hume had long
since concluded that, "of all the Writers that are or ever were in
Europe," Rousseau "is the man who has acquird the most enthusiastic and most passionate Admirers." He never found reason to alter
that opinion.

Though most of Hume's friends at first opposed publication, they
soon began to change their minds. On July 21 D'Alembert, writing
in the name of the Paris group, voiced this change: "The public is
now too much concerned with your quarrel, and things have advanced too far for you not to give them the plain unvarnished
facts." [43] Hume had three copies made of his narrative, one for
D'Alembert, one for Lord Hertford, the third for himself. His letter of August 12 to Trudaine de Montigny announced the sending

[43] *Ibid.*, II, 413.

of the packet to Paris and explained: "It is nothing to dispute my Style or my Abilities as an Historian or a Philosopher; My Books ought to answer for themselves, or they are not worth the defending: To fifty Writers, who have attacked me on this head, I never made the least Reply: But this is a different Case: Imputations are here thrown on my Morals and my Conduct."

In London, the King and Queen expressed a desire to see the documents. "They read them with avidity," says Hume, "and entertain the same sentiments that must strike every one." In Paris, D'Alembert, granted discretionary power, ultimately elected to publish. And in October appeared *Exposé succinct de la contestation qui s'est élevée entre M. Hume et M. Rousseau, avec les pièces justicatives*, with an anonymous Preface extolling Hume's well-known virtues and a signed Postscript by D'Alembert denying Rousseau's charge that he had been implicated in the fictitious King-of-Prussia letter. Hume immediately arranged for an English edition, which appeared the next month as *A Concise and Genuine Account of the Dispute between Mr. Hume and Mr. Rousseau; with the Letters That Passed between Them during Their Controversy. As Also, the Letters of the Hon. Mr. Walpole, and Mr. D'Alembert, Relative to This Extraordinary Affair.*

In order to safeguard the original documents, Hume sent them to the British Museum with the comment: "As M. Rousseau had wrote to several of his Correspondents abroad, that I never dared to publish the Letters, which he had wrote me; or if I published them, they wou'd be so falsify'd, that they wou'd not be the same, I was obliged to say in my Preface, that the Originals wou'd be consigned to the Musæum: I hope you have no Objection to the receiving them. . . . Be so good as to give them the Corner of any Drawer." After the lapse of three months the papers were returned with the information that the Trustees did not think it proper to receive them.

"I cannot imagine," Hume told his printer, Thomas Becket, "that a Piece wrote on so silly a Subject as mine will ever come to a second Edition." Like the careful man of letters that he was, however, he was fully prepared, adding, "but if it shoud, please order the following Corrections to be made." One of the corrections that were never made clears up a minor mystery in Rousseau's letter of July 10, where he had charged that only Hume could have supplied the information for two attacks in the *St. James's Chronicle*. In the *Concise Account* Hume had merely remarked that he knew nothing whatsoever about them. But on November 27 he received a letter from Georges Deyverdun, an unknown young Swiss living in London, confessing that it was he who had written them and offering to make public acknowledgment if Hume deemed it necessary. Hume was satisfied with sending a copy of the letter to Davenport, requesting him to turn it over to Rousseau.

IX

The controversy was over. Hume was sorry that it had happened and sorry that he had had to publish. "I forsaw," he acknowledged on December 20, "that many wou'd doubt of the Propriety of my Conduct: But I was told, that many, from want of Information, believd me to have been a Calumniator and a false perfidious Friend. You will own that there was no Proportion between the one blame & the other." Yet he admitted candidly, "I have a mortal Aversion to these Publications." [44] Rousseau, for his part, was sorry that he had been persecuted, and was still being persecuted, and would always be persecuted by Hume and by others like him. But justice would be done: "If I knew that Mr. Hume would not be unmasked before his death, I should find it hard to retain belief in Providence." [45]

All the world but a few ardent Rousseauists, however, was convinced, in the words of the Marquis de Chastellux, that "David Hume can do no wrong," [46] that he was and always had been *le bon David*. And so he was, for his patronage of Rousseau never abated. In February, 1767, Rousseau, urged on by Davenport, allowed that gentleman to apply to General Conway for the royal pension, which he would be proud to accept if Hume had nothing to do with it.[47] Conway, of course, immediately consulted Hume who had recently become Undersecretary of State. David "exhorted him to do so

[44] Hume, MS letter, Victoria and Albert Museum, London.
[45] *Corr. gén.*, XVI, 35. [46] *Calendar of Hume MSS*, IV, 22.
[47] *Corr. gén.*, XVI, 276-77.

charitable an Action." The benignant King did not need to be long persuaded; and the transaction was soon concluded, Conway officially informing Davenport on March 18, 1767.

But before any payments were made, Rousseau had fled from Wooton. The circumstances [48] may be related as told by Hume to Turgot on May 22:

I know not, whether you have heard of the late Incidents which have happened to the poor unfortunate Rousseau, who is now plainly delirious and an Object of the greatest Compassion. About three Weeks ago, he ran off, without giving the least Warning, from Mr Davenport's, carrying only his Gouvernante along with him, leaving most of his Baggage, and above thirty Guineas of Money: There was also a Letter found on his Table, abusing his Land-lord, and reproaching him as an Accomplice with me in the Project of ruining and affronting him. He took the Road towards London; and Mr Davenport begged me to find him out, and to discover how his Money and Baggage might be sent after him. He was never heard of for a fortnight; till at last a most extravagant Letter of his was delivered to the Chancellor, dated at Spalding in the County of Lincoln. He there tells the Magistrate that he was on his Road to Dover, in order to leave the Kingdom (tho' Spalding is entirely out of the Road). But he dares not proceed a Step farther, nor stir out of the House; for fear of his Enemies: He entreats therefore the Chancellor to send him an authorized Guide to conduct him; and this he demands as the last Act of Hospitality from the Nation towards him. A few days after, I learned from Mr Davenport that he had received a new Letter from Rousseau dated still at Spalding, in which he expresses great Contrition, speaks of his miserable and unhappy Condition, and marks his Intention of returning to his former Retreat at Wootton. I was then hopeful, that he had now recovered his Senses; when behold! a few hours after, General Conway received a Letter from him dated at Dover above two hundred Miles distant from Spalding: This great Journey he had made in about two days. Nothing can be more frenzical than this Letter: He supposes himself to be a Prisoner of State in the hands of the General at my Suggestion, entreats for Leave to depart the Kingdom, represents the Danger of assassinating him in private, and while he owns that he has been rendered infamous in England during his Life he fortells that his Memory will be justifyed after his Death. He says that he has composed a Volume of Memoirs, chiefly with regard to the Treatment he has met

[48] See Note L, below.

with in England, and the State of Captivity, in which he has been detained; and if the General will fairly give him Permission to depart, this Volume, which is deposited in safe hands, shall be delivered to him, and nothing ever appear to the Disgrace of the Nation or of its Ministers. He adds, as if a Ray of Reason then broke in upon his Soul, speaking of himself in the third Person: *He abandons forever the project of writing his life and his memoirs; he will never let slip, orally or in writing, a single word of complaint about the misfortunes that he met with in England; he will never speak of Mr. Hume, or will speak of him only with honor; and when pressed to explain those indiscreet accusations that he sometimes made at the height of his sufferings, he will blame them without further ado on his melancholy disposition, which inclined to distrust and suspicion, by this unhappy bent, the product of his misfortunes, now completes them.*

The letter to Turgot and a similar one to the Comtesse de Boufflers were not written simply to give information; they were pleas for clemency. "The poor Man," Hume informed Turgot, "is absolutely lunatic and consequently cannot be the Object of any Laws or civil Punishment." Would all the good people in Paris please exert their influence to see that he is not persecuted any more and, if possible, to settle him somewhere in the country "under a discreet Keeper"? The very day that Hume penned his letters of compassion Rousseau landed joyfully at Calais, having experienced as he put it, "many bizarre adventures." [49]

Rousseau's later life was truly one long, bizarre adventure, the result of persecution mania. Why he never extended the *Confessions* to include the quarrel with Hume is probably not ascertainable. Perhaps the weird promise to General Conway had something to do with it. Perhaps not. At any rate, it was not because he either recognized his own mistake about Hume or forgave Hume for his alleged betrayal. Even in France as late as 1768,[50] he detected Hume's persecuting hand. But by then Rousseau had found new and more tangible evidence, the full meaning of which was not worked out until 1770 after nearly four years of brooding. This was the matter of the Ramsay portraits.[51] Jean-Jacques, it would seem, who really was

[49] *Corr. gén.*, XVII, 65.   [50] *Ibid.*, XVIII, 150.
[51] See Note M, below.

handsome, had been given the face of a Cyclops; David, who really had the face of a Cyclops, had been given a charming air.

In *Rousseau, Judge of Jean-Jacques*, that extraordinary anatomy of self, the affair of the paintings is discussed in detail. Hume had schemed it out of pure malice. "He desired this portrait," avows Rousseau the Judge, "as ardently as a deeply smitten lover desires his mistress's. Through importunities he extorted the consent of Jean-Jacques. That same Jean-Jacques was made to wear a deep black cap and a deep brown garment; he was posed in a dark spot; and, in order to paint him seated, he was made to stand up, stooped over, supported by one hand on a low table, in an attitude where highly strained muscles altered the very contours of his face." And the result? "This terrible portrait"! "The face of a frightful Cyclops"! All the machination of David Hume! And the purpose? To distribute engravings throughout Europe so that Rousseau would become known as ugly and Hume as handsome.

Poor Allan Ramsay, who had painted his masterpieces. Poor Jean-Jacques, who had worn his accustomed Armenian robe and fur cap. Poor David, who had worn a beautiful scarlet coat with gold lace and who had innocently sent engravings of his "pupil" to Rousseau's absent friends. The two Ramsay paintings hung in Hume's parlor in Edinburgh until his death, serving as pieces of art no doubt, but also, one surmises, as reminders of how *le bon David* had won and lost a friend.

The friendship had assuredly ended unhappily, but no one was to blame. Rousseau was not to blame, for he could not help feeling persecuted. Hume was not to blame, for he could not pass by virtue in distress. They were both geniuses. They were both well intentioned. They were both sincere. And if they had never met, there is every reason to believe that they would have remained friends.

PART IV

THE JOHNSONIANS

Hume would never have written History, had not Voltaire written it before him. He is an echo of Voltaire.—JOHNSON TO BOSWELL, SPRING, 1768

I have not read Hume.—JOHNSON TO BOSWELL, APRIL 30, 1773

CHAPTER 7

HUME AND BOSWELL

D AVID HUME had no Boswell, which is a great loss to the modern lover of biography. The few surviving glimpses of this strikingly original Inquirer after truth are tantalizing in their failure to reveal more of his personality. Yet it is possibly well for Hume's philosophical reputation that no ardent disciple recorded the commonplaces of daily conversation. For if Dr. Johnson is more beloved as a man through the efforts of James Boswell, he is certainly less respected as a thinker through the disclosure of his habit of "talking for victory." No hero is perfectly heroical to his valet, and no philosopher perfectly philosophical to his Boswell. But, though Hume had no Boswell, he nearly had *the* Boswell. Less paradoxically, James Boswell, while a young man in search of a hero, seriously considered the worship of Hume.

Yet against all the allurements drawing Boswell to Hume—his international preëminence in literature, his patronage of Scottish talent, his character of *le bon David*—one opposing factor remained insuperable, his religious skepticism. This skepticism peculiarly distressed Boswell and was the deciding consideration that impelled him to seek out Dr. Johnson as a fitter hero. He erred, however, in believing that even the stalwart faith of a Johnson could serve him to any ultimate avail. For Boswell's sense of morality was fundamentally unstable: an insatiable appetite for alcohol and for women stimulated an active conscience that could be lulled only momentarily in religion. Many years later when a devoted follower of Dr. Johnson's, he had the honesty to state the issue, though not the courage to face it: "How inconsistent is it for me to be making a pilgrimage to meet Dr. Johnson, and licentiously loving wenches by the way." [1]

[1] Boswell, *Private Papers*, XIII, 16. Cited hereafter as *P. P.*

Essentially, Boswell was not religious in temperament. It is true that he tried in turn several Christian sects ranging from Presbyterianism to Roman Catholicism and then back to Anglicanism after flirting momentarily with infidelity. And although he doubtless leaned more to High than to Low Church, the particular form of religious service was of but secondary importance. Nor, as with many, was it ethical value that he was seeking. Boswell approached religion fundamentally neither for worship nor for ethics. Religion was of supreme value to him because it answered one overwhelming emotional yearning. Christianity held out the promise of immortality, the guarantee to the faithful against annihilation, against that most terrible and yet most pervasive of all thoughts that he, James Boswell, would one day pass forever out of existence.

Though, in consequence, Hume's infidelity violently repelled Boswell, it also strangely attracted him. He was seized with a strong curiosity to discover the key to Hume's ethical existence: Why did not his skepticism of religion, the reputed foundation of morality, make of him an immoral man? And immoral Hume was not. On the contrary, he was the very soul of virtue: calm, honest, fair, tolerant, friendly, and generous—in short, *le bon David*. He was, moreover, the boon companion of an ever increasing number of Moderates among the Edinburgh clergy, the ablest and most distinguished ministers of the Church of Scotland.

Boswell was frankly puzzled. Moral imperatives may be imperative, yet—he was compelled to admit—they do not always carry conviction. That virtue and infidelity are irreconcilable, he did not seriously doubt; but the consequences were not entirely clear: If Hume was not a Christian, he must secretly be wicked? Or, if Hume was good, he must secretly be a Christian? Which alternative offered the more suitable explanation? One or the other, he felt, must be true. But which? Boswell's mind was confused, as many a more speculative mind than his has been confused, both before and since. The problem weighed on him mightily.

This, then, was the ethical enigma that vexed Boswell periodically while Hume was in full career, that demented him temporarily while Hume lay dying in the summer of 1776, and that continued to harry him for some years afterwards until it finally worked itself off through psychological purgation. The history of this mental fixation provides important evidence concerning the character of Hume and suggests a new and hitherto untested guide to the still uncharted regions of the biographer's complex mind. The fantastic tale of the dual role played by Hume, Great Infidel as well as *le bon David*, in the consciousness of James Boswell may now be told in sober fact with little need of conjecture and none of embellishment. The outline is in the hand of a great artist, Boswell himself, in his *Letters* and *Private Papers*, records among the most intimate that any man has ever dared to bequeath to posterity.

I

In the summer of 1758 James Boswell, not yet eighteen years old, presented a letter of introduction to David Hume in Edinburgh. Kindly received, he was at once favorably impressed with his host: "a most discreet, affable man as ever I met with, and has realy a great deal of learning, and a choice collection of books. He is indeed an extraordinary man, few such people are to be met with nowadays." Momentarily Boswell lost his misgivings and assured the donor of the introduction: "Mr. Hume, I think, is a very proper person for a young man to cultivate an acquaintance with; though he has not, perhaps, the most delicate taste, yet he has apply'd himself with great attention to the study of the ancients, and is likeways a great historian, so that you are not only entertained in his company, but may reap a great deal of usefull instruction. I own myself much obliged to you, dear Sir, for procuring me the pleasure of his acquaintance." [2]

This first meeting represents the triumph of Hume's personal charm over Boswell's latent prejudice. The cleavage between dread of the consequences of religious infidelity and pleasure in the company of Hume was not ultimately to be ignored; but for the time being, Boswell was flushed with success. Hume was the first literary lion of distinction that he had bagged, and his pride knew no limits. Indeed, until after he attached himself, like the proverbial Scottish burr, to Dr. Johnson in May, 1763, he accepted Hume unreservedly as "the greatest Writer in Brittain." [3]

The first impressions of Hume were long remembered by Bos-

[2] Boswell, *Letters*, I, 2.   [3] *P. P.*, I, 130.

well, particularly what seemed to be the discrepancy between the philosopher's keenness of mind and broadness of brogue. While traveling with Henry Home, Lord Kames, in October, 1762, the young lion-hunter had a bad night's sleep in an uncomfortable rustic inn. In the morning, "I got up stupid and discontented enough," he admits. "I was reduced to that ebb of Understanding as to produce the following compositions which I wrote with a diamond pen upon a window":

> David Hume, the Historian, on Christmas did eat
> A rabbit alive as it stood on it's feet.
> T. SMOLLETT M.D.

> Howt owt Tobie Smallet maun ye lauch at me
> Tho' ye in your garret be liken to dee.
> D. HUME

> Gentlemen, I am no Poet but I laugh at you both.
> H. HOME

"Alas! alas!" laments Boswell, "am I reduced to this state!" [4]

Before meeting Dr. Johnson, Boswell paid another visit to Hume and records in his journal under November 4, 1762, a sample of what a Boswell might have done for the philosopher. It is an intimate scene that he pictures. Hume was "in his house in James's Court, in a good room newly fitted up hung round with Strange's Prints. He was sitting at his ease reading Homer." Boswell, on this occasion, discovered his extraordinary talent for conducting an interview: "We payed him a few compliments in pleasant mirth. Thus did an hour and a half of our Existence move along. We were very happy. I showed away, started subjects and now and then spoke tollerably, much better than my knowledge entitles me to do. I have remembered the heads and the very words of a great part of Mr. Hume's conversation with us." The young hero-worshiper made no effort to conceal his admiration: "I asked Mr. Hume to write more. He said he had done enough and was allmost ashamed to see his own bulk on a Shelf." [5]

The interview is further remarkable in baring the perennial antagonism between Hume and Johnson, an antagonism that Bos-

---

[4] *Ibid.*, I, 102-3.   [5] *Ibid.*, I, 126-29.

well himself was to play a part in heightening. The "character" of the great lexicographer that Hume drew at Boswell's instigation is not wholly unfair, and it is notable for self-revelation: "Mr. Samuel Johnson has got a Pension of £300 a year. Indeed his Dictionary was a kind of a national Work so he has a kind of claim to the Patronage of the state. His stile is particular and pedantic. He is a man of enthusiasm and antiquated notions, a keen Jacobite yet hates the Scotch. Holds the Episcopal Hierarchy in supreme veneration and said he would stand before a battery of cannon to have the Convocation restored to it's full powers. He holds Mr. Hume in abhorrence and left a company one night upon his coming in."

Soon after, Boswell displayed his sharpness of observation in venturing at a party to entertain the ladies with a mimicry of Hume. "Indeed it was not an imitation," he modestly explains, "but the very Man. I had not only his external address, but his sentiments and mode of expression." [6] The mimicry was carried on in good humor and with genuine respect. Respect is also shown in a penetrating remark of 1764: "David Hume, who has thought as much as any man, who has been tortured on the metaphysical rack, who has walked the wilds of the speculation, wisely and calmly concludes that the business of ordinary life is the proper employment of man." [7] A wise and a calm sentiment that would have made a happier man of James Boswell had he been capable of following it.

Under the influence of Dr. Johnson, however, Boswell's original respect for Hume began to wane. For the venerated moralist was forthright in detestation of Hume as of all skeptics. "Truth," he thundered at one of the early sessions with Boswell, "will not afford sufficient food to their vanity; so they have betaken themselves to errour." He continued, toying with the idea: "Truth, Sir, is a cow that will yield such people no more milk, and so they are gone to milk the bull." [8] Boswell shortly came to adopt one of Johnson's most vigorously held principles, that any means of discommoding an antagonist in argument is legitimate, and that if the antagonist is an infidel, rudeness is proper. Ostentatiously to leave a company upon the entrance of a known infidel is the least a man can do to

---

[6] *Ibid.*, I, 135-36.   [7] Boswell, *Letters*, I, 50.
[8] *Life of Johnson*, I, 444.

demonstrate his orthodoxy! In the course of time, Boswell became so much an exponent of this principle as to take to task Dr. William Adams, Master of Pembroke College, Oxford, for "the politeness with which he treats the Infidel," David Hume.[9] But it was only behind his back that Boswell himself was impolite to the Scottish infidel. Hume's friendship he continued to court because he was ever eager to fathom the ethical enigma that was Hume.

II

During the decade and a half following 1758 Boswell heard much of Hume, talked much against him, but was always pleased to tell strangers of their friendship. While traveling on the Continent from 1763 to 1766 before settling down as an advocate in Edinburgh, he found that the name of Hume attracted attention. And he was by no means averse to being the center of attention. After his remarkable early success with Hume and Johnson, Boswell had become an incorrigible literary lion-hunter, a veritable Tartarin of the *salons*. In Europe he added to the spoils of the chase in rapid succession a distinguished trio, Rousseau, Voltaire, and Paoli. General Paoli was an ardent religionist and bitter contemnor of Hume. Voltaire was his equally ardent admirer; Hume is *"Un vraye Philosophe,"* he instructed the audacious young Scot.[10] And Rousseau was Hume's "pupil."

When Hume brought Rousseau to England in 1766, Boswell, as has been seen, shared in the undertaking. He was entrusted with the delicate mission of escorting Thérèse Le Vasseur. Of how little Boswell was fit to be trusted with any woman, the native simplicity of the Citizen of the World had no suspicion. Yet in the *affaire* of the passage from Paris to London, Thérèse was surely as much at fault as Jamie. And once safe in England that worthy was no little relieved to hand over to Jean-Jacques his indefatigable *gouvernante*.

If Rousseau had not known his Boswell, Hume had. Immediately on learning that Thérèse was in his custody, Hume warned the Comtesse de Boufflers. Though bantering in tone, his letter displays insight into the character of Boswell as well as prescience: "I

[9] *P. P.*, XI, 169. [10] *Ibid.*, IV, 130.

learn that Mademoiselle sets out post, in company with a friend of
mine; a young gentleman, very good-humoured, very agreeable, and
very mad. He visited Rousseau in his mountains, who gave him a
recommendation to Paoli, the King of Corsica; where this gentleman, whose name is Boswell, went last summer, in search of adventures. He has such a rage for literature, that I dread some event
fatal to our friend's honour. You remember the story of Terentia,
who was first married to Cicero, then to Sallust, and at last, in her
old age, married a young nobleman, who imagined that she must
possess some secret, which would convey to him eloquence and
genius."

In London, joyously babbling to Dr. Johnson about his Continental exploits, Boswell innocently mentioned Rousseau. Johnson
waxed sarcastic, "It seems, Sir, you have kept very good company
abroad. . . ." Boswell rose to the defense: "My dear Sir, you don't
call Rousseau bad company. Do you really think *him* a bad man?"
Johnson: "Sir, if you are talking jestingly of this, I don't talk with
you. If you mean to be serious, I think him one of the worst of
men; a rascal, who ought to be hunted out of society, as he has been.
Three or four nations have expelled him; and it is a shame that he
is protected in this country. . . . Rousseau, Sir, is a very bad man. I
would sooner sign a sentence for his transportation, than that of any
felon who has gone from the Old Bailey these many years. Yes, I
should like to have him work in the plantations." [11]

"This violence seemed very strange to me," remarked Boswell—
to himself. At the moment, he must also have been wondering how
much more violent Johnson might have been had he known of the
letter of January 4. "I am going to give myself the exquisite pleasure," Boswell had written to Rousseau, his "Illustrious philosopher,"
"of making you acquainted with Mr. Johnson, of whom I spoke so
much at Motiers, and of whom you said: *I would like that man, I
would respect him,* and that after having heard that he did not at
all respect you. But I know you both, and although the one employs
his forces to support the wisdom of the ages, and the other to support the visions of his sublime and unique genius, I am sure that

[11] *Life of Johnson,* II, 11-12.

your great souls will recognize one another with warmth." [12] How little Boswell had really known his Johnson!

While Rousseau was in England, Boswell let no opportunity pass to display his journalistic talents. Seizing the occasion of the subsequent "literary tragi-comedy," as he well named it, he suggested the idea for a ludicrous print exposing the ingrate Rousseau as *The Savage Man*. Unaware of its origin, Hume described the print to the Comtesse de Boufflers: "M. Rousseau is represented as a Yahoo, newly caught in the woods; I am represented as a farmer, who caresses him and offers him some oats to eat, which he refuses in a rage; Voltaire and D'Alembert are whipping him up behind; and Horace Walpole making him horns of *papier maché*. The idea is not altogether absurd." Boswell also took the side of Hume in various squibs in the newspapers, both prose and verse.

The residence of Hume in London from 1767 to 1769 as Undersecretary of State deprived him of the company of Boswell except when down for a spree in between sessions of the Edinburgh courts. On such occasions that irrepressible spirit exulted inordinately in having close at hand his first two tamed lions. "I am really the *Great Man* now," he boasted in 1768. "I have had David Hume in the forenoon and Mr. Johnson in the afternoon of the same day visiting me." [13] Capitalizing on their proximity, he soon learned to play off the one against the other. He would leave the company of the infidel to pass to that of the moralist, whom he would bait with what he had just heard. The refutations offered by Johnson of the remarks made by Hume, he treasured up to provide consolation when consolation was most needed. But about Johnson's general attitude toward Hume he had no illusions, observing once when the subject arose, "Hume I knew he would abuse." [14]

Yet Johnson was hypersensitive about Hume, as Boswell also learned: "I repeated to him from Temple's letter the expostulation how 'he would not say my *pious*, but my *moral* friend' could 'support barbarous measures of administration which they had not the face to ask even their Infidel Pensioner Hume to defend.' This made more impression upon him than almost any thing that I ever wit-

---

[12] Boswell, *Letters*, I, 87. The original is in French.
[13] *Ibid.*, I, 160.   [14] *P. P.*, VII, 175.

nessed. Indeed I can make no exception. However firm in his own sentiments, it might affect him a little seriously to find in what a light his conduct could be viewed by others." [15] On a later occasion Boswell tried the same remark on Hume, but naturally without drawing the same fire. Hume merely thought it ungentlemanly.

Boswell had known well enough in advance that explosion was sure to result from this placing of the infidel above the moralist; but he liked danger. Bored with easy success in ordinary literary sport, he cultivated the more exotic taste of hunting lions in pairs, uncongenial pairs—and the more uncongenial the better. The achievement in 1776 of seating Dr. Johnson and the infidel Whig statesman, John Wilkes, side by side at the dinner table and having Johnson remain affably in the room was the triumph of his life. "There was nothing to equal it in the whole history of the *Corps Diplomatique*," complimented Edmund Burke.[16] Only one other feat could possibly have surpassed it in daring, the bringing together of Johnson and Hume. But even Boswell realized that there are limits in lion-baiting.

For a lion, as well as a worm, will turn. A typical altercation with Johnson is described by his tormentor: "You was of his opinion, but to be more fully confirm'd you was going on. He thought you was going to push him with contrariety, and called out, 'My dear Bosé, let us have no more of this. It is extremely disagreable to me. You are making nothing of this argument. I had rather you'd whistle me a Scotch Tune.' " [17] Hume also could turn. His taunt that "it required great goodness of disposition to withstand the baleful effects of Christianity" [18] was a palpable hit against the exponent of rough methods with the heterodox. And Hume could maul in true Johnsonian fashion, as the time he buffeted Boswell into a fury by offering to give him half a crown for every page in Johnson's *Dictionary* in which he could not find an absurdity, if Boswell would give him half a crown for every page in which he did find one.

On the whole, as the years passed, the friendship between Hume and Boswell increased in intimacy. Hume delighted in acting as literary patron to the younger man. In 1767 he attempted to arrange

[15] *Ibid.*, X, 178.   [16] *Life of Johnson*, III, 79.
[17] *P. P.*, VII, 74.   [18] *Ibid.*, VII, 189.

for the publication of the *Account of Corsica* and was later solicitous in bringing to the author reports of its good reception. He outlined at his request a course of study in modern history. He sought to persuade him to write an account of the union of Scotland with England, "which might be a neat popular piece of History." [19] He pampered and uncled him with much evident fondness.

Boswell's affectionate nature responded to the friendliness of *le bon David*. "I was very hearty with him here this winter," he acknowledged in 1767.[20] Two years later he wrote to his fiancée most ingratiatingly soon before their marriage: "Mr. David Hume was with me this morning, and gave a philosophical opinion that our marriage must be a happy one. Were it not for his infidel writings, every body would love him. He is a plain, obliging, kind-hearted man." [21] The future Mrs. Boswell was to learn considerably more about the character of her husband than either of his distinguished friends, the philosopher or the moralist, even dimly suspected. But she, poor woman, also wisely learned to keep a secret.

Boswell, a little later, became Hume's tenant in Edinburgh, and the two were drawn even closer together. Boswell has a story about an intimate gathering of the literati at the house of "the northern Epicurus," where an "elegant supper" was served, with "three sorts of ice-creams." [22] The tenant's half-yearly visits to the landlord for the payment of rent are models of literary and friendly ceremonies. That of March, 1775, is worthy of comparison with the best between Boswell and Johnson. The subject of Ossian supplied the pretext for the continuation of the perennial Johnson-Hume bout. And Boswell, if not exactly a fair, was certainly an expert, referee.

"*Monday 6 March.* . . . Drank tea with David Hume, having half a year's rent of his house to pay him. He spoke of Mr. Johnson's *Journey* in terms so slighting that it could have no effect but to shew his resentment. He however agreed with him perfectly as to Ossian. But then he disbelieved not so much for want of testimony, as from the nature of the thing according to his apprehension. He said if fifty barea——d highlanders should say that *Fingal* was an

[19] *Ibid.*, X, 42.
[21] *P. P.*, VIII, 227.
[20] Boswell, *Letters*, I, 103.
[22] Boswell, *Letters*, I, 233.

ancient Poem, he would not believe them. He said it was not to be believed that a people who were continually concerned to keep themselves from starving or from being hanged, should preserve in their memories a Poem in six books. He said that Homer had once been written, which made a great difference. . . . He said that the extensive fame of Ossian was owing to the notion that the poems were so ancient; that if McPherson had given them as his own, nobody would have read them to an end. He acknowledged that there were some good passages in them, and perhaps there might be some small parts ancient. He said the highlanders, who had been famed as a warlike people, were so much flattered to have it thought that they had a great Poet among them that they all tried to support the fact, and their wish to have it so made them even ready to persuade themselves into it. I told him Mr. Johnson's saying that he could undertake to write an epick poem on the story of Robinhood which the half of the people of England should say they had heard in their youth. Mr. Hume said the people of England would not be so ready to support such a story. They had not the same temptation with the highlanders, there being many excellent english Poets." [23]

More poignantly than ever during this period of increasing personal affection for Hume was Boswell prepossessed with the horror of annihilation. One incident is of high significance in revealing the latent skepticism of his essentially unreligious mind and in anticipating the greatest upheaval of his moral life the following year over the death of Hume. It happened during a church service in November, 1775. The sermon was on the text, "O death, where is thy sting?" and the lesson emphasized the consolations of Christianity. "A strange thought struck me," confides Boswell, "that I would apply to David Hume, telling him that at present I was happy in having pious faith. But in case of it's failing me by some unexpected revolution in my mind, it would be humane in him to furnish me with reflections by which a man of sense and feeling could support his spirit as an Infidel. I was really serious in this thought. I wonder what David can suggest." [24]

Several weeks later of a Sunday, and well fortified with both

[23] *P. P.*, X, 109-11.   [24] *Ibid.*, XI, 5.

morning and afternoon sermons, Boswell, the man of little faith, ventured to call on Hume. The philosopher was just finishing dinner with his sister and nephew. "He had on a White nightcap and a hat above it. He called for a fresh bottle of port, which he and I drank, all but a single glass that his Nephew took. I indeed took the largest share." Though somewhat ailing in health, Hume was in fine intellectual fettle; and Boswell drew him out expertly, *vini causa,* over the chief literary themes of the day and elicited from him biographical information. "I had really a good chat with him this afternoon. I thought also of writing his life."

The subject of religious skepticism Boswell did not broach. Yet it was clearly in his mind when he reflected: "It was curious to see David such a civil, sensible, comfortable looking man, and to recollect this is the Great Infidel. Beleif or want of Belief is not absolutely connected with practice. How many surly men are teachers of the Gospel of peace!" [25] Boswell had proceeded a considerable way toward the solution of the problem of the moral imperatives. He was, indeed, on the brink of decision.

III

That Johnson and Hume were the opposite faces of the moral medallion, good and evil, Boswell had long been striving to convince himself, but without success. Hume, despite his convictions or lack of convictions, was patently good; he was *le bon David.* And Boswell at long last was satisfied that there was nothing fruitful in the moral imperative: If Hume was not a Christian, he must secretly be wicked. Much more fascinating was the alternative: If Hume was good, he must secretly be a Christian! This was a hope that Boswell earnestly cherished. He had once hinted it pretty broadly: "David is really amiable. I allways regret to him his unlucky principles and he smiles at my faith. But I have a hope which he has not, or pretends not to have." [26] He longed for the chance to test out this alluring hypothesis fairly and fully and so settle the problem once and for all. The opportunity came in the summer of 1776. After a year of failing heath, Hume lay dying. This, then, was the grand moment, in fact, the last moment. The time for jocularity was past. All pre-

[25] *Ibid.,* XI, 40-42.   [26] Boswell, *Letters,* I, 160.

tense would now be over and Hume would tell the truth. Boswell was determined to see it through.

The deathbed interview [27] of July 7, 1776, between Boswell and Hume holds a dual interest. It is, to begin with, an exceptionally brilliant piece of reporting. Boswell always had a flair for news, and now he outdid himself. As journalism it is the most sensational "scoop" of the eighteenth century, although unpublished until the twentieth. But it is more than the graphic record of the dying thoughts of a great philosopher. It is also the graphic record of a moral crisis in the mind of a most unphilosophical reporter. The interview belongs, therefore, to the autobiography of James Boswell as well as to the biography of David Hume.

"Annihilation" was the theme set by Boswell to which he relentlessly forced Hume to return time and again when the conversation threatened to flow into other channels. Though lean and ghastly, Hume "seemed to be placid and even cheerful. He said he was just approaching to his end. I think these were his words. I know not how I contrived to get the subject of Immortality introduced. He said he never had entertained any beleif in Religion since he began to read Locke and Clarke. I asked him if he was not religious when he was young. He said he was. . . . He then said flatly that the Morality of every Religion was bad, and, I really thought, was not jocular when he said 'that when he heard a man was religious, he concluded he was a rascal, though he had known some instances of very good men being religious.' . . . I asked him if it was not possible that there might be a future state. He answered It was possible that a piece of coal put upon the fire would not burn; and he added that it was a most unreasonable fancy that we should exist for ever. . . . I asked him if the thought of Annihilation never gave him any uneasiness. He said not the least; no more than the thought that he had not been, as Lucretius observes. . . . I tried him . . . saying that a future state was surely a pleasing idea. He said No, for that it was allways seen through a gloomy medium; there was allways a Phlegethon or a Hell. . . . I said, 'If I were you, I should regret Annihilation. Had I written such an admirable History, I should be sorry to leave it.' He said, 'I shall leave that history, of

[27] *P. P.*, XII, 227-32.

which you are pleased to speak so favourably, as perfect as I can.' . . .
He said he had no pain, but was wasting away."

Hume's part in the interview needs no interpretation. He was
dying as the ideal Inquirer, calm, detached, and thoughtful. He was
also dying as he had lived, *le bon David*. He recognized the serious
intent of Boswell and was pained to have to check so bluntly those
eager illusions. Boswell, on his side, recognized Hume's honesty:
"I had a strong curiosity to be satisfied if he persisted in disbeleiving
a future state even when he had death before his eyes. I was persuaded from what he now said, and from his manner of saying it,
that he did persist."

But Boswell, himself, was completely crushed by this very persuasion. The hope that he had been nursing for so long was shattered. His mind was in a turmoil: "I . . . felt a degree of horrour,
mixed with a sort of wild, strange, hurrying recollection of My
excellent Mother's pious instructions, of Dr. Johnson's noble lessons,
and of my religious sentiments and affections during the course of
my life. I was like a man in sudden danger eagerly seeking his defen-
sive arms; and I could not but be assailed by momentary doubts
while I had actually before me a man of such strong abilities and
extensive inquiry dying in the persuasion of being annihilated. . . .
I left him with impressions which disturbed me for some time."

The shock was more than disturbing; it was stunning. For months
Boswell was a sadly chastened and bewildered man, paralyzed with
the horror, now seemingly so certain, of extinction. "From a kind of
curiosity and selftormenting inclination," he forced himself to go to
the Advocates' Library, where Hume had been Keeper, to read
"his worst Essays." [28] Eagerly he sought out the company of
those who could be relied on to defend the concept of immortality.
Helplessly he resorted to the now too well-known consolations of
alcohol and of women.

During the succeeding weeks until the end of August while the
noble spirit of Hume was valiantly facing death, Boswell haunted
his door in the vain hope that a change of mind might yet be indicated. On the twelfth of August he "called . . . at Mr. David
Hume's. His Housekeeper, who I have reason to beleive was his

[28] *Ibid.*, XII, 25-26.

concubine, appeared to be crying, and told me he had seen nobody for two days, and had said he would never be down stairs again to meals." And on the twenty-first, having eluded his wife, who attempted to keep him at home until the effects of his wine were slept off, he "walked to the New town, called at Mr. David Hume's, wishing to converse with him while I was elevated with liquor, but was told he was very ill." Little wonder after this pitiful and disgraceful exhibition that he felt a tinge of remorse: "I was shocked at the consciousness of my own situation"! [29]

And then on August 25 Hume died. "This struck me a good deal," noted Boswell. "I went and called at his door, and was told by his servant that he died very easily." The day of the funeral was wet, and Boswell dedicated it to self-abasement. Early in the morning he went to the Calton Hill Cemetery to inspect the open grave, and when the carriages approached, "stood concealed behind a wall," and viewed "the procession of the corpse carried to the grave." In desperate torment he plodded once more to the Advocates' Library to read further into Hume's essays, "his Epicurean, his Stoick, his Sceptick, and on Natural Religion." When night came he went to bed "somewhat dejected in mind" and woke up the next morning still "not right." For penance and for solace he resolved to write a letter to Dr. Johnson.[30] Slowly the tension began to ease.

I V

The half year following the last interview with Hume saw Boswell through a mental crisis during which he sounded the depths of moral degradation. Even then he was not completely cured, but time assuages pain. The ethical enigma that was Hume was not solved; it was only shelved. Boswell became expert at eluding what he could not forget. Three chief devices he learned to employ. The first was to display anger when anyone ventured to defend Hume. The second was to maintain that Hume's mind had been in a stupor on the subject of immortality. And the third was to pretend that Hume had all his life deceived the world. None of these methods was genuinely satisfying—which added to his discomfiture.

Adam Smith was the most distinguished victim of the Boswellian

[29] *Ibid.*, XII, 27, 30-31.　　　　[30] *Ibid.*, XII, 34-35.

wrath. Smith's open letter describing Hume's last days was published as a Preface to the philosopher's *My Own Life* in 1777. The concluding sentence of this letter is a touching tribute to the character of *le bon David:* "Upon the whole, I have always considered him, both in his lifetime, and since his death, as approaching as nearly to the idea of a perfectly wise and virtuous man, as perhaps the nature of human frailty will admit." [31] Boswell was righteously indignant. He wrote to Dr. Johnson, endeavoring to engage him to "knock Hume's and Smith's heads together, and make vain and ostentatious infidelity exceedingly ridiculous. Would it not be worth your while to crush such noxious weeds in the moral garden?" [32] Apparently it was not, but Boswell did not easily forget or forgive.

More than two years later he was still resentful. One day at the customs house in Edinburgh he accidentally came across the economist, who inquired why they never met any more. "I fairly told him," admits Boswell, "that I did not like his having praised David Hume so much. He went off to the board huffed, yet affecting to treat my censure as foolish. I did not care how he took it. Since his absurd eulogium on Hume and his ignorant, ungrateful attack on the English University education, I have had no desire to be much with him." [33] Social nature finally got the better of petulance, however, and Boswell resumed the acquaintanceship with Smith, though on cooler terms.

The notion that Hume had simply found it impossible to think clearly on the subject of immortality was comforting to Boswell. It had occurred to him shortly after Hume's death and was elaborated in a letter of August 30, 1776, to Mrs. Thrale: "It has shocked me to think of his persisting in Infidelity. Gray in one of the letters published by Mason represents Hume as a child. I cannot agree with him. Hume had certainly considerable abilities. My notion is that he had by long study in one view, brought a *stupor* upon his mind as to futurity. He had pored upon the earth, till he could not look up to heaven. He was like one of the Bramins who, we are told, by a rigid perseverance in maintaining a certain posture, become

[31] Smith to Strahan in Hume, *Letters*, II, 452. See also Chapter 8, sec. IV, below.

[32] Boswell, *Letters*, I, 264.   [33] *P. P.*, XIII, 287.

unable to change it. Or may we not with propriety compare him to the woman in the Gospel, who 'was bowed down, and could in no wise lift herself up,' till healed by our SAVIOUR who describes her as one 'whom Satan hath bound lo these eight years.' Hume told me about six weeks before his death, that he had been steady in his then sentiments above forty years. I should like to hear Dr. Johnson upon this." [34]

The idea of the "stupor" was particularly intriguing to Boswell because it enabled him to retain his early belief in the high intellectual powers of Hume. It might even have ultimately induced him to pity the philosopher, and so have brought posthumous reconciliation through sympathy. But Boswell was much more struck with a third answer, the suggestion of Dr. Johnson, to whom he had appealed.

Johnson's was a short and easy method. When Boswell mentioned Hume's assertion that "he was quite easy at the thought of Annihilation," "He lied," retorted Dr. Johnson. "He had a vanity in being thought easy. It is more probable that he lied than that so very improbable a thing should be as a Man not afraid of death; of going into an unknown state and not being uneasy at leaving all that he knew. And you are to consider that upon his own principle of Annihilation he had no motive not to lie."

At the moment, however, Boswell was less struck with the oddness of the logic than with the earnestness of the speaker. "The horrour for Death which I have allways observed in Dr. Johnson appeared strong tonight. I said that I had been for moments in my life not afraid of death; therefore I could suppose another Man in that state of mind for a considerable span of time. He said he never had a moment in which death was not terrible to him. . . . It was humbling to find that even the powerful mind of Dr. Johnson was foiled by Futurity. I felt my own mind much firmer than formerly, so that I was not depressed tonight; and even the gloom of uncertainty in solemn religious Speculation, being mingled with hope, was much more consolatory than the emptiness of infidelity." [35]

[34] Boswell, MS letter, National Library of Scotland, MS Acc. No. 1371. The version in Boswell, *Letters*, is inaccurate and incomplete.
[35] *P. P.*, XIII, 23-24.

The crass crudity of the Johnsonian "He lied" at first made it difficult for Boswell to accept. Moreover, Johnson's skepticism sounded strangely familiar. It was, Boswell told himself, the gist of Hume's own argument against miracles! Summoning courage a few days afterwards, he taxed his friend: "Sir, you come near Hume's argument against Miracles: that it is more probable Men should lye or be mistaken, than that they should happen." "Hume," acknowledged Dr. Johnson, "taking the proposition simply, is right. But the Christian Revelation is not proved by miracles alone, but as connected with prophecies and with the doctrines in confirmation of which they were wrought." [36]

Here was a new consideration to tone down the seeming crudity of the original rebuttal. Hume's intellect, Boswell had always respected. But if Hume's belief in annihilation could be demonstrated to be wrong on his own principles, what was he to think? That Hume was actually convicted of loose logic, or that he had harbored an ulterior motive? Suppose Hume could be proved to have been deliberately concealing something? Suppose: If Hume was good, he must secretly be a Christian? Boswell was back again at the second moral imperative, but now with renewed hope. The possibility intrigued him. He brooded over it more than ever. Finally the answer came. It took the form of a revelation.

During the night of January 9, 1784, Boswell had a dream: "Awaked after a very agreable dream that I had found a Diary kept by David Hume, from which it appeared that though his vanity made him publish treatises of skepticism and infidelity, he was in reality a Christian and a very pious Man. He had, I imagined, quieted his mind by thinking that whatever he might appear to the World to show his talents, his religion was between GOD and his own conscience. (I cannot be sure if this thought was in sleep.) I thought I read some beautiful passages in his Diary. I am not certain whether I had this dream on thursday or friday night. But after I awaked, it dwelt so upon my mind that I could not for some time perceive that it was only a fiction." [37]

The catharsis had come. The mind of Boswell was purged of a fixation of over a quarter of a century's duration, and greatly inten-

[36] *Ibid.*, XIII, 54.   [37] *Ibid.*, XVI, 20-21.

sified since the death of Hume. The final "solution" of the enigma, to be sure, has nothing to do with philosophy, for philosophy demands evidence and coherence. It has just as little to do with common sense, for common sense demands that issues other than the practical be dropped immediately. Boswell's Christianization of *le bon David* was only the rest demanded by a troubled spirit. Wishful thinking undoubtedly, but there is little need to call names. Boswell, himself, was no fool; he recognized Hume's "confession" as a fiction. The important thing is that it brought good through enduring peace.

Nevermore did Boswell rack his brain over the paradox of Hume, the virtuous infidel. He was free now to view *le bon David* with a detachment hitherto impossible. In 1785 he could even suffer the Rev. William Mason to remark in his presence that, "one such Christian as Johnson did more hurt to Religion than many Humes," without flying into a rage.[38] And when he began to create out of his enormous collections of notes the great biography of that great man, Dr. Samuel Johnson, his emancipation in art from the enigma in ethics becomes clearly discernible.

A comparison of the two biographical studies, the *Journal of a Tour to the Hebrides* and the *Life of Johnson,* with the *Private Papers* indicates that Hume, who plays a background role in all three, is treated with considerable restraint and even fairness in the published works. Some of Johnson's abuse is omitted altogether; much more is softened. And Boswell took the occasion in the *Journal of a Tour* to state his mature position, venturing to rebuke Dr. John-son for discourtesy to the philosopher: "Violence is, in my opinion, not suitable to the Christian cause."

Boswell then proceeded to explain that, "I always lived on good terms with Mr. Hume, though I have frankly told him, I was not clear that it was right in me to keep company with him. 'But, (said I) how much better are you than your books!' He was cheerful, obliging, and instructive; he was charitable to the poor; and many an agreeable hour have I passed with him: I have preserved some entertaining and interesting memoirs of him, particularly when he knew himself to be dying, which I may some time or other communicate to the world. I shall not, however, extol him so very highly

[38] *Ibid.,* XVI, 149.

as Dr. Adam Smith does. . . . When I read this sentence delivered by my old *Professor of Moral Philosophy*, I could not help exclaiming with the *Psalmist*, 'Surely I have now more understanding than my teachers!'" [39] And so Adam Smith suffers rebuke for overmuch praise, just as Dr. Johnson does for overmuch abuse of Hume. The Boswellian balance, itself, had been achieved only at great cost and, above all else, had to be preserved.

The Boswell of these late years, though never free from the hypochondria that Hume had always discerned in him, is yet to some degree, a new Boswell.[40] And this new Boswell is reminiscent of that "young gentleman, very good-humoured, very agreeable, and very mad," who in 1758 had first sought out the great philosopher. The cycle was now complete. After all, Hume was Boswell's first lion; and hunters, especially big-game hunters, have long memories.

[39] *Boswell and Johnson Tour*, pp. 177-78.   [40] See Note N, below.

CHAPTER 8

HUME AND JOHNSON

IF—like Rousseau—Boswell had dreamed his dream about Hume while that philosopher was still alive, and if—like Rousseau again—he had later convinced himself that that dream was true, then he would almost certainly have attempted to bring about a friendly meeting between Hume and Johnson. There can be no doubt that the reconciliation of the heads of the Scottish and the English literary circles might have had important consequences. There can also be no doubt that Boswell was the man to effect it, and that it was precisely the double-barreled sport of lion-hunting that he himself had invented and practised so skillfully. Moreover, Hume and Johnson were his two most important prizes, and he was on the best of terms with both. Lacking, however, the inner conviction that Hume was "in reality a Christian and a very pious Man," Boswell made no move. And when Johnson visited Edinburgh in 1773, Hume was not invited to meet him. Boswell had not forgotten Johnson's outburst at the mere mention of Rousseau!

Hume would certainly have made no objection to meeting Johnson. True to the principles of his philosophy, that kindly skeptic was always willing to meet those who disagreed with him. Several years after the friendly controversy with Wallace, he had requested Thomas Cadell, the London publisher, to introduce him to his leading opponents. To Cadell's literary dinner in honor of Hume, the learned doctors and divines came, saw, and were conquered. The personal charm of *le bon David* won the good will of Drs. Adams, Douglas, and Price, just as the disinterested intellect of the Inquirer had previously won their respect.

The major obstacle to a reconciliation with Johnson was, of course, that "very good hater," Johnson himself, of whose reaction to anything regarding Hume, Boswell could predict only that it would be violent. Witness the time that he repeated Hume's anecdote of Johnson's veneration for the episcopal hierarchy, doubtless in the expectancy of provoking an onslaught against Hume, only to find himself bearing the brunt of the storm:

Wed. Aug. 3, 1763: I mentioned to him how common it was in the world to tell absurd stories of him, and to ascribe to him very strange sayings. *Johnson.* "What do they make me say, Sir?" *Boswell.* "Why, Sir, as an instance very strange indeed, (laughing heartily as I spoke,) David Hume told me, you said that you would stand before a battery of cannon, to restore the Convocation to its full powers."—Little did I apprehend that he had actually said this: but I was soon convinced of my errour; for, with a determined look, he thundered out, "And would I not, Sir? Shall the Presbyterian *Kirk* of Scotland have its General Assembly, and the Church of England be denied its Convocation?" He was walking up and down the room while I told him the anecdote; but when he uttered this explosion of high-church zeal, he had come close to my chair, and his eyes flashed with indignation. I bowed to the storm and diverted the force of it, by leading him to expatiate on the influence which religion derived from maintaining the church with great external respectability.[1]

Dr. Johnson, furthermore, shared the common prejudice against the Scots in his own personal and crotchety way. Decidedly not political in tone, his anti-Caledonianism was, to be sure, un-Whiggish but nevertheless intense. However obscured in origin and however good-humored on occasion, it was yet deep-seated. After Boswell had negotiated the famous meeting with Wilkes, infidel as well as Whig, gibes at the Scots afforded the strangely assorted pair the safest topic for conversation. Johnson's *Journey to the Western Islands of Scotland* is an unsympathetic and hypercritical account of a traveler more surprised than pleased upon discovering civilization and culture where he had anticipated only barrenness and ignorance. And there is a measure of truth in "Peter Pindar's" accusation against Boswell:

> Thou jackal, leading lion Johnson forth
> To eat Macpherson 'midst his native North;
> To frighten grave professors with his roar,
> And shake the Hebrides from shore to shore.

[1] *Life of Johnson*, I, 464.

David Hume, for his part, was the acknowledged leader of the Caledonian party. But his attitude differed fundamentally from Johnson's. The product of circumstance rather than of prejudice, it was but distantly related to his genuine love for the homeland, which of itself would never have turned him against the English. For Hume had long waged war against provincialism in thought, in language, and in letters. Chauvinism, however, begets chauvinisms; and the very violence of the anti-Scottish current compelled him to become actively anti-English. And eventually Hume learned to roar as loud as Johnson.

On the fence as usual, Boswell was in the unique position of being able to act as moderator between the English and the Scottish literary factions. For the "clubable" Jamie, though he threw in his weight with the English, was always acceptable to both camps. As late as 1774, however, he was not without misgivings over his defection from Scotland, arguing with himself in the privacy of his diary: "It is true Hume, Robertson, and other greater Geniuses than I am, prefer Scotland. But they have neither that peculiar and permanent love of London and all it's circumstances which I have; nor are they so much in unison with the English as I am, which I have clearly perceived and of which Mr. Johnson has assured me." [2] And three years later Boswell was still enough the Scot to chide Dr. Johnson for his illiberality: "I ventured to mention a person who was as violent a Scotsman as he was an Englishman; and literally had the same contempt for an Englishman compared with a Scotsman, that he had for a Scotsman compared with an Englishman; and that he would say of Dr. Johnson, 'Damned rascal! to talk as he does of the Scotch.' This seemed, for a moment, 'to give him pause.' It, perhaps, presented his extreme prejudice against the Scotch in a point of view somewhat new to him, by the effect of *contrast*." [3]

Moderator though he occasionally was, Boswell more customarily fanned the flames of animosity by retailing literary gossip as he flitted back and forth between Edinburgh and London. So, for a multiplicity of reasons, factional differences between England and Scotland were not allowed to be forgotten; on the contrary, as time went on, they heightened. The perfect awareness by Hume and

[2] *P. P.*, IX, 128.   [3] *Life of Johnson*, III, 170.

Johnson of their rival positions as national spokesmen is indicated through a contrast of some typical pronouncements:

If Johnson professed to lament that the Scots love Scotland better than truth, Hume professed to lament how much the English have declined in literature during his time.

If Johnson belittled the Scots as too unlearned for the dignity of literature, Hume belittled the English as barbarians who inhabit the banks of the Thames.

If Johnson boasted of the English as maintaining the capital of literature, Hume boasted of the Scots as the people most distinguished for literature in Europe.

If Johnson found Hume's style French rather than English, Hume found Johnson's style a peculiar and enormous variety of English.

If Johnson decried Hume as a blockhead and a rogue, Hume decried Johnson as a man of enthusiasm and antiquated notions.[4]

But this mutual antipathy need not be labored since it is sufficiently obvious. What is more to the point is to attempt an evaluation of it through a systematic survey of the characters, beliefs, careers, and reputations of the two men. Full comprehension of these factors may possibly reveal implications of more than personal import.

I

Hume and Johnson had several traits of character in common. They were both sociable, fond of good company, of hearty food, of a bit of horseplay, and of intellectual stimulation. They were both capable of making intimate and enduring friendships, with women as well as with men. They were both charitable and compassionate and never happier than when relieving the needy and the oppressed. Although Hume was distinctly more urbane, neither was polished in manners; and both were occasionally subjected to unseemly ridicule on the part of snobs. Yet Hume and Johnson were gentlemen by nature and, in the best sense of the term, men of the world, wide in experience and deep in wisdom. Finally, inspiring others to follow, they were both leaders.

[4] See Note O, below.

These similarities, however, were almost completely obscured by more striking differences. In temperament the Scotsman was serene, courteous, and dispassionate; the Englishman, irritable, magisterial, and disputatious. In debate Hume talked to discuss, Johnson talked to win; Hume was reserved, Johnson was domineering; Hume insinuated, Johnson bludgeoned. The arguments of the one were always rational and philosophical, his rebuttals evidential; the arguments of the other were frequently emotional and subjective, his rebuttals retaliatory. The immediate effect of Hume was more profound, of Johnson more dramatic. The lasting effect of Hume was of keen penetration; the lasting effect of Johnson was of rugged strength.

Their beliefs were likewise radically dissimilar, Hume being utilitarian and Johnson authoritarian. As an "unbeliever," Hume dissociated morality from religious faith and faced death with philosophical composure. Johnson was pious, reverent, firm in orthodox Christianity, High Church in outlook, fearful of damnation, and obsessed with the dread of death. Though both were externally Tory in politics, Hume was essentially liberal and never a Jacobite; Johnson essentially reactionary and always a sentimental Jacobite. In fine, Hume was systematic, searching, and tentative in his convictions; Johnson personal, apologetic, and positive.

The similarities and dissimilarities in characters and beliefs are reflected in the literary careers. Regarding the dignity of literature, the two were in complete accord. Hume's famous dictum, "Such a superiority do the pursuits of literature possess above every other occupation, that even he who attains but a mediocrity in them, merits the preëminence above those that excel the most in the common and vulgar professions," was matched by Johnson's equally famous dictum, "The chief glory of every people arises from its authors." [5] Men of letters, both, in the broadest eighteenth-century sense, Hume and Johnson were also agreed on the necessity of maintaining intellectual integrity through financial independence and, to that end, of making strict frugality suffice for lack of patrimony. The younger son of country gentry, Hume received but a

[5] Hume, *History of England*, VI, 197; Johnson, Preface to *Dictionary*, *Works*, II, 65.

small inheritance; yet small as it was, it gave him a decided initial advantage over Johnson, who inherited even less. And although Johnson was senior by two years and began to publish considerably before Hume, the latter was the first to achieve distinction in his literary ventures. "Slow rises worth by poverty depress'd."

Hume's earlier success, however, is actually less attributable to greater financial security than to a positive intellectual program. Unlike Johnson, Hume had a message to put before the world, a scheme whereby to carry it into execution, and a plan for his career. Johnson was willing to turn his hand to any literary undertaking whereby he might earn an honest penny. Hume dictated the outlines of his career, filling in the details according to inclination.

Planning to write, in turn, works on logic, psychology, ethics, political science, economics, history, and criticism, Hume was content to fill in with the positions of private tutor, Advocate General to a military expedition, secretary to an embassy to Turin, librarian in Edinburgh, Secretary to the British Embassy in Paris, chargé d'affaires in Paris, and Undersecretary of State in England. With no definite program other than the maintaining of a high moral and literary standard, Johnson let fortune and the booksellers name the specific nature of miscellaneous hackwork—cataloguing and review-ing of books, translating, journalistic accounts of Parliamentary de-bates—resting content to seize available opportunities for compiling a dictionary, conducting divers periodicals, editing Shakespeare, com-posing occasional verses, essays, political tracts, a novel, a tragedy, a travelogue, and a series of biographies.

Just as Hume's intellectual outlook was wider than Johnson's, so, when both were well established each after his own fashion, Hume's reputation was international and Johnson's insular. Hume was a Citizen of the World; Johnson was John Bull. With the publication of his *Political Discourses* in 1752, Hume was honored in France, Germany, and Italy as Britain's leading man of letters, in all Europe the only worthy inheritor of the soon to be vacated throne of Montesquieu. The Continent has never been able to com-prehend the provincialism of Johnson and the prestige accorded him at home as a literary figure.

In 1755 when his *Dictionary* brought Johnson belated recognition in the learned world, Hume was already Britain's most brilliant—if not her most acceptable—philosopher, her most influential thinker in political science and in economics, her first national historian, and one of her foremost critics of fine letters. And in 1762 when Johnson finally won the long battle against poverty by the grant of a governmental pension, Hume had already earned a substantial fortune by his publications, which shattered all previous sales records. His governmental pension of 1763 was but a minor increment. In sober truth, it must be put on the record that, with a single important exception, Johnson's imposing literary production did not equal Hume's, whether in quality, in scope, or in influence. The exception was the *Dictionary*.

With his recognition as the greatest authority on the English language, Dr. Johnson at once began to exert a literary influence unexampled for a lexicographer, "a harmless drudge"—an influence that was further extended through personal contacts with the organization of "The Club" in 1764. Hume, too, maintained close contacts with the world of letters; and a comparison of the Humian and the Johnsonian circles is at once indicated. The antagonism in the characters, beliefs, careers, and reputations of the two men of letters is not unnaturally mirrored in their respective circles.

II

"The Club" in London bore from the beginning the indelible stamp of its spiritual head, Dr. Johnson. The belief in subordination which made him Jacobite in politics and High Church in religion also cast him unmistakably for the role of literary dictator. The office descended to him in a direct line of inheritance from earlier dictators, Ben Jonson, Dryden, and Addison. The "tribe" of Ben, the "court" of Dryden, the "little senate" of Addison were all governed from on high; but never was literary authoritarianism carried further than in "The Club."

"As Alexander and Cæsar were born for conquest, so was Johnson for the office of a symposiarch, to preside in all conversations; and I never yet saw the man who would venture to contest his right." So wrote Sir John Hawkins,[6] charter member of "The Club" and

---

[6] Hawkins, *Life of Johnson*, p. 258.

loyal friend of its dictator. Though the Great Lexicographer might professionally define "club" as "an assembly of good fellows meeting under certain conditions," those conditions in the Johnsonian practice inevitably involved constraint. Literature in the Johnsonian understanding was always the "universal *monarchy* of wit." "The Club" was the court of the "great Cham of literature."

Dr. Johnson ruled his court with imperial authority, imposing his opinions and crushing resistance. The members were disciplined to follow the leader, and perceptively even the most independent learned to do so. The spread of Johnson's dogmatic intolerance affords a prime instance, as his conspicuous rudeness to Hume set the example for his followers. It was caught up by Boswell, as has already been observed, in his impudent reproof of Dr. Adams. It encouraged Edmund Burke to explain sanctimoniously that speaking to an infidel, however socially expedient, was morally unjustifiable. It led David Garrick to remonstrate concerning Dr. Robertson's friendly defense of Hume against the overzealous abuse of Dr. Beattie. And it induced Sir Joshua Reynolds to degrade himself and his art by introducing into his grandiose allegorical portrait of that same James Beattie a crouching and cringing figure in the recognizable shape of David Hume.[7]

This dire picture of the inner mind of "The Club" must not, however, be overpointed. There were shining lights among the shadows. The gentle Oliver Goldsmith had the fortitude to withstand the oppressive tide, and his reprimand of Reynolds is memorable. Once, at least, Johnson went too far even for the belligerent Boswell, who felt compelled to suppress a remark of the master's about Hume as "something much too rough."[8] Nevertheless, intolerance pervaded the circle of Johnson and, while assuredly not his responsibility alone, was yet fostered by his deliberate indoctrination. Certain patterns of thought were encouraged while other patterns of thought were discouraged. Freedom of expression was not guaranteed. Intimidation and chastisement were not unknown. Thus overawed and overpowered by one supreme oracle, the London circle lay at the opposite social and intellectual poles from the Edinburgh circle.

[7] See Note P, below.   [8] *Boswell and Johnson Tour*, p. 177.

No exact counterpart of "The Club," to be sure, existed in the "Athens of the North." The Select Society of Edinburgh, instituted in 1754 by the painter Allan Ramsay on Continental rather than on English models, was for some ten years a highly successful instrument of the Scottish Enlightenment. But as it increasingly tended to become less select, it also became less stimulating and finally broke up. During the first several years of its existence, Hume acted as treasurer, was a member of the steering committee, and twice took his turn as chairman. His influence was always felt, and the list of topics adopted for formal debate reads like the table of contents to his *Essays and Treatises*. But never once did he enter into the discussions from the floor. The Select Society did not suit Hume's taste because it lacked the intimacy he deemed vital.

A greater degree of fellowship was attained in other ventures such as the Griskin Club, formed to promote John Home's *Douglas*, and the Poker Club, formed to promote Scottish nationalism; but none of these adequately filled the bill of a genuine literary society. So far as Hume personally was concerned, no organized club ever did, as the very act of organization tended to stifle free exchange of opinion in close discussion—what he himself described as "the company of a few select companions, with whom I can, calmly and peaceably, enjoy the feast of reason, and try the justness of every reflection, whether gay or serious, that may occur to me." [9]

In quest of the feast of reason, Hume and the Scots turned again to the Continent, finding their model this time in the French *salon intime*. The intimate—as distinguished from the grand—*salon* was the society of a few choice spirits, warm in friendship and mutual respect, animated in intellect, and appreciative of good food and good wine. No hard drinking, however, for as Hume expressly warned, a gathering kept from dullness only by that means will soon find the remedy worse than the disease. The Rev. Alexander Carlyle writes glowingly of "warm suppers and excellent claret," adding that "it was those meetings in particular that rubbed off all corners, as we call it, by collision, and made the *literati* of Edinburgh less captious and pedantic than they were elsewhere" [10]—meaning, of course, London.

[9] *Phil. Works*, III, 194*n*.   [10] Carlyle, *Autobiography*, p. 312.

An especial feature of the Edinburgh literary life was the informal exchange of suppers from home to home. An added feature was the occasional invitations extended to distinguished outsiders, travelers from England, the Continent, and America. In eschewing formality the Edinburgh literary life warmly embraced hospitality. When Mrs. Elizabeth Montagu, Queen of the London Bluestockings, visited the Scottish capital in 1766, she was astonished, she wrote back to Mrs. Vesey, by the pleasant contrast afforded with English "ignorance or brutality." The Scots, she exulted, "live in ye french way, des petits soupers fins, & they have ye easy address of the french. The lettered sage & rural Gentleman is in Scotland a polite man." [11]

The easy address of the French was the pattern of the Edinburgh circle into which Hume fitted so well and of which he was the undisputed leader. During the period of his residence in the city from 1751 to 1763, Hume had been fond of dining at home with literary friends; and returning in 1769 from his various governmental offices to settle down permanently, he reassumed old interests with intensified pleasure. "He liked to eat," testifies Henry Mackenzie, "and still more to give his friends a good dinner." [12] In France, Hume had acquired a choice stock of personally selected and tested recipes. Now, he sensibly reduced the number to suit the capacity of Peggy Irvine, his devoted old servant. Hume might, indeed, jest about "my great Talent for Cookery, the Science to which I intend to addict the remaining Years of my Life"; but his *petits soupers fins*, embellished with rare old claret, were the source of genuine pride. They became justly famous, earning for him from Boswell the title of "the northern Epicurus." Never merely gastronomic, however, these occasions stressed sociability and the free exchange of ideas. They were, in fact, the center of the Scottish intellectual life.

The spirit of tolerance illumined the Edinburgh circle. Though many of the literati were clergymen, all were enlightened. To them, the Great Infidel presented no insurmountable problem of ethics. While they reprobated Hume's religious opinions, they were yet able to distinguish between the opinions and the man; and if they

[11] Montagu, MS letter, Huntington Library, MSS MO uncat., EM 1766.
[12] Mackenzie, *Anecdotes and Egotisms*, p. 172.

abhorred the first, they loved the second. Dr. John Gregory, the eminent and pious physician, explained this nice distinction to Mrs. Montagu: "I detest Mr Hume's Philosophy as destructive of every principle interesting to Mankind & I think the general Spirit that breathes in his History unfavourable both to Religion & Liberty, tho in other Respects one of the most animated, entertaining & instructive Historys I have ever read. But I love Mr Hume personally as a Worthy agreeable Man in private Life, & as I believe he does not know & cannot feel the mischief his writings have done, it hurts me extremely to see him harshly used." [13] The Rev. Hugh Blair put the issue of toleration more pointedly in urging *le bon David* to a speedy return from London: "We would even be content to bear a little persecution for the sake of it. *Usque ad aras,* is the word." [14]

The ideal of the Scottish circle, attested by the pervasive toleration accorded all persons and all ideas, was democratic. The spirit achieved was what Lord Shaftesbury a half century earlier had so aptly termed, *"Liberty of the Club,* and that sort of Freedom which is taken amongst Gentlemen and Friends, who know one another well." The Scottish Enlightenment discovered its literary instrument, not in despotism benevolent or otherwise, but in a genuine republic of letters. The social standard was fraternity, and the personal motto of Dr. Robertson was the implicit motto of all: *Vita sine literis mors est.*

After the publication of Boswell's *Life of Johnson* in 1791 had made available the details of the London set, the comparison with Edinburgh was demanded. Henry Mackenzie offers an eyewitness account of "the free and cordial communication of sentiments, the natural play of fancy and good humour, which prevailed among the circle" in Edinburgh during the epoch of David Hume, when as a boy he himself had been a sort of literary page. Mackenzie's national bias is patent, especially as the literary leadership had descended to him upon the death of Adam Smith in 1790. Nevertheless, he was possessed of the facts, and his comparison is instructive.

The spirit of Edinburgh, declared Mackenzie, "was very dif-

---

[13] Gregory, MS letter, Huntington Library, MSS MO uncat.
[14] Blair, MS letter, Royal Society of Edinburgh, Hume MSS, III, 56.

ferent from that display of learning—that prize-fighting of wit, which distinguished a literary circle of our sister country, of which we have some authentic and curious records. There all ease of intercourse was changed for the pride of victory; and the victors, like some savage combatants, gave no quarter to the vanquished. This may, perhaps, be accounted for more from the situation than the dispositions of the principal members of that society. The literary circle of London was a sort of sect, a *caste* separate from the ordinary professions and habits of common life. They were traders in talent and learning, and brought, like other traders, samples of their goods into company, with a jealousy of competition which prevented their enjoying, as much as otherwise they might, any excellence in their competitors." [15] Scottish freedom and English restraint was Mackenzie's thesis. Whatever may be thought of his more elaborate explanation of the major distinctions between the rival circles, it is timely to examine into their membership until the death of Hume in 1776.

"The Club," in addition to Dr. Johnson, was distinguished chiefly by Edmund Burke, Sir Joshua Reynolds, Oliver Goldsmith, David Garrick, Charles James Fox, and James Boswell, of whom two were Irish and one Scottish. Edward Gibbon made several appearances after his election only to sit uncomfortably silent before the Johnsonian truculence. Adam Smith, admitted in 1775 over the vigorous protests of his fellow Scot Boswell, would not placidly endure insolence, and open quarrel with Johnson not infrequently resulted. Other scholars and men of letters included Dr. Thomas Barnard, Sir Robert Chambers, George Colman, Samuel Dyer, Sir John Hawkins, Sir William Jones, Bennet Langton, Dr. Thomas Percy, and George Steevens. Among men of affairs and society were to be found Topham Beauclerk, Sir Charles Bunbury, Anthony Chamier, Lord Charlemont, Dr. George Fordyce, Dr. Christopher Nugent, and Agmondesham Vesey.[16]

The more fluid and less formalized Edinburgh circle around Hume, Scotsmen all, achieved its distinction through Adam Smith, William Robertson, Adam Ferguson, and Hugh Blair. The names of Alexander Carlyle, Robert Henry, John Home, Henry Macken-

<hr/>

[15] Mackenzie, *Life of Home*, pp. 22-23.   [16] *Annals of The Club, passim.*

zie, Robert Wallace, and William Wilkie were prominent in the literature of their day. Lord Monboddo, Lord Kames, Lord Hailes, Lord Elibank, and Sir Gilbert Elliot were all learned in the law. Drs. Joseph Black, William Cullen, and John Gregory were famous scientists. Others of the local clergy, members of Dr. Robertson's Moderate Party, were the Rev. John Drysdale and John Jardine. And lastly, of course, there was James Boswell, who was never excluded.

Comparisons may sometimes be odious but, along with analogies, are requisite to all thinking concerning matters of fact. Yet it would be futile as well as odious to attempt any precise measure of the Edinburgh and the London groups. Suffice it to say, both were distinguished, although distinguished in quite different ways. The literary merit of "The Club" need not be rehearsed here as it is justly famous and customarily receives its due meed of praise. It was undeniably great. But the literary merit of the Edinburgh circle is neglected today—perhaps unduly so. In the eighteenth century, however, such was not the case; in fact, more frequently the reverse was true.

In 1758 Horace Walpole, who as son of the great Whig statesman would hardly have been suspected of a leaning toward the Scots, publicly proclaimed Scotland, "the most accomplished nation in Europe; the nation to which, if any one country is endowed with a superior partition of sense, I should be inclined to give the preference in that particular." [17] A few years later Professor Carlo Denina, in commenting upon the decline in English literature since the age of Pope and Swift, Addison and Steele, praised the ascendancy of the Scots and took the occasion for a smart thrust at the vanity of the Johnsonian coterie:

> The good writers in our day bear no proportion to those who adorned England thirty years ago. But this deficiency in England is amply compensated by the many eminent authors who at present make such a distinguished figure in Scotland. . . .
>
> It is now an incontestable fact, that the principal authors who have adorned the British literature in these latter times, or do honour to it in the present days, have received their birth and education in Scotland. . . .

[17] Walpole, *Catalogue of Royal and Noble Authors*, in *Works*, I, 492.

Some people, infatuated with the pride and vanity of being born in
the metropolis of a nation, persuade themselves that they alone are capable
of writing their own language; and of course will scarcely believe that the
Scotch bid fair to carry off the prize of language even from the English
themselves.[18]

Voltaire's egregious sneer at Lord Kames's *Elements of Criticism* was in reality a concealed eulogy of the Scottish Enlightenment:
"It is an admirable result of the progress of the human spirit that
at the present time it is from Scotland we receive rules of taste in
all the arts—from the epic poem to gardening." [19] In 1781 Tieman,
a literary Hungarian writing from Paris, awarded to Scotland the
unqualified accolade: "Whenever the English mention *Scotchmen* to
me in that contemptuous tone they sometimes affect, I advise them
to go to Edinburgh to learn how to live and how to be men. Your
learned men, Robertson, Black, and Hume are looked upon here as
geniuses of the first rank. Only two days ago, I saw the Comte de
Buffon, who named them all to me at his finger's tip, just as you
might name Newton and Locke." [20]

Voltaire and Buffon were speaking for France; and France,
speaking for Europe, was enjoying an age of Anglomania. To that
age, the Scottish literary achievement rose superior to the English:
Anglomania found its model inspiration in the Edinburgh circle
around Hume. The British Enlightenment might write English
with clarity and vigor, but it spoke English with a burr. Guileless,
indeed, was that honest Scot, Tobias Smollett, in pointing with pride
to Edinburgh as "a hot-bed of genius," with "the two Humes,
Robertson, Smith, Wallace, Blair, Ferguson, Wilkie, etc." [21]

III

"The two half-men of their time" Thomas Carlyle found Hume
and Johnson: Hume with his "intrepid Candor and decisive scientific Clearness," Johnson with his "Reverence, Love, and devout
Humility." And until England can produce one "whole-man" com-

[18] Quoted in *Scots Magazine*, XXVI (1764), 465-66, 467.
[19] Quoted by Hume Brown in *History of Scotland*, III, 371.
[20] Quoted by Thompson in *A Scottish Man of Feeling*, p. 185, in French.
[21] Smollett, *Humphrey Clinker*, letter of Matthew Bramble, Aug. 8.

bining the best features of both, Carlyle will be happy with "half-men worthy to tie the shoe-latchets of these, resembling these even from afar!" [22] The idea of the Sage of Chelsea that Hume and Johnson were complementary in character—clearly more suggestive than Boswell's first reading of them as the moral antipodes—deserves examination. It is half true and half false.

As men of letters, Johnson and Hume represent two distinct and divergent traditions. Johnson is the finest surviving example in the later eighteenth century of Christian Humanism. He is the spiritual heir of the early Protestant Reformation. His intellectual individualism is as yet untempered by the sense of historical change and by the significance of the New Science. He revels in the freedom to think as he chooses but glories in his affinities with the great Latin-Christian and Anglo-Catholic traditions. To disengage the mind of Johnson from the principle of prescription is to lose that which is most inherently Johnsonian. His intellectual individualism and his religious authoritarianism combine to a single purpose, the dominant moral purpose of all his literary endeavor. They combine to lend stability to his world, a world that he urgently feels lacking in stability.

Hume, too, desired stability for his world. But Hume's conception of stability was not to be reached through intellectual individualism and religious authoritarianism. Hume's stability was to be the product of creative skepticism: To challenge accepted dogmas and beliefs, to test the validity of each, to reject the false—that is the way to stabilize the true and to build afresh upon surer foundations. While Johnson sought stability through spiritual retrogression, Hume sought stability through spiritual revolution. The one pointed to the grand old world, the other to the brave new world; and as Johnson's mind was of the Reformation, Hume's was of the Enlightenment.

Yet it will not suffice merely to say that Johnson looked backward and Hume forward. Johnson was not completely confident that looking backward would salvage his world, and Hume was not completely confident that looking forward would create his. Neither was a confirmed optimist, subscribing to the "idea of progress";

[22] Carlyle, *Essay on Johnson*, the close.

neither was a confirmed pessimist, subscribing to the "idea of decline." Both were too firmly rooted in a sense of reality, in a sense
of struggle, in life itself, to be carried away by catch-words or by
catch-thoughts. There was far too much of the skeptic in both.

For it will not suffice, again, merely to say that Hume was skeptical and Johnson authoritarian. While there was no suspicion of
the authoritarian in Hume, there was considerable of the skeptic in
Johnson. A born authoritarian, Johnson was also a born skeptic.
The paradox is more ostensible than real because the most skeptical
of minds are occasionally the most authoritarian. Complete departmentalization of the intellect does occur, and the most radical skepticism in one department does not necessarily carry over into the
others. Among minds of unexceptionable genius, Pascal affords the
best example in the century preceding Johnson, Newman in the
century following. The parallel also suggests that, typically, it is in
the religious realm that the skeptical breakdown occurs. Certainly it
was in religion that the Johnsonian skepticism disintegrated.

Regarding the descriptive powers of the blind poet Blacklock,
Johnson vigorously denounced the specious reasoning of "that foolish fellow, Spence." Regarding the authenticity of the poems of
Ossian, Johnson brusquely demanded of Macpherson, "Where are
the manuscripts?" Regarding temporal questions in general, Johnson
was consistently incredulous, sometimes, indeed, beyond all reason.
He is reputed, for instance, to have taken six months to credit the
fact of the 1755 Lisbon earthquake. But, on the whole, his reluctance to believe the wonderful was salutary. Echoing Horace's *incredulus odi*, he habitually rejected whatever smacked of pretense or of
humbug. "Clear your mind of cant" remains the core of Johnson's
worldly teaching and is what makes him the living symbol of common sense.

But there is another side to Johnson's common-sense skepticism,
no less genuine. This appears in his attitude to spiritual questions
where, for instance, he advisedly took pains to investigate alleged
instances of ghosts and of second sight. Hume, for his part, would
never have concerned himself with such psychical researches because
his luminous scientific skepticism attributed to that very class of
phenomena such a low degree of probability as to render the effort

unfruitful. "Does a man of sense," he inquired, "run after every silly tale of witches or hobgoblins or fairies, and canvass particularly the evidence? I never knew any one, that examined and deliberated about nonsense who did not believe it before the end of his inquiries." Johnson, however, canvassed the evidence of the Cock-lane ghost and of Highland second sight because he wished to believe in them. The fact that, in the event, he actually laid the goblin and hedged concerning second sight does not alter the other fact that in that particular class of phenomena he had the "will to believe."

Religion, it must be recalled, had not so long since relinquished witches upon their being legally exorcized by Act of Parliament in 1736. But the inner convictions of the devoutly religious were not immediately quashed by that juridical change. As late as 1768 so important a figure in the history of religion as John Wesley grievously lamented "that the English in general, and indeed most of the men of learning in Europe, have given up all accounts of witches and apparitions as mere old wives' fables. I am sorry for it; and I willingly take this opportunity of entering my solemn protest against this violent compliment which so many that believe the Bible pay to those who do not believe it." He then gravely warned, "that the giving up witchcraft is, in effect, giving up the Bible." But most interesting of all is Wesley's revelation of why he wished to accept ghosts and apparitions: "If but one account of the intercourse of men with separate spirits be admitted, their [the unbelievers'] whole castle in the air (Deism, atheism, materialism) falls to the ground." [23]

Like Wesley in this respect, if in few others, Johnson did not relish giving up popular superstitions so long associated with religion. No aspect of religion did he choose to doubt because religion alone provides mankind with the ability to suffer this life by faith in the life everlasting. Whatever attacks religion, therefore, attacks immortality; and without that hope, without that surety, life in this world would be unendurable. As Christian Stoic, Johnson poignantly and forcefully depicts the *Vanity of Human Wishes* without religious faith:

[23] Wesley, *Journal*, V, 265.

Where then shall Hope and Fear their objects find?
Must dull Suspence corrupt the stagnant mind?
Must helpless man, in ignorance sedate,
Roll darkling down the torrent of his fate?
Must no dislike alarm, no wishes rise,
No cries attempt the mercies of the skies?
Enquirer, cease, petitions yet remain,
Which heav'n may hear, nor deem religion vain.
Still raise for good the supplicating voice,
But leave to heav'n the measure and the choice,
Safe in his pow'r, whose eyes discern afar
The secret ambush of a specious pray'r.
Implore his aid, in his decisions rest,
Secure whate'er he gives, he gives the best.
Yet when the sense of sacred presence fires,
And strong devotion to the skies aspires,
Pour forth thy fervours for a healthful mind,
Obedient passions, and a will resign'd;
For love, which scarce collective man can fill;
For patience sov'reign o'er transmuted ill;
For faith, that panting for a happier seat,
Counts death kind Nature's signal of retreat:
These goods for man the laws of heav'n ordain,
These goods he grants, who grants the pow'r to gain;
With these celestial wisdom calms the mind,
And makes the happiness she does not find.

In Johnson's religious skepticism, subdued but never extinguished, lies the secret of his consuming hatred of Hume, a hatred that seemed to him a good hatred. Johnson hated Hume because he recognized in him a kindred spirit, and one capable moreover of pushing inquiry fearlessly to its logical conclusions. When Boswell told him of Hume's religious doubts, Johnson snapped: "If I could have allowed myself to gratify my vanity at the expence of truth, what fame might I have acquired. Every thing which Hume has advanced against Christianity had passed through my mind long before he wrote."[24] Contemporary recognition of Johnson's repressed religious skepticism is cited by Richard Porson: "A very old

[24] *Life of Johnson*, I, 444.

gentleman, who had known Johnson intimately, assured me that the bent of his mind was decidedly towards skepticism! that he was literally afraid to examine his own thoughts on religious matters; and that hence partly arose his hatred of Hume and other such writers." [25]

Johnson's hatred of Hume was grounded on fear—on the fear that Hume might conceivably be right, and if right, that immortality itself was unsure. Johnson's religious skepticism, therefore, became the strength of his religious faith: the more he doubted, the more desperately he believed. Yet never, he morbidly confessed to Boswell, for one moment of his life did he not fear death. Ardently religious though he was, Johnson did not find the promised happiness in religion; solace, at best, but never happiness. His Christianity was thus exceptional, although he liked to think that it was representative, as when he protested that "There are many good men whose fear of GOD predominates over their love." [26]

Though Carlyle was right in viewing Hume and Johnson as essentially complementary in character, Carlyle was wrong in supposing that a superman would be the happy result of the combination of those "two half-men of their time." For in human nature addition is not always simple arithmetic. Sometimes it is geometrical increment. Sometimes it is annihilation. Sometimes it is sheer impossibility. Psychologically speaking, the constituent features of Hume and Johnson do not appear together. There is no reason to believe that they ever will. There is no valid reason to hope that they ever will. Good men both, each after his fashion, Hume and Johnson are the two whole-men of all time, the one inspiring respect, the other veneration. And it is not meet to depreciate either in order to exalt the other, for the world needs both. Hume, imbued with the "will to doubt," is the Inquirer, philosopher or scientist; Johnson, imbued with the "will to believe," is the Consoler, priest or lay preacher.

IV

Hume and Johnson are more than ideal types; they are also men prominent historically. Johnson is greatly beloved by many

[25] "Porsoniana" in *Table-Talk of Samuel Rogers*, p. 348.
[26] *Life of Johnson*, III, 339.

readers today because he still seems alive. He is, in fact, the best known of any literary figure because he, happily, had his Boswell; and vitality, no matter how imperfect the man, is ever thrilling. That other Johnson, the not so lovable exponent of intolerance and bigotry, the man who cannot bear to lose, that melancholy figure also exists to obscure the picture of the ideal Johnson, the Consoler. Both combine to form the true composite, Samuel Johnson, the distinguished English man of letters of the eighteenth century. Carlyle's choice of this historical figure as his representative Hero as Man of Letters was a one-sided judgment, for assuredly it was the Consoler rather than the human being, the ideal rather than the man, that excited Carlyle's transcendental hero worship.

Regrettably, the only Hume that is widely known today is the Inquirer. The intellect is much alive; but, lacking a contemporary Boswell, the man is forgotten. Yet as the accounts of Hume's contacts with his contemporaries become better known, he too begins to thrill into life. And it is proper to insist that this historical Hume is the equal of Johnson, morally as good, humanly as lovable. That eminently human and lovable clergyman and sentimental traveler, Laurence Sterne, valued Hume as the most amiable of men. "I should," he insisted, "be most exceedingly surprized to hear that David ever had unpleasant contention with any man;—and if I should be made to believe that such an event had happened, nothing would persuade me that his opponent was not in the wrong; for in my life did I never meet with a being of a more placid and gentle nature." [27]

Yorick's high estimate of the amiability of Hume was heartily endorsed by Adam Smith, but Smith also discerned superior qualities. His final and mature judgment remains the fullest contemporary statement, uncontrovertible today after more than a century and a half:

Thus died our most excellent, and never-to-be-forgotten friend; concerning whose philosophical opinions men will no doubt judge variously, every one approving or condemning them according as they happen to coincide, or disagree with his own; but concerning whose character and conduct there can scarce be a difference of opinion. His temper, indeed,

[27] Cross, *Life and Times of Sterne*, II, 34.

seemed to be more happily balanced, if I may be allowed such an expression, than that perhaps of any other man I have ever known. Even in the lowest state of his fortune, his great and necessary frugality never hindered him from exercising, upon proper occasions, acts both of charity and generosity. It was a frugality founded not upon avarice, but upon the love of independency. The extreme gentleness of his nature never weakened either the firmness of his mind, or the steadiness of his resolutions. His constant pleasantry was the genuine effusion of good nature and good humour, tempered with delicacy and modesty, and without even the slightest tincture of malignity, so frequently the disagreeable source of what is called wit in other men. It never was the meaning of his raillery to mortify; and therefore, far from offending, it seldom failed to please and delight even those who were the objects of it. To his friends, who were frequently the objects of it, there was not perhaps any one of all his great and amiable qualities which contributed more to endear his conversation. And that gaiety of temper, so agreeable in society, but which is so often accompanied with frivolous and superficial qualities, was in him certainly attended with the most severe application, the most extensive learning, the greatest depth of thought, and a capacity in every respect the most comprehensive. Upon the whole, I have always considered him, both in his lifetime, and since his death, as approaching as nearly to the idea of a perfectly wise and virtuous man, as perhaps the nature of human frailty will admit.[28]

Beyond all cavil, David Hume was the ideal Inquirer just as Samuel Johnson was the ideal Consoler. Let it be remembered that Hume was also *le bon David*.

[28] Smith to Strahan in Hume, *Letters*, II, 452.

CHAPTER 9

·

AFTERWORD

THE MIND of Hume was the catalyst of the Enlightenment, quickening every reaction. Intellectually, the age was Hume's. "Amongst the learned in Europe, who does not know the celebrated works of David Hume?" inquired Denina [1] in 1764; and the question carried its own answer. In English literature, on the contrary, the age was Johnson's, though—despite the *Dictionary*—less for what he published, than for the man he was. So the later eighteenth century is typified by the mind of Hume and by the personality of Johnson, a distinction between ideas and persons that would certainly have been acceptable to the philosopher. Hume would also have been willing to acknowledge that ideas are much less apt to hold general attention than persons.

When Boswell asserted that he had "*Johnsonised* the land," [2] he was thus making no idle boast nor talking vain philosophy. Through Boswell, Johnson had become *the* personality.

> Triumphant thou through Time's vast gulf shall sail,
> The pilot of our literary whale—

sang "Peter Pindar" to Bozzy, and with more truth than poetry— but still with only half the truth. For, if England was to be "Johnsonised," the whale had to have his pilot, his Boswell.

Lacking a hero-worshiper, or pilot, or Boswell, Hume stood no chance of becoming *the* personality. Yet it is doubtful, in any event, if he would ever have rivaled Johnson. Johnson might be canonized the ideal Consoler and his human foibles forgiven or even enhanced into "glorious prejudices," as his very lack of emotional restraint is a source of popular appeal. Hume, aside from nationalistic con-

---

[1] Quoted in *Scots Magazine*, XXVI (1764), 467.
[2] Advertisement to second edition of *Life of Johnson* (1793).

siderations which would always have ruled him out, might be presented as the ideal Inquirer; but the vast majority of his contemporaries were simply incredulous of *le bon David*. Such humanity, such benevolence, such goodness were not to be associated with any skeptic, let alone with the Great Infidel.

In 1770 Hugh Blair had been unable to convince James Beattie that Hume was a "Worthy, humane, good natured man." [3] In 1777 Adam Smith had made a similar effort in the published "character" of the philosopher and had also failed. The only readers to accept that appraisal at its face value were those who were already convinced through personal experience. Blair, for instance, wrote William Strahan, to whom Smith's letter had been addressed: "Poor David! What an irreparable blank does he make amongst us here. Taking him all in all, we shall never see the like. Indeed I cannot but agree with what Adam Smith says of him in the last sentence of his printed letter to you." [4]

Yet after ten years Smith was still embittered over the public reaction to that friendly effort. "A single, and as I thought, a very harmless Sheet of paper," he complained, "which I happened to write concerning the death of our late friend, Mr Hume, brought upon me ten times more abuse than the very violent attack I had made upon the whole commercial system of Great Britain." [5] Toleration, according to Voltaire, is the consequence of humanity; but the hardest lesson to be learned by mankind is humanity. The dispassionate search for truth seldom has a wide appeal, and rigorous thinking is not infrequently stigmatized in the popular mind as "cold philosophy." Hume the ideal Inquirer was, therefore, not to be humanized. And, rejected by the Age of Johnson, *le bon David* shortly became the forgotten Hume.

With the passing of a century and a half, however, it may now be possible to appraise the character of Hume with justice and to place the humanity, the benevolence, and the goodness of the great Inquirer beyond controversy. His had, indeed, been the good life,

[3] Blair, MS letter, King's College Library, Aberdeen, MS C.33.
[4] Blair, MS letter. Photostats in University of Chicago Library of MS in possession of the Earl of Rosebery.
[5] Quoted by Scott in *Adam Smith as Student and Professor*, p. 283.

perfectly fulfilling the ideal implied in the motto inscribed on his personal seal: [6] TRUE TO THE END. To establish that fact has been the broad purpose of this book through the portrayal of its hero in his relations with contemporaries, particularly with close associates. The received opinion of those who knew and appreciated him best was classically phrased by Earl Marischal of Scotland, George Keith. Doubtless that affectionate tribute [7] pleased Hume in 1767 as Keith's benediction after the lamentable quarrel with Rousseau. Finally reconciling the philosopher with the man, it is a tribute that will please Hume's admirers always: "To the highflyers you are therefor a sad whig, to the whigs an hidden Jacobite, and to reasonable men *le bon David*, a Lover of truth."

[6] Hume, Seal, National Library of Scotland, MS 1703A. See tailpiece below.
[7] *Calendar of Hume MSS*, V, 116.

DISCURSIVE NOTES

DISCURSIVE NOTES

A. HUME'S FIRST MEETING WITH BLACKLOCK

"The first time I had ever seen or heard of Mr Blacklock was about twelve years ago," Hume informed Spence in 1754. That would make it about 1742. Greig, therefore, was certainly rash in assigning letter No. 89 [Hume, *Letters*, I, 183] as from Hume to Blacklock in 1753, with the comment: "It would appear that this letter marks the beginning of Hume's friendship with, and patronage of, him." Hume, furthermore, [I, 204] specifically disclaimed having seen Blacklock's 1754 edition "till it was printed." As letter No. 89 is undated, as well as unaddressed, and refers only to an unspecified preface—presumably, but not certainly—to an unknown volume of poetry, I will not at present conjecture as to the addressee.

B. BLACKLOCK'S LETTER TO BEATTIE CONCERNING HIS FRIENDSHIP WITH HUME

Sir William Forbes [*Life of Beattie*, I, 135n] writes: "I find among Dr Beattie's papers a long letter to him from Dr Blacklock, giving a detail of the intercourse between him and Mr Hume, from its commencement to its close." Forbes did not print the letter nor date it explicitly, although it obviously belongs to the 1769-70 period. Dr. L. W. Sharp, the librarian at Edinburgh University, was kind enough to conduct a search for this letter on my behalf. He reports that it is not to be found in his own University Library, in the National Library of Scotland, or in the Aberdeen University Library where the bulk of the Beattie MSS are deposited.

C. HUME ON SHAKESPEARE'S PUNS

Maclaurin's note reads: "*David Hume*, Esq; in his history of *Great Britain*, vol. I. in a note, has these words ['What could *Shakespear* have said worse?']." When Hume's comment is read in its proper context, it will be observed how invidious is Maclaurin's use of it:

"The name of Polynices, one of Oedipus's sons, means in the original *much quarrelling*. In the altercations between the two brothers, in Aeschylus, Sophocles, and Euripides, this conceit is employed: and it is remarkable, that so poor a conundrum could not have been rejected by any of these three poets, so justly celebrated for their taste and simplicity. What could Shakespeare have done worse? Terence has his *inceptio est amentium, non amantium.* Many similar instances will occur to the learned. It is well known that Aristotle treats very seriously of puns, divides them into several classes, and recommends the use of them to orators" [*History of England,* VI, 190*n*].

D. HUME'S TWO SUPPRESSED ESSAYS OF 1757

References in the pamphlet literature of 1757 concerning *Douglas* indicate that Hume's *Of Suicide* and *Of the Immortality of the Soul* were by no means unknown. Just how this happened is not perfectly clear. In 1764 John Wilkes admitted to Hume that he had been given a copy of *Five Dissertations* by Andrew Millar, Hume's printer. Wilkes claimed, however, to have taken the precaution, after reading the volume, of tearing out "the two obnoxious Dissertations"! Millar denied Wilkes's story, but it seems a safe guess that he allowed other copies to get out. In 1770, apparently unknown to Hume, the two essays turned up in French translation in a collection published under the auspices of Baron d'Holbach. It is perhaps significant that Wilkes had earlier visited Holbach and had become his good friend. For further remarks on this bibliographical problem, see Hume, *Letters,* I, 444 and note, II, 346; and Rudolf Metz, "Les Amitiés françaises de Hume et le mouvement des idées," *Revue de littérature comparée,* IX (1929), 710-11.

E. PIGEON-SHOOTING AND THE EPIGONIAD

A nice critical point, unaccountably overlooked by the Age of Enlightenment, has been called to my attention by a waggish colleague. If, as Hume says, Wilkie composed most of the poem out in the fields while acting as a scare-pigeon, is it possible to determine in the versification when he "rose up, ran towards them, & fir'd at them"? Any critic who may care to study the 5,782 lines—my count—for a possible staccato effect, will, I am confident, reap a just reward. I hereby solemnly affirm that I have no intention of following eminent precedent in founding an *Epigoniad Club* to consist of those who have had the temerity to read the entire epic.

F. HUME ON OSSIAN

That Hume's Ossianic critique was directly inspired by Johnson's *Journey to the Western Islands of Scotland* has not, I believe, been previously noted. Indeed, the intense rivalry, personal and literary, between the two leaders of national letters has been strangely neglected. A fuller treatment of the significance of that rivalry will be found in Chapters 8 and 9.

G. POPULATION CONTROVERSY

In a letter of April 18, 1750, Hume singled out Vossius and Montesquieu as the outstanding representatives of the theory of decline as applied to population. In 1685 Vossius had included in a volume entitled *Variarum observationum liber* an essay, "De antiquae Romae magnitudine." Montesquieu had twice discussed the subject at considerable length: first in the *Lettres persanes* (1721), Lettres CXIII-CXXIII, and later in *L'Esprit des loix* (1748), Livre XXIII, cap. 17-19. Further observations on Hume's use of both the idea of decline and the idea of progress will be found in Chapter 8, section III.

H. WALLACE AND THE DOUGLAS CONTROVERSY

Ramsay of Ochtertyre's statement that Wallace opposed those "who went openly to the playhouse when 'Douglas' was acted" [*Scotland and Scotsmen*, I, 48], is expressly contradicted by Carlyle's testimony referred to in the text and also by Mackenzie's [*Life of Home*, p. 48]. It would seem entirely out of keeping with the character of Wallace as evidenced in many actions, especially in the defense of Hume against the same Highflying set.

I. FURTHER HUME-WALLACE RELATIONSHIPS

Among the Hume manuscripts in the Royal Society of Edinburgh is a short paper on mathematical principles said to be in the handwriting of Wallace. Under what circumstances it got there and what Hume had to do with it remain unknown. The paper is an attempt to circumvent Hume's denial of the existence of abstract universal ideas in so far as mathematics is concerned [*Calendar of Hume MSS*, XIII, 40].

J. HUME AND WALPOLE'S KING-OF-PRUSSIA LETTER

The desire to implicate Hume in the King-of-Prussia letter has been the motivating principle of a long line of Rousseau apologists. The nineteenth-century mistranslation that made Hume acknowledge his complicity is retained in the twentieth-century *Correspondance générale*, providing the editor with the opportunity for denouncing Hume's later prevarications. The case is worth citation in full. Hume wrote to the Marquise de Barbentane, February 16, 1766 [*Letters*, II, 16]: "Please tell Madame de Boufflers that I received her letter the day after I wrote mine. Assure her that Horace Walpole's letter was not founded on any pleasantry of mine: the only pleasantry in that letter came from his own mouth, in my company, at Lord Ossory's table; which my Lord remembers very well." This appears in French [*Corr. gén.*, XIV, 16] as: "Dites à Mme de Boufflers que la seule plaisanterie que je me sois permise relativement à la prétendue lettre du roi de Prusse, fut faite par moi à la table de Lord Ossory." This false confession was detected by Burton in 1846 [II, 322*n*], but apparently went unnoticed by many Rousseauists until the publication of Greig's edition of Hume's *Letters* in 1932.

The desire to implicate Hume in Walpole's letter has not, however, entirely been given up. Roddier, for instance, who acknowledges the facts, is seemingly content to build up a new case against Hume without facts. Hume, he argues, loved pleasantry and sociability. Several of his compatriots were in Paris, and he doubtless met them frequently and doubtless also joined in the pleasantries at the expense of Rousseau. His denials and those of Walpole carry no weight because the British will stick together to preserve the social amenities. Now, on the basis of this seemingly unimportant—and certainly unsubstantiated—hypothesis, Roddier proceeds to interpret Hume's later conduct. It is to be understood in the light of a certain sense of guilt that he felt concerning Rousseau. The peccadillo was small enough, to be sure, but the guilt was there. When Rousseau made the first vague accusations against him, it was this consciousness of guilt that distressed Hume so greatly. When Rousseau later specified the charges without directly involving him in the pleasantries giving rise to Walpole's letter, Hume was vastly relieved: that was the one point on which his conduct had not been perfectly exemplary. He could, therefore, affect righteous indignation and even brutal anger. Thus is Hume convicted of cruelty and inhumanity. Thus is Hume not *le bon David*.

Roddier's reasoning is of a piece with Rousseau's own on the same King-of-Prussia letter. Before seeing it, Rousseau suspected—shrewdly enough, to be sure—that Voltaire was the author. But after seeing it, he *knew*, just as surely as if he had actually watched him writing it, that D'Alembert was the author. And Walpole? Oh, he was nobody; he had merely permitted his name to be used as a screen to protect Rousseau's enemies, the *philosophes*. This alleged alliance of Walpole with the *philosophes* is, in point of fact, the only real pleasantry in the whole affair!

In view of all this feeling, this intuiting of facts, it might be well to recall that in the court of justice—and surely also in the court of scholarship—motive and opportunity are not sufficient to convict. Evidence is always the primary consideration. To speak plainly: there is not the slightest shred of evidence that Hume had any hand whatsoever in the letter, either before or after its composition. The facts stated in the text above are all verifiable as testimony.

Evidence against Hume is entirely lacking. Opportunity, of course, he had along with everyone else in Paris. But what of motive? As indicated in the text, Hume had been carrying on a personal campaign to assist Rousseau since the spring of 1765, at least eight months before that philosopher reached Paris. The patron, it might readily be supposed, would be the last person in the world to discredit his protégé. To raise funds for Rousseau by a campaign of sneering at him would be a strange procedure indeed! Moreover, the known character of *le bon David* is additional and important evidence that his raillery was never intended to mortify. The new case against Hume, therefore, is as implausible as the old case was spurious.

K. HUME'S CONSULTATION WITH MME DE VERDELIN

Conceivably it was after the farewell visit to Holbach—rather than before, as stated in the text—that Hume sought the advice of Mme de Verdelin. Yet as the Holbach visit is supposed to have taken place the eve of the departure from Paris, the time would have been exceedingly short. It seems likely enough that others of the *philosophes* had retailed stories concerning Rousseau at an earlier date, perhaps in December after the proposed trip to England became known. So far as the actual Rousseau-Hume quarrel is concerned, however, the problem is purely academic.

L. ROUSSEAU'S LAST WEEKS IN ENGLAND, 1767

The following unpublished MS letters in the National Library of Scotland deal with the close of Rousseau's stay in England:

Hume to Davenport: MS 1005, ff. 11-12: March 20, 1767.
Davenport to Hume: MS 1798, ff. 68-69: May 13, 1767; ff. 70-71: May 18, 1767; ff. 72-73: [undated]; ff. 74-75: July 4, 1767; ff. 76-77: July 6, 1767.

Unfortunately these letters have been declared inaccessible for the duration and were not used in the text above.

M. THE RAMSAY PORTRAIT OF ROUSSEAU

The facts concerning this painting, upon which the narrative in the **text is based**, are to be found as follows: Hume: *Letters*, II, 27, 45, 116,

386; *Concise Account*, p. 38*n*. Rousseau: *Corr. gén.*, XV, 125, 129, 301; XIX, 129, 196, 317; *Œuvres*, XXI, 248, 252-53, 257-58.

N. BOSWELL AND THE HUME FIXATION

In Chapter 7 I have attempted merely to record the facts of the Hume fixation as evidenced in Boswell's *Letters* and *Private Papers* and have rigorously restricted myself to as few hypotheses as possible. The closing suggestion that that fixation may be susceptible of wider application is admittedly cavalier. Yet I hope that the student of Boswell will test it out and that it may at least prompt him to other, and possibly more fruitful, psychological approaches.

O. HUME-JOHNSON ANTAGONISMS

Hume:
> The English decline in literature during his time: *Letters*, II, 312.
> The English as barbarians who inhabit the banks of the Thames: *Ibid.*, I, 436.
> The Scots as the people most distinguished for literature in Europe: *Ibid.*, I, 255.
> Johnson's style, a peculiar and enormous variety of English: *Ibid.*, II, 240.
> Johnson, a man of enthusiasm and antiquated notions: *P. P.*, I, 128.

Johnson:
> The Scots love Scotland better than truth: *Boswell and Johnson Tour*, p. 108.
> The Scots too unlearned for the dignity of literature: [The corrected version was kindly supplied me by Dr. James L. Clifford, who is engaged in editing the *Diary* of Dr. Thomas Campbell, its source. It appears also in *Johnsonian Miscellanies*, II, 48.]
> The English maintaining the capital of literature: *Works*, XII, 317.
> Hume's style French rather than English: *Life of Johnson*, I, 439.
> Hume, a blockhead and a rogue: *P. P.*, I, 128. [This is the passage suppressed by Boswell as "something much too rough." See *Boswell and Johnson Tour*, p. 177.]

I am well aware that since the time of Birkbeck Hill, it has been customary for scholars to gloze over Johnson's prejudices against Scotland. I regret that I cannot agree. It seems to me just as certain that Johnson entertained such prejudices as that, from the 1750's onwards, Hume entertained anti-English prejudices. The evidence of this nationalistic rivalry is available to all who will see it; and there is no good to be gained by suppressing facts, even regrettable facts.

P. THE REYNOLDS PORTRAIT OF BEATTIE

An interesting discussion of this allegorical painting, the "Triumph of Truth over Error," is afforded by Edgar Wind, "Humanitätsidee und heroisiertes Porträt in der englischen Kultur des 18. Jahrhunderts," *Vorträge der Bibliothek Warburg* (1932), 195-99. The comparison of Reynolds's technique on Beattie with Ramsay's on Hume is particularly illuminating.

AUTHORITIES

CRITICAL BIBLIOGRAPHY

I. HUME

MANUSCRIPTS

Eight letters to Wallace. Edinburgh University Library, MSS Laing, II, 96. [Only the first is dated, but all belong to the period 1751-53. See also under Heinemann, below.]

Corrections on the proof sheets of Wallace's *Dissertation*. Edinburgh University Library, MSS Laing, II, 96.

Letter of Feb. 27, 1754. Harvard College Library, insertion in T. P. 2050.50.2. [Unaddressed, but almost certainly to Adam Smith.]

Letter of Oct. 19 [14?], 1754. Victoria and Albert Museum, London. [Unaddressed, but certainly to Robert Dodsley.]

Receipt of March 20, 1756. Edinburgh University Library, MSS Laing, II, 508.

Letter of May 5, 1757. National Library of Scotland, MS 1810, No. 83.

Letter of Sept. 29, 1757. National Library of Scotland, MS 1005.

Letter of Dec. 20, 1766. Victoria and Albert Museum, London.

Letter of June 9, 1775. National Library of Scotland, MS 1034, No. 100.

Letter of Feb. 8, 1776. Edinburgh University Library, MSS Laing, II, 173.

Personal seal. National Library of Scotland, MS 1703A. [Description: Initials "DH," surrounded by a strap and buckle bearing the motto, "TRUE TO THE END," and surmounted by a lion's head.]

PUBLICATIONS

Calendar of Hume MSS in the Possession of the Royal Society of Edinburgh, compiled by J. Y. T. Greig and Harold Beynon. Edinburgh, 1932. [Includes letters addressed to Hume and other MSS that came into his possession.]

Letters, edited by J. Y. T. Greig. Oxford, 1932. 2 vols. [The source of all Hume quotations in the text unless otherwise noted.]

Philosophical Works, edited by T. H. Green and T. H. Grose. London, 1874-75. 4 vols.

Concise and Genuine Account of the Dispute between Mr. Hume and
Mr. Rousseau; with the Letters that Passed between Them during
Their Controversy. As Also, the Letters of the Hon. Mr. Walpole,
and Mr. D'Alembert, Relative to This Extraordinary Affair. London, 1766.

Exposé succinct de la contestation qui s'est élevée entre M. Hume et M.
Rousseau avec les pièces justicatives. London [Paris], 1766.

Four Dissertations. London, 1757.

History of England. Edinburgh, 1792. 8 vols.

"Letter to the Authors of the *Critical Review*," in *Crit. Rev.*, VII
(1759), 323-34. [Anon. Reprinted in *Phil. Works*, IV, 425-37.]

"Of the Authenticity of Ossian's Poems," in *Phil. Works*, IV, 415-24.

Political Discourses. Edinburgh, 1752.

True Account of the Behaviour and Conduct of Archibald Stewart, Esq;
Late Lord Provost of Edinburgh, in a Letter to a Friend. London,
1748. [Anon.]

II. GENERAL

Adam, R. B., Library Relating to Dr. Samuel Johnson and His Era.
London and New York, 1929-30. 4 vols.

Annals of The Club, 1764-1914. London, 1914.

Beattie, James. Poems. In *Chalmers*, Vol. XVIII.

Blacklock, Thomas. "Blindness," article in *Encyclopaedia Britannica*,
2d ed.

———— A Collection of Original Poems. By the Rev. Mr Blacklock, and
Other Scotch Gentlemen. Edinburgh, 1760. [Blacklock did not contribute to Vol. II, Edinburgh, 1762.]

———— Paraclesis; or, Consolations Deduced from Natural and Revealed
Religion: in Two Dissertations. The First Supposed to Have Been
Composed by Cicero; Now Rendered into English: the Last Originally
Written by Thomas Blacklock, D.D. Edinburgh, 1767.

———— Poems. In *Chalmers*, Vol. XVIII.

———— Poems by the Late Reverend Dr. Thomas Blacklock. Edited by
Henry Mackenzie. Edinburgh, 1793.

———— Poems on Several Occasions. Glasgow, 1746. [Anon.]

———— Poems on Several Occasions. Edinburgh, 1754.

———— Poems; to Which Is Prefix'd, an Account of the Life, Character,
and Writings, of the Author, by the Reverend Mr. Spence, Late Professor of Poetry, at Oxford. The Third Edition. London, 1756.

——— Two Discourses on the Spirit and Evidences of Christianity. Translated from the Original French of the Rev. Mr. James Armand, Minister of the Walloon Church in Hanau. Edinburgh, 1768.

Blair, Hugh. MS letter of July 1, 1764. Royal Society of Edinburgh, Hume MSS, III, 53.

——— MS letter of Feb. 24, 1766. Royal Society of Edinburgh, Hume MSS, III, 56.

——— MS letter of July 10, 1766. Royal Society of Edinburgh, Hume MSS, III, 59.

——— MS letter of May 14, 1770. King's College Library, Aberdeen, MS C.33.

——— MS letter of April 10, 1778. Photostats in University of Chicago Library of MS in possession of the Earl of Rosebery.

——— A Critical Dissertation on the Poems of Ossian, the Son of Fingal. London, 1763. [Appendix to this dissertation appeared in *Works of Ossian*, 3d ed., 1765, II, 445-60.]

——— Preface to Macpherson's *Fragments of Ancient Poetry*. [Anon.]

Bonar, James. Theories of Population from Raleigh to Arthur Young. London, 1931.

Boswell, James. MS letter of Aug. 30, 1775. National Library of Scotland, MS Acc. No. 1371.

——— Boswelliana, edited by Charles Rogers. London, 1874.

——— Journal of a Tour to the Hebrides, in *Johnson's Journey to the Western Islands of Scotland and Boswell's Journal of a Tour to the Hebrides*, edited by R. W. Chapman. London, 1934. [Cited as *Boswell and Johnson Tour*.]

——— Letters, edited by C. B. Tinker. Oxford, 1924. 2 vols.

——— Life of Johnson, edited by G. B. Hill; revised and enlarged by L. F. Powell. Oxford, 1934——. 4 vols.

——— Private Papers from Malahide Castle, edited by G. Scott and F. A. Pottle. Privately printed, New York, 1928-34. 18 vols. [Cited as *Private Papers* and in Chapters 7 and 8 as *P.P.*]

Brougham, Henry. Lives of Men of Letters and Science, Who Flourished in the Time of George III. London, 1845-46. 2 vols.

Brown, P. Hume. History of Scotland. Cambridge, 1899-1909. 3 vols.

Burke, Edmund. Works. London, 1900-1901. 8 vols.

Burns, Robert. Letters, edited by J. De Lancey Ferguson. Oxford, 1931. 2 vols.

Burns, Robert. Poetical Works, edited by J. L. Robertson. London, 1939.

Burton, John Hill. Life and Correspondence of David Hume. Edinburgh, 1846. 2 vols. [Cited as *Burton*. Still invaluable, although textually superceded by Greig's edition of Hume's *Letters*.]

Caldwell Papers. Glasgow, 1854.

Carlyle, Alexander. Autobiography, edited by John Hill Burton. London and Edinburgh, 1910.

———— An Argument to Prove That the Tragedy of Douglas Ought to Be Publickly Burnt by the Hands of the Hangman. Edinburgh, 1757. [Anon.]

———— A Full and True History of the Bloody Tragedy of Douglas, as It Is Now to Be Seen Acting in the Theatre at the Canongate. [Edinburgh, 1757. Anon.]

Carlyle, Thomas. Essay on Burns.

———— Essay on Johnson.

Chastellux, François Jean, Marquis de. An Essay on Public Happiness, Investigating the State of Human Nature, under Each of Its Particular Appearances, through the Several Periods of History to the Present Times. London, 1774. 2 vols. [Translated from the French edition, Amsterdam, 1772. 2 vols. Anon.]

Churchill, Charles. Poems, edited by James Laver. London, 1933. 2 vols.

Courtois, Louis-J. Séjour de Jean-Jacques Rousseau en Angleterre (1766-1767); Lettres et documents inédits. Annales de la Société Jean-Jacques Rousseau, Vol. VI. Geneva, 1910. [Detailed and accurate account of Rousseau's actions and whereabouts in England with no attempt at interpretation of the quarrel.]

Critical Essay on the Epigoniad; Wherein the Author's Horrid Abuse of Milton Is Examined. Edinburgh, 1757. [Anon.]

Critical Review.

Cross, Wilbur L. Life and Times of Laurence Sterne. A new edition. New Haven, 1925. 2 vols.

Dempster, George. Letters to Sir Adam Fergusson, edited by James Fergusson. London, 1934.

Doering, J. F. "Hume and the Theory of Tragedy," *Publications of the Modern Language Society of America*, LII (1937), 1130-34. [A sound beginning.]

Douglas Tracts. [The largest collection is in the Huntington Library, a smaller collection in Harvard College Library.]

Dryden, John. Poems.

Ebert, Hermann. Jean-Jacques Rousseau und David Hume. Versuch einer psychologischen Darstellung ihrer persönlichen Beziehungen. Würzburg, 1936. [Makes small contribution and seems inexcusably ignorant of Greig.]

Ferguson, Adam. The Morality of Stage-Plays Seriously Considered. Edinburgh, 1757.

Fergusson, Robert. Works. London, 1807.

Forbes, Margaret. Beattie and His Friends. London, 1904.

Forbes, William. An Account of the Life and Writings of James Beattie, LL.D. Edinburgh, 1806. 2 vols.

Fraser, G. M. "The Truth about Macpherson's 'Ossian,' " Quarterly Review, CCXLV (1925), 331-45. [Sums up the work "as one of the most remarkable literary impostures that has happened in Britain in modern times."]

Gerard, Alexander. The Influence of the Pastoral Office on the Character Examined; with a View, Especially, to Mr. Hume's Representation of the Spirit of That Office. Aberdeen, 1760.

Gibbon, Edward. Decline and Fall of the Roman Empire. Vol. I. London, 1776.

——— Memoirs, edited by O. F. Emerson. Boston, 1898.

Gipson, Alice E. John Home; a Study of His Life and Works with Special Reference to His Tragedy of Douglas and the Controversies Which Followed Its First Representation. Privately printed, 1916. [The best study of Home. Includes a section, though not very complete, on Hume's part in the Douglas controversy.]

Gray, Thomas. Correspondence, edited by the late Paget Toynbee and Leonard Whibley. Oxford, 1935. 3 vols.

Gray, W. Forbes. "The 'Discoverer' of Burns," Cornhill Magazine, CXLIX (1934), 26-35. [Interesting account of the later career, but sketchy on the connections with Hume.]

Gregory, John. MS letter of June 3, 1770. Huntington Library, MSS MO uncat.

Hawkins, John. Life of Samuel Johnson, LL.D. 2d ed., revised and corrected. London, 1787.

Heinemann, F. H. David Hume; the Man and His Science of Man. Containing Some Unpublished Letters of Hume. "Actualités Scientifiques et Industrielles," No. 860. Paris, 1940. [The first section of this pamphlet, pp. 7-22, is entitled, "David Hume and Robert Wallace." It offers a brief sketch of their relationship and prints the full texts of the eight Hume letters and of the single Wallace draft letter; the two Wallace MSS concerning Hume are little more than mentioned. Chapter 5, above, was written before I was able to get a copy of Heinemann's pamphlet; and as it proved to cover the ground much more completely than his, there was no reason to suppress it. I have carefully collated Heinemann's version of the MS quotations with my own and am completely satisfied that mine are more accurate.]

Home, John.   Epigrams, in *A Collection of Poems by Scotch Gentlemen*, Vol. II.   Edinburgh, 1762.

————— Works, edited by Henry Mackenzie.   Edinburgh, 1822. 3 vols.

Johnson, Samuel.   Journey to the Western Islands of Scotland, in *Johnson's Journey to the Western Islands of Scotland and Boswell's Journal of a Tour to the Hebrides*, edited by R. W. Chapman.   London, 1934. [Cited as *Boswell and Johnson Tour*.]

————— Lives of the English Poets, edited by G. B. Hill.   Oxford, 1905. 3 vols.

————— Miscellanies, arranged and edited by G. B. Hill.   London, 1897. 2 vols.

————— Works, edited by Arthur Murphy.   London, 1801. 12 vols.

Kant, Immanuel.   Prolegomena.

Lamb, Charles.   Letters, edited by E. V. Lucas.   New Haven, 1935. 3 vols.

Landor, Walter S.   Works, edited by T. E. Welby and S. Wheeler. London, 1927-36. 16 vols.

Letters of Eminent Persons Addressed to David Hume, edited by John Hill Burton.   Edinburgh and London, 1849. [Cited as *Eminent Persons*. Useful, but textually untrustworthy.]

Lévy-Bruhl, L.   "Quelques Mots sur la querelle de Hume et de Rousseau," *Revue de métaphysique et de morale*, XX (1912), 417-28. [Best short summary of the affair. The interpretation, however, is oversimplified and therefore somewhat misleading.]

Locke, John.   Essay concerning Human Understanding.

Lockhart, J. G.   Life of Scott.   London, 1900. 5 vols.

Mackenzie, Henry.   Anecdotes and Egotisms, edited by H. W. Thompson.   London, 1927.

————— Life of Blacklock, Preface to Blacklock's *Poems*.   Edinburgh, 1793.

————— Life of John Home.   Edinburgh, 1822.

————— Report of the Committee of the Highland Society of Scotland,

Appointed to Inquire into the Nature and the Authenticity of the Poems of Ossian. Edinburgh, 1805.

———— Works. Edinburgh and London, 1808. 8 vols.

Maclaurin, John. Apology for the Writers against the Tragedy of Douglas. Edinburgh, 1757. [Anon.]

———— The Philosopher's Opera. [Edinburgh, 1757. Anon.]

Macpherson, James. Fingal; an Ancient Epic Poem, in Six Books: Together with Several Other Poems, Composed by Ossian, the Son of Fingal. Translated from the Galic Language. London, 1762. [Appeared late in 1761.]

———— Fragments of Ancient Poetry, Collected in the Highlands of Scotland, and Translated from the Galic or Erse Language. Edinburgh, 1760. [Anon., with anonymous Preface by Blair.]

———— The History of Great Britain, from the Restoration, to the Accession of the House of Hannover. London, 1775. 2 vols.

———— The Iliad of Homer, translated by James Macpherson. London, 1773. 2 vols.

———— An Introduction to the History of Great Britain and Ireland. London, 1771.

———— Original Papers; Containing the Secret History of Great Britain, from the Restoration, to the Accession of the House of Hannover. To Which Is Prefixed Extracts from the Life of James II as Written by Himself. The Whole Arranged and Published by James Macpherson. London, 1775. 2 vols.

———— Temora; an Ancient Epic Poem, in Eight Books: Together with Several Other Poems, Composed by Ossian, the Son of Fingal. Translated from the Galic Language. London, 1763.

———— The Works of Ossian, the Son of Fingal. The Third Edition. London, 1765. 2 vols.

Malthus, Thomas R. An Essay on the Principle of Population as It Affects the Future Improvement of Society. London, 1798.

Marmontel, Jean François. Mémoires, edited by Maurice Tourneaux. Paris, 1891. 3 vols.

Metz, Rudolf. "Les Amitiés françaises de Hume et le mouvement des idées," Revue de littérature comparée, IX (1929), 644-713.

Miller, Frank. "Dr. Blacklock's Manuscripts," Scottish Historical Review, X (1913), 369-76. [Notes on the Blacklock collection in the Annan Public Library.]

———— "Unpublished Topical Poem by Dr. Blacklock," Scottish Historical Review, IV (1907), 205-12. [Text of Pistapolis.]

Mirabeau, the Elder. L'Ami des hommes. 5th ed. Hamburg, 1760.

Monod-Cassidy, Hélène. Un Voyageur-Philosophe au XVIIIᵉ siècle; L Abbé Jean-Bernard Le Blanc. Cambridge, Mass., 1940.

Montagu, Elizabeth. MS letter of Oct. 20, 1766. Huntington Library, MSS MO uncat., EM 1766.

Montesquieu. Correspondance. Bordeaux, 1914. 2 vols.

Monthly Review.

Morellet, André. Mémoires. Paris, 1823. 2 vols.

Mossner, Ernest C. "Hume and the Scottish Shakespeare," *Huntington Library Quarterly,* III (1940), 419-41. [Chapter 3, above, represents a considerable expansion and revision of this article.]

——— "Hume as Literary Patron; a Suppressed Review of Robert Henry's *History of Great Britain,* 1773," *Modern Philology,* XXXIX (1942), 361-82.

——— "Rousseau Hero-Worship," *Modern Language Notes,* LV (1940), 449-51. [First publication of the Robert Liston letter of Jan. 13, 1766. In the article, the letter is printed precisely as in the MS. In Chapter 6, above, quotation marks and paragraphing have been introduced.]

Peoples, Margaret. La Querelle Rousseau-Hume. Annales de la Société Jean-Jacques Rousseau, Vol. XVIII. Geneva, 1928. [A remarkably full study which, though pressing the case hard against Hume, sticks to the then available facts. Unfortunately, Greig's corrected texts were unavailable. For the Continental repercussions, this work remains authoritative.]

Pottle, Frederick A. "The Part Played by Horace Walpole and James Boswell in the Quarrel between Rousseau and Hume," *Philological Quarterly,* XV (1925), 351-62. [Reprints from the *St. James's Chronicle* of 1766-67, several items pertinent to the affair. Some of the interpretations expressed are no longer acceptable to Professor Pottle.]

Ramsay, John, of Ochtertyre. Scotland and Scotsmen in the Eighteenth Century, edited by Alexander Allardyce. Edinburgh and London, 1885. 2 vols.

Reimarus, Hermann S. The Principal Truths of Natural Religion Defended and Illustrated, translated by R. Wynne. London, 1766.

Ridpath, George. Diary, edited by Sir James Balfour Paul. Edinburgh, 1922.

Roddier, Henri. "A Propos de la Querelle Rousseau-Hume; Précisions chronologiques," *Revue d'histoire littéraire de la France,* CDLXIX

(1939), 211-14. [Makes several minor corrections in the dating of letters.]

———— "La Querelle Rousseau-Hume," *Revue de littérature comparée*, XVIII (1938), 452-77. [The first Rousseauist to use Greig and to correct many earlier factual errors, but is conspicuous for new and unwarrantable inferences to the discredit of Hume. See Note J, above.]

Rogers, Samuel, Recollections of the Table-Talk of, edited by Alexander Dyce. London, 1887.

Rousseau, Jean-Jacques. Collection complète des œuvres. Geneva, 1782-89. 33 vols.

———— Correspondance générale. Paris, 1924-34. 20 vols. [Cited in Chapter 6 as *Corr. gén.* Texts of the letters of both Rousseau and Hume are not always trustworthy; the notes relative to Hume and the quarrel seldom are. Most of Rousseau's letters to Hume were printed accurately by Greig, and translation has, therefore, been made from that work whenever possible.]

Saunders, Bailey. Life and Letters of James Macpherson. London and New York, 1894. [Still the standard life.]

Schinz, Albert. Etat présent des travaux sur J.-J. Rousseau. New York, 1941. [Critical bibliography. Considers Roddier as "définitif sur la question" Rousseau-Hume (pp. 343-44). See Note J, above.]

———— "La Querelle Rousseau-Hume; Un Document inédit," with Appendices by Frederick A. Pottle. Annales de la Société Jean-Jacques Rousseau, Vol. XVII. Geneva, 1926. [The text of Hume's letter of July 25, 1766, to Mme la Présidente de Meinières as the basis for an extended commentary. The Appendices list the items relating to Rousseau and Hume from the *St. James's Chronicle.*]

Scots Magazine.

Scott, W. R. Adam Smith as Student and Professor. Glasgow, 1937.

Scott, Walter. Review of Mackenzie's *Report*, in *Edinburgh Review*, VI (1806), 429-62.

———— Review of Mackenzie's edition of *Works of John Home*, in *Quarterly Review*, XXXVI (1827), 167-216.

Shenstone, William. Letters, edited by Duncan Mallam. Minneapolis, 1939.

Smart, J. S. James Macpherson; an Episode in Literature. London, 1905. [Severe attack on Macpherson by an eminent folklorist.]

Smollett, Tobias. Humphrey Clinker.

———— Letters, edited by E. S. Noyes. Cambridge, Mass., 1926.

Snyder, F. B. Life of Robert Burns. New York, 1932.

Somerville, Thomas. My Own Life and Times, 1741-1814. Edinburgh, 1861.

Spence, Joseph. An Account of the Life, Character, and Poems of Mr. Blacklock; Student of Philosophy, in the University of Edinburgh. London, 1754. [See also under Blacklock, above.]

———— Anecdotes, Observations, and Characters, of Books and Men, edited by Samuel W. Singer. London, 1820.

Straus, Ralph. Robert Dodsley. London, 1910.

Thompson, Harold W. A Scottish Man of Feeling; Some Account of Henry Mackenzie, Esq. of Edinburgh and of the Golden Age of Burns and Scott. London and New York, 1931. [Actually the fullest history of Scottish literature in the late eighteenth and early nineteenth centuries. Contains valuable bibliographies.]

Tytler, Alexander F. Memoirs of the Life and Writings of the Honourable Henry Home of Kames. Edinburgh, 1807. 2 vols.

Voltaire. Le Caffé; ou, L'Ecossaise, comédie par Mr. Hume pasteur de l'Eglise d'Edimbourg. Traduite en Français. London [Geneva], 1760. [Anon.]

Wallace, Robert. MS draft in Wallace's hand of letter of Sept. 26, 1751. Edinburgh University Library, MSS Laing, II, 96.

———— MS essay. "A Letter from a Moderate Freethinker to David Hume Esquire concerning the Profession of the Clergy. In Which It Is Shewed That Their Vices Whatever They Are Are Owing to Their Disposition and Not to the Bad Influence of Their Profession." Edinburgh University Library, MSS Laing, II, 97. [The MS is in eleven pages, the sheets being folded in half. Because of Wallace's vicious habit of inserting most of the punctuation only on the proof sheets, the necessary additions have been made in the extracts printed in Chapter 5, above. A few editorial guesses at his wretched handwriting have been placed within square brackets.]

———— MS essay. "The Necessity or Expediency of the Churches Inquiring into the Writings of David Hume Esquire and Calling the Author to Answer before the Spiritual Courts. Considered with Some Reflections on Christians Being Occasionally in Company with Scepticall or Infidell Writers. In Which There Are Some Animadversions on the Account in the Scotch Magazine for June. 1756 of the Debates in the Committee of Overtures of the Generall Assembly 1756 concerning These Subjects. Printed Edinburgh 1756." Edinburgh University Library, MSS Laing, II, 97. [Never published by Wallace. The MS is in sixty-six pages, the sheets being folded in half. Punctuation has been inserted as above.]

———— MS essay. "Of Venery; or, The Naturall Commerce of the 2 Sexes & Proposalls to Prevent Debauchery & Render Marriage More Happy." Edinburgh University Library, MSS Laing, II, 620, No. 12.

———— Characteristics of the Present Political State of Great Britain. Dublin, 1758. [This edition was probably pirated from the London edition of the same year.]

———— A Dissertation on the Numbers of Mankind in Antient and Modern Times; in Which the Superior Populousness of Antiquity Is Maintained. With an Appendix, Containing Additional Observations on the Same Subject, and Some Remarks on Mr. Hume's Political Discourse, Of the Populousness of Antient Nations. Edinburgh, 1753. [Anon. A second edition appeared at Edinburgh in 1809 after the second edition of Malthus's essay.]

———— Ignorance and Superstition a Source of Violence and Cruelty, and in Particular the Cause of the Present Rebellion; a Sermon Preached in the High Church of Edinburgh, Monday, January 6, 1745-46. Edinburgh, 1746.

———— Various Prospects of Mankind, Nature, and Providence. London, 1761.

Walpole, Horace. Letters, edited by Mrs. Paget Toynbee. Oxford, 1904. 16 vols.

———— Works. London, 1798-1825. 9 vols.

Wesley, John. Journal, edited by Nehemiah Curnock. London, 1906-16. 8 vols.

Wilkes, John. The North Briton, revised and corrected by the Author. Dublin, 1766. 2 vols.

Wilkie, William. The Epigoniad; a Poem. In Nine Books. Edinburgh, 1757. [Anon.]

———— The Epigoniad; a Poem. In Nine Books. The Second Edition, Carefully Corrected and Improved. To Which Is Added, a Dream. In the Manner of Spenser. London and Edinburgh, 1759.

———— Fables. London, 1768.

Wind, Edgar. "Humanitätsidee und heroisiertes Porträt in der englischen Kultur des 18. Jahrhunderts," *Vorträge der Bibliothek Warburg* (1932), pp. 156-229.

Witherspoon, John. A Serious Inquiry into the Nature and Effects of the Stage. Glasgow, 1757.

Wolcot, John. Works of Peter Pindar, Esq. London, 1809. 4 vols.

Wright, Austin. "Life and Works of Joseph Spence." Unpublished Ph.D. dissertation, Harvard University, 1930. 2 vols. [Not very illuminating on the Spence-Blacklock-Hume issue (pp. 162-66): Is inclined to believe that Hume was seeking publicity for his patronage of Blacklock! Has no good excuse to offer for Spence's discourtesy to Hume, and seems unaware of their later reconcilement.]

INDEX

INDEX

Account of Blacklock (Spence), 22, 23, 26

Account of Corsica (Boswell), 178

Adams, William, 174, 189, 196

Addison, Joseph, 47, 52, 195, 201

Advocates' Library, Hume in charge of, 6, 194; his dispute with the curators, 27; salary given to Blacklock, 28; Hume's successor, 51; made free of access to Hume's friends, 123; Boswell reads Hume's essays in, 182, 183

Agis (Home), 41, 43, 47

Alembert, Jean d', 159, 162, 176, 218; quoted, 161

Analogy of Religion (Butler), 29

Anderson, George, 118

Anglomania in France, 202

Annandale, Marquess of, 4

Annihilation, Boswell's attitude toward, 170, 179, 182, 185; Hume's, 181, 193; Dr. Johnson's, 185, 193

Apology for the Writers against the Tragedy of Douglas (Maclaurin), 51, 52, 215-16

"Appendix Containing . . . Observations concerning the Numbers of Mankind . . ." (Wallace), 114, 115

Argument . . . [on] the Tragedy of Douglas (Carlyle), 51

Argyle, Duke of, 43

Augustan Age of Scottish literature, 16, 36

Authoritarianism and skepticism, 204

Authorities, bibliographical, 225-36

Ballads occasioned by *Douglas*, with excerpts, 54-58

Barbentane, Marquise de, 150, 218

Barnard, Thomas, 200

Beattie, James, 196, 211; relations with Blacklock, 32-36, 37, 215; superficial philosophic character of, 34-36; antagonism toward Hume, 35, 36; the Reynolds portrait of, 36, 196, 221

Beauclerk, Topham, 200

Becket, Thomas, 162

Behn, Aphra, 58

Berkeley, George, 14, 34, 107

Bibliography, 225-36

Black, Joseph, 201, 202

Blacklock, Thomas, the Scottish Pindar, xiii, 13-37, 82, 101, 102, 204; Hume's friendship, and efforts to help, 13, 18, 20 ff., 28, 30, 215; literary efforts, 14, 19, 20 ff., 26, 28, 31, 33, 34; widespread interest in blindness of, and other factors contributing to receptive attitude toward, 14, 16, 17; relations with Spence, 15, 18, 22 ff., 28, 33; high moral character, 17; birth, 17; early life, 18; licensed to preach, 28; wife, 28 f., 31; opposition to his ministry, 30; retirement, 31; relations with Beattie, 32-36, 37, 215; estrangement from Hume, 32-36; literary import: recognition of Burns and Scott, 36 f.

Blacklock, Sarah Johnston (Mrs. Thomas), 28 f., 31

Blair, Hugh, 31, 35, 38, 39, 40, 106, 118, 125, 200, 202; quoted, 84, 199, 211; attitude toward Macpherson's Ossianic poems, 88-95 *passim*, 98; a leading figure among Moderates, 106, 118; the Hume-Rousseau correspondence, 140, 148, 151, 156, 157, 159, text, 158

Blair, Robert, 41

Blindness, interest of psychologists in, 14

Blind poet, *see* Blacklock, Thomas
Bolingbroke, Lord, 57
Bondeli, Julie, quoted, 63
Booksellers, Hume's complaint against, 75
Boswell, James, xiv, 34, 62, 63, 89, 93, 97, 127, 147, 167, 190, 200, 201, 203; dream about Hume, xi, 186-87, 189; conduct as escort of Rousseau's mistress, 149, 174; relations with Hume, 169-88; as literary lion-hunter, 169, 174, 176, 188, 189; why he chose Dr. Johnson a fitter hero than Hume, 169; Johnson's reputation perpetuated by, 169, 208, 210; appetite for drink, 169, 182; for women, 169, 174, 182; what religion meant to, 170; mental fixation regarding the paradox of Hume as a virtuous infidel, 170, 179 ff., 220; fear of annihilation, 170, 179, 182; first meetings with, and impressions of, Hume, 171 ff.; double-faced attitude toward him, 173 f.; adopts Johnson's rude attitudes, 173, 196; baiting of Johnson, 176, 177; journalistic talents, 176, 181; takes Hume's side in the Rousseau quarrel, 176; wife, 178, 183; deathbed interview with Hume, 180 ff.; during mental crisis, sounded depths of moral degradation, 183; treatment of Hume in published works, 187; made no effort to reconcile Hume and Johnson, 189; attitude toward English and Scotch, 191
Boswell, Mrs. James, 178, 183
Boufflers, Comtesse de, 63, 65; and the Hume-Rousseau relationship, 133, 134, 135, 136, 141, 143, 146, 149, 151, 155, 157, 158, 165, 174, 176, 218
Brown, John, 123
Buffon, Comte de, 202
Bunbury, Charles, 200
Burke, Edmund, 14, 35, 91, 196, 200; quoted, 15, 177

Burns, Robert, 80; Golden Age of Scott and, 13, 36, 66; encouraged by Blacklock, 36; epistle "To Dr. Blacklock," text, 37; quoted, 64
Burton, J. H., xii
Bute, Lord, 50, 86, 89, 92
Butler, Joseph, 29

Cadell, Thomas, 1, 189
Caffé, Le . . . (Voltaire), 63
Caledonian Enlightenment, 67, 105, 197, 199
Calvinists, *see* Church and clergy
Campbell, George, tribute to Hume, 103
Campbell, Thomas, 220
Canongate Theatre, 43, 51
Carlyle, Alexander, 30, 35, 38, 51, 58, 70, 106, 200, 217; quoted, 38, 46, 48, 70, 197; action against, for attendance at play, 119, 217
Carlyle, Thomas, description of Hume, xi; comparison of Hume and Johnson, 202, 207, 208
Caroline, Queen, 106
Cato (Addison), 47
Chambers, Robert, 200
Chamier, Anthony, 200
Characteristics of the Present Political State of Great Britain (Wallace), 123
Charlemont, Lord, 200
Charles I, 6, 123
Chastellux, Jean, Marquis de, 127, 129, 163
Chesterfield, Lord, 76, 79
Church and clergy, Scottish: contest over Blacklock, 30; attitude toward theatre, 44 f., 119, 217; attitude toward a clergyman's writing or seeing a play, 44; continued persecution of John Home and his drama, 48; efforts against Hume defeated, 46, 118 ff., 135-36, 217; patronage, 106, 125 f.; Hume's excoriating analysis of, 108; Wallace's refutation, excerpts, 108-11; Gerard's, 111; clergymen subject to

Church censure if seen in company of an infidel, 113, 119, 122; out for infidel blood, 118 ff.; fight of Hume and Wallace against bigotry, 123; enlightened clergymen among literati, 198; *see also* Moderates

Churchill, Charles, quoted, 63, 87

Clairaut, Alexis-Claude, 138, 139

Clarke, Samuel, 181

Cleghorn, Dr., 32

Clephane, John, 22, 25

Clergy, *see* Church and clergy

Clifford, James L., 220

"Club, The," Dr. Johnson and earlier literary dictators, 195; leading members, 196, 200; intolerant attitudes, 196; no counterpart of, in Edinburgh, 197

Clubs, of London, 195 f.; of Edinburgh, 107, 115, 128, 197 f.; French *salon*, 197

Cockburn, Mrs. Alison, quoted, 147

Collection of Original Poems, A (Blacklock and others), 34

Collins, William, 42, 83

Colman, George, 200

Color-associations of the blind, 15

Concise and Genuine Account of the Dispute between Mr. Hume and Mr. Rousseau, A, (Hume), 162

Condillac, Étienne de, 14

Confessions (Rousseau), 105, 132, 161, 165

Conti, Prince de, 140

Controversies of Hume, *see* Johnson, Samuel; Rousseau, J.-J.; Wallace, Robert

Conway, General, 8, 9, 126; and the Rousseau pension, 155, 156, 157, 163, 164, 165

Critical Dissertation on the Poems of Ossian . . . (Blair), 88, 89, 93, 95

Critical Essay on the Epigoniad, A . . . (anon.), 72

Critical Review, 86; excerpts, 60, 72; Hume's letter to, about *Epigoniad,* 76, 79, 102; excerpt, 77 f.

Cullen, William, 201

Davenport, Richard, and Rousseau, 150, 151, 157, 159, 160, 163, 164, 219

David, le bon, Hume's reputation as, xi-xii, xiii, 98, 131, 211, 212

David Hume (Greig), xiii

Death, attitude of Boswell, 170, 179, 182, 185; of Hume, 181, 193; of Dr. Johnson, 185, 193

Decline, idea of, 203, 217

Decline and Fall of the Roman Empire (Gibbon), xiv, 100

Demography, *see* Population controversy

Denina, Carlo G. M., 14; quoted, 13, 80, 201, 210

Departmentalization of intellect, 204

Deposition, The . . . (anon.), 54

De Somno (Cleghorn), 32

Deyverdun, Georges, 163

Dick, Sir Alexander, 27

Dictionary (Johnson), 173, 177, 194, 210

Dictionary of Music (Rousseau), 139

Diderot, Denis, 14

Digges in *Douglas,* 58*n*

Discourses . . . of Rousseau, 133

Dissertation on the Numbers of Mankind . . . (Wallace), 105, 112, 114, 115, 117, 128

Divine Order in the Changes of the Human Race . . . (Süssmilch), 130

Dodsley, Robert and James, 21, 22, 23, 24, 26, 34

Douglas, John, 189

Douglas; a Tragedy (Home), 42-66; *see entries under* Home, John

Dryden, John, 17, 195; quoted, 67

Drysdale, John, 126, 201

Dundas, Robert, 27

Dyer, George, 80

Dyer, Samuel, 200

Edinburgh, defense of, during Rebellion, 40 f., 70; staging and reception of *Douglas* at, 43 ff.

Edinburgh Evening Courant, review of *Essay on Truth* in, 36

Edinburgh literati, efforts to inspire in poetry the exalted qualities attained by prose, 13, 16; influence throughout Europe, 16; learned societies and clubs, 107, 115, 128, 197 f. (*see also* Select Society); finical about Scotticisms, 116; hospitality modeled on *salon intime*, 197 f.; spirit of tolerance, 198; democratic ideal: leaders, 199; compared with London's, 199 ff.; prominent persons in circle around Hume, 200; *see also* Scottish literature

Edmonstoune, Colonel, 75, 138

Elements of Criticism (Kames), 202

Elibank, Lord, 93, 201

Elliot, Gilbert, 11, 68, 74, 75, 139, 201

Emile (Rousseau), 133, 140

English literature, struggle between Scottish and English factions, 64, 191; London literati, 195 f.; culture and literature of Scotland and, compared, 199 ff.

Epics, writers of, 67, 68 ff., 82 ff.

Epigoniad (Wilkie), 71-82; *see entries under* Wilkie, William

Erskine, Sir Harry, 5

Essay on Miracles (Hume), 97

Essay on Public Happiness, An . . . (Chastellux), 129

Essay on the Origin and Immutability of Truth . . . (Beattie), 34, 36

Essay on the Principles of Population (Malthus), 131

Essays, Moral and Political (Hume), 5, 107

Essays and Treatises (Hume), 63, 197

Estimate of the Manners and Principles of the Times (Brown), 123

Ethics disassociated from religion, 170, 180, 181, 193

Exposé succinct de la contestation qui s'est élévee entre M. Hume et M. Rousseau . . . (Hume), 162

Fables (Wilkie), 81

Falconar, Sir David, 3

Ferguson, Adam, 36, 38, 50, 92, 95, 106, 200, 202

Fergusson, Robert, quoted, 80

Fingal; an Ancient Epic Poem . . . Composed by Ossian . . . tr. by James Macpherson, 86, 88, 89, 178

"Five Dissertations" (Hume), 48, 216

Forbes, Sir William, 215

Fordyce, George, 200

Four Dissertations (Hume), 48; Dedication, 45n, 47, 48 f., 51, 58 ff., 63, 66, 102

Fox, Charles James, 200

Fragments of Ancient Poetry, Collected in the Highlands of Scotland . . . , brought out by James Macpherson (*q.v.*), 83, 86, 89; cited, 84-85

France, literati's lack of interest in *Douglas*, 63; Anglomania of, found inspiration in Edinburgh literati, 202; *see also* Paris

Frederick the Great and Rousseau, 135, 136, 140, 146; Walpole's feigned King-of-Prussia letter, 143, 153, 217, text, 142

Free Inquiry (Middleton), 5

Friend of Humanity, The . . . (Mirabeau), 129

Garrick, David, 28, 41, 43, 44, 48, 61, 148, 150, 196, 200

Gay, John, 95n

George III, 134, 148, 162; pension for Rousseau, 146, 150, 154, 155, 156, 164

Gerard, Alexander, 76, 111

Ghost, The (Churchill), 88

Gibbon, Edward, xiv, 100, 200

"Gil Morrice" ballad, 46, 101

Golden Age of Burns and Scott, 13, 36, 66

Goldsmith, Oliver, 196, 200; quoted, 60, 73

Gordon, Gilbert, 20

Grant, General, 5

Gray, Thomas, 85, 106, 184; quoted, 65

Gregory, John, 201; opinion of Hume, 199

Greig, J. Y. T., xiii, xiv, 215, 218

Griffiths, Ralph, quoted, 73

Griskin Club, 197

Hailes, Lord, 201

Halkerton, Lord, 3

Hawkins, Sir John, 200; quoted, 195

Henry, Robert, 99, 200

Herring, Thomas, 7

Hertford, Lord, 8, 9, 137, 157, 161

Highflyers, against drama, 44, 119, 217; out for infidel blood, 118 ff.; see also Church and clergy

Highlander, The (Macpherson), 83

Hill, George Birkbeck, 220

History of England (Hume), 20, 27, 67, 76, 123, 133, 215; plan of writing, 6; its reception, 6 f., 8; sales records, 8

History of Great Britain (Henry), 99

History of Great Britain . . . (Macpherson), 97

Holbach, Baron d', 144, 145, 156, 216, 219

Home, Henry, see Kames, Lord

Home, John, the Scottish Shakespeare, xiii, 36, 38-66, 70, 82, 95, 98, 101, 102, 149, 200; quoted, 36, 62; intimacy with Hume, 38 ff., 63, 67; personality, 38; birth: early life, 40; ordained, 41; failure of first drama, 41; his *Douglas; a Tragedy*, 42 ff.; Hume's efforts in behalf of the tragedy, 43, 44 ff.; resulting controversies, 44 ff.; victim of religious bigotry, 44, 119, 217; Hume's dedication to, 45, 47, 48 f., 51, 58 ff., 63, 66; *Douglas* founded on ballad of "Gil Morrice," 46, 101; the Scottish literati's attacks and defense of *Douglas* and of Hume, 50-58; resigned ministry, 50; awarded medal and pension, 50; reaction to tragedy and controversy, in London, 58-63; in France,

63; import to Scottish literature, 64-66; the discoverer of Macpherson, 83; Griskin Club formed to promote *Douglas*, 197

Home, John (David's brother), 3, 148

Home, Joseph (David's nephew), 31

Homer, allusion to fall of Thebes, 71; imitations of *Iliad*, 71, 80; Macpherson's translation, 92

Homers, the Scottish, 67-102; see Macpherson, James; Wilkie, William

Hospitality of Edinburgh literati, 197, 198

Hume, David, *My Own Life*, xiii, text, 3-10; reputation established throughout Europe, xiii, 131; letters to Adam Smith, 1, 20, 28, 49, 76, 92, 98; ancestry: family, 3; early life, 3 ff.; financial status, 3, 5, 8, 9, 195; belief in superiority of the pursuits of literature, 4, 193; his own account of the publication and reception of his works, 4 ff.; with military embassy in Vienna and Turin, 5; resolution never to reply to literary squabbles, 6, 103; as librarian of Advocates' Library, 6, 27, 28, 51, 123, 194; assailed for showing sympathy for Charles I, 6; discouragement over reception of his *History*, 7; Tory sympathies, 7, 123, 193; book sales shatter all previous records, 8, 195; an important public figure while Secretary to British Embassy in Paris, 8, 124, 137; declining health, 9, 180; own estimate of his character and conduct, 9; efforts in behalf of Scottish poetry, 13, 16, 102; friendship with, and patronage of, Blacklock, 13, 18, 20 ff., 28, 30, 215; Edinburgh literary circle of, 16, 200 (see also Edinburgh literati); relations with Spence, 22, 23 ff., 27; end of friendship with Blacklock, 32-36; Beattie's antagonism, 35; relations with Moderates of the

Hume, David (*Continued*)

clergy, 38, 46, 48, 118 ff., 170 (*see also* Moderates); intimacy with John Home, 38 ff., 63; efforts in behalf of Home's *Douglas*: resulting counterattacks, 38, 43, 44 ff.; dedication of the *Four Dissertations* to Home, 45, 47, 48 f., 51, 58 ff., 63, 66; why qualified to combat intolerance, 46; Britain's most influential man of letters, 46, 125, 171, 194; Maclaurin's attacks against, 51-54; on Shakespeare's puns, 52, 215; gibes at physique of, 55; two suppressed essays, 56, 216; struggle between Scottish and English intellectuals dignified by, 64, 191; lent dignity to controversies over the Scottish Shakespeare, 64; and Scottish Homers, 65; as a judge of poetry, 65; part in the Scottish Declaration of Literary Independence, 66, 102; estimate of Milton's genius, 67; account of William Wilkie, text, 68-70; efforts to interest public in Wilkie's *Epigoniad*, 68, 74-79; complaint against booksellers, 75; letter to the *Critical Review*, 76, 79, excerpt, 77 f.; role as guardian of Scottish literary integrity in the Ossian affair of James Macpherson, 82, 85, 88-102 *passim,* 178, 216; shocked by Dr. Johnson's abuse of Scotland, 94; resulting efforts to clear the national character, 95, 97 ff.; why his *Of the Authenticity of Ossian's Poems* was never published, 97-99; perennial conflict between the two aspects of his character, the Inquirer after truth and *le bon David*, 98; Adam Smith his literary executor, 99; failures and valuable by-products of program for Scottish poetry sponsored by, 102; tributes to character of, texts, 103, 208, 212; the friendship-in-controversy between Wallace and, 105-31; gen-

erosity and humanity evidenced, 105; their population controversy, 105, 112-17, 124, 127-31, 217; paper on population, 105, 112, 115, 116, 117; excoriating analysis of clergymen, 108; Wallace's refutation, 108-11; Gerard's, 111; scrupulous of injuring the good name of another by associating it with that of an infidel, 112; Secretary to Philosophical Society, 115; finical about Scotticisms, 116; Presbytery's attack on, 118 ff., 135-36, 217; association with Wallace in fight against bigotry and for literature and humanity, 123; other relationships between them, 123-27, 217; steered church patronage to the Moderates, 125; Mirabeau and, 129; the Rousseau quarrel, 132-66; quarrel omitted from autobiography, 132; character displayed in connection with Rousseau affair, 132; careers of the two men compared, 133; campaign to bring them together, 133 ff.; Rousseau's analysis of difference between them, 134; won over to Rousseau, 138; efforts to assist him, 138 ff., 146, 147, 154, 155, 163; Walpole's King-of-Prussia letter, 143, 154, 217; information he and Rousseau had about each other, 144; Rousseau's suspicions of, and campaign against, 146, 151, 152 ff., 165; their journey to England, 146; in London, 147; Ramsay's portrait of, 148, 165, 219, 221; growing difficulties with his charge, 149; reaction to Rousseau's charges against him, 156 ff.; account of their relationship published in England and France, 162; pleads clemency for Rousseau, 164, 165; lack of a Boswell to perpetuate reputation of, 169, 208, 210; relations with Boswell, 169-88; ethical and moral nature as seen by Boswell, 170, 180, 187; Boswell's first meetings with and impressions of, 171 ff.; his mental fixation regarding the paradox of, as a virtuous infidel, 171, 183 ff., 220; perennial antagonism between Dr. Johnson and, 172, 173, 176 f., 187, 220; character he drew of Dr. Johnson notable for self-revelation, 173; Boswell's double-faced attitude toward, 173 f.; Boswell on the side of, in Rousseau quarrel, 176; hospitality, 178, 198; Boswell's deathbed interview with, 180 ff.; considered morality of religions bad, 181; attitude toward death, 181, 193; death, 183; Adam Smith's tribute to character of, 184, 211 (text, 208 f.); treatment of, in Boswell's published works, 187; willingness to meet Johnson, 189; survey of characters, beliefs, careers, and reputations of Johnson and, 189-210; war against provincialism: finally compelled to become anti-English, 191; typical pronouncements showing rival positions of Johnson and, as national spokesmen, 192, 220; caricatured in the Reynolds portrait of Beattie, 196, 221; and the Edinburgh literary groups, 197 ff.; prominent persons in circle around, 200; Carlyle's view of Johnson and, as complementary in character, 202, 207, 208; reputation in Europe as a genius, 202, 210; known today only as the Inquirer: the man forgotten, xi, 208; mind of, the catalyst of the Enlightenment, 210; appraised after a century and a half: why forgotten, 211 f.; motto on seal, 212; Ossianic critique directly inspired by Johnson's *Journey* . . . , 216; works: *see titles beginning with* Essay; Essays; Five; Four; History; Inquiry; Letter; My; Natural; Of; Political; Treatise

Hurd, Richard, 7

Ideas, of progress and of decline, 203, 217; distinction between persons and, in Hume and Johnson, 210; exemplified in relation to mathematics, 217

Ignorance and Superstition . . . (Wallace), 106

Iliad (Homer), 71, 80; Macpherson's translation, 92

Imaginary Conversations (Landor), 64

Infidels, Hume known as an infidel, 112, 178, 180; clergymen not to be seen in company of, 113, 119, 122; Presbytery's attacks upon, 118 ff.; ethics and morality, 170, 180 f.; Boswell's paradox of Hume as a virtuous infidel, 171, 183 ff., 220; rudeness to, approved by Johnson and Boswell, 173

Influence of the Pastoral Office . . . *The* (Gerard), 111

Inquirer, Hume known as, xi, 98, 208

Inquiry concerning Human Understanding (Hume), 5

Inquiry concerning the Principles of Morals (Hume), 5, 6, 55, 113

Inquiry into the Human Mind . . . (Reid), 124

Introduction to the History of Great Britain and Ireland (Macpherson), 92

Irene (Johnson), 47

Irvine, Peggy (Hume's housekeeper), 182-83, 198

Jardine, John, 201

Johnson, Samuel, xiv, 14, 29, 35, 47; attitude toward Blacklock, 15, 16, 17, 204; quoted, 22, 167; criticism of Home's *Douglas*, 62; repudiation of Macpherson and his Ossianic poems, 93 ff., 101, 204; tour of, and book on, Scotland, 93, 190, 216; abuse of the Scots, 94, 97; Hume's reaction, 95, 97, 216; reputation perpetuated by Boswell, 169, 208, 210; perennial antagonism between

Johnson, Samuel (*Continued*)
Hume and, 172, 173, 176 f., 185,
187, 189, 220; Hume's evaluation
of, 173; opinion of Rousseau, 175;
Boswell's baiting of, 176, 177; religion based on fear, 185, 187,
205-7; attitude toward death, 185,
193; survey of characters, beliefs,
careers, and reputations of Hume
and, 189-210; anti-Caledonianism
deep-seated, 190; typical pronouncements showing rival positions
of Hume and, as national spokesmen, 192, 220; rule of "The
Club," 195 f.; authority and influence through *Dictionary*, 195;
Carlyle's view of, 202, 207, 208;
secret of his consuming hatred of
Hume, 206; the Enlightenment,
the age of, in English literature,
210
Johnston, Sarah, 28
Jones, William, 200
Jonson, Ben, 195
*Journal of a Tour to the Hebrides
. . .* (Boswell), 187
Journey, The (Churchill), 63
*Journey to the Western Islands of
Scotland* (Johnson), 93, 97, 178,
190, 216
Judgment of Paris, The (Beattie), 34

Kames, Lord, 118, 127, 172, 201,
202; quoted, 98
Kant, Immanuel, quoted, 35
Keith, George, Earl Marischal of
Scotland, 105; and Rousseau, 135-
37, 146, 154, 155; tribute to
Hume, 212
King-of-Prussia letter, *see* Walpole,
Horace

Lamb, Charles, quoted, 80
Landor, Walter Savage, 64
Langton, Bennet, 200
Lawrie, George, 37
Le Blanc, Abbé, 22, 47, 128, 129
Leibniz, G. W. von, 14

Leslie, Alexander, 124, 125
Letters (Boswell), 171, 220
Letters from the Mountain (Rous-
seau), 138
Letters of David Hume (Greig, ed.),
xiv
*Letter to Mr. David Hume, A, on the
Tragedy of Douglas . . .* (anon.),
61
"Letter to the *Critical Review*"
(Hume), 76, 79, 102; excerpt,
77 f.
Le Vasseur, Thérèse, 140, 153; and
Rousseau, 140, 149, 150, 160; re-
lations with Boswell, 149, 174
Library, *see* Advocates' Library
*Life and Correspondence of David
Hume* (Burton), xii
Life of Johnson (Boswell), 187, 199
Liston, Robert, on Rousseau and
Hume, 140-41
Literature, *see* English literature; Scot-
tish literature
Locke, John, 14, 15, 34, 181, 202
London, staging of *Douglas* and re-
sulting controversy, 58-63; attitude
toward Rousseau, 147, 148; "The
Club," 195 f.
London Chronicle, excerpts, 58, 59
London literati, 195 f.; compared with
those of Edinburgh, 199 ff.
Luze, J.-J. de, 145, 149
Lyttleton, George, 24, 43, 160

Mackenzie, Henry, 19, 36, 200, 217;
quoted, 80, 106, 198, 199; investigation of Ossian, 100, 101; literary
leadership in Edinburgh, 199
Maclaurin, John, attacks against Hume,
Home, and the Select Society, 51,
excerpts, 52-54; cited, 215
Macpherson, James, Scottish Homer,
xiii, 82-102; early life, 83; publishes his *Fragments of Ancient Poetry . . .* , 83; the first fragment,
"Shilric . . . ," text, 84; publishes
the supposedly Ossianic epics, *Fingal*
and *Temora*, 86; resulting contro-

versy over value and authenticity of poems, 86 ff.; Hume's skeptical attitude toward his Ossian translations, 82, 85, 88-102 *passim*, 178 f., 216; translation of *Iliad*, 92; histories by, 92, 97; Dr. Johnson's repudiation of, 93 ff., 204; reactions of other intellectuals, 99-101; why his Ossian rejected and forgotten, 101, 102

Malthus, Thomas, 131

Marischal, Lord, *see* Keith, George

Mason, William, 184, 187

Mathematics and abstract universal ideas, 217

Metz, Rudolf, 216

Middleton, Conyers, 5

Millar, Andrew, 5, 7, 49, 59, 74, 75, 76, 216

Milton, John, 14, 17, 67, 72, 88

Mirabeau, Victor, Marquis de, 127, 129

Miracles, 186

Moderates of Scottish clergy, Hume's relations with, 38, 48, 118-19, 170; defeat efforts of Presbytery against the infidel Hume, 46, 118 ff.; philosophy: leaders among, 106; church patronage steered to, by Hume, 125; enlightened clergy among, 198; *see also* Church and clergy

"Molly Mog" (Gay), 95

Monboddo, Lord, 201

Montagu, Elizabeth, 98, 198, 199

Montesquieu, 112, 127 f., 194, 217

Monthly Review, excerpts, 59, 62, 73, 86

Morality disassociated from religion, 170, 180, 181, 193

Morton, Lord, 115, 128

Mure, William, 30, 49

My Own Life (Hume), xiii, 1; text, 3-10; omission of Rousseau controversy, 132; Smith's Preface, 184

Natural History of Religion (Hume), 7

"Necessity or Expediency of the Churches Inquiring into the Writings of David Hume . . . The" (Wallace), 119; Advertisement, text, 120

New Heloise (Rousseau), 133

Newman, John H., 204

Newton, Isaac, 202

Nugent, Christopher, 200

Nuneham, Lord, 153

Ode on the Popular Superstitions of the Highlands of Scotland, An . . . (Collins), 42, 83

Of National Characters (Hume), 107

Of Suicide (Hume), 48, 56, 216

Of the Authenticity of Ossian's Poems (Hume), 95, 97-99, 100, 102; excerpts, 95, 96 f.

Of the Immortality of the Soul (Hume), 48, 56, 216

Of the Populousness of Antient Nations (Hume), 105, 112, 115, 116, 117

Of the Standard of Taste (Hume), 48

Of Tragedy (Hume), 47

On the Immortality of the Soul (Blacklock), 26

Original Papers (Macpherson), 97

Ossian, Macpherson's imitations, or translations, of poems by, with resulting controversy, 82-102; *see entries under* Macpherson, James

Ossory, Lord, 143, 218

Oswald, James, 35

Paoli, General, 174, 175

Paraclesis . . . (Blacklock), 33

Paris, Hume with British Embassy at, 8, 124, 137; hero worship of Rousseau, 140, 145; *salon intime*, 197; *see also* France

Pascal, Blaise, 204

Percy, Thomas, 79, 200

Persons and ideas, distinction between, exemplified in Hume and Johnson, 210

"Peter Pindar" (John Wolcot), quoted, 190, 210

Philosopher's Opera, The (Maclaurin), 53

Philosophical Inquiry into . . . Ideas of the Sublime and Beautiful (Burke), 15, 91

Philosophical Society of Edinburgh, 107, 111, 115, 128

Pindar, the Scottish, 13-37; *see* Blacklock, Thomas

"Pistapolis . . ." (Blacklock), 31

Pitt, William, 43

Players Scourge . . . (anon.), 51

Poems (Blacklock), 14n, 19, 20 ff.

Poems . . . (Burns), 36

Poetry, *see* Scottish poetry

Poetry Professors, The (Wilkes), 87

Poker Club, 197

Political Discourses (Hume), 5, 6, 112, 114, 123, 128, 133, 194

Pope, Alexander, 17, 18, 67, 72, 74, 76, 201; quoted, 19, 71

Population controversy, 105, 112-17, 124, 217; interest of French liberals in, 127-30; of Germans, 130; work of Malthus, 130 f.; *see also* Hume, David; Wallace, Robert

Porson, Richard, on Johnson, 206

Presbytery, *see* Church and clergy

Price, Richard, 189

Priestley, Joseph, 35

Principal Truths of Natural Religion, The . . . (Reimarus), 130

Private Papers (Boswell), 171, 187, 220

Progress, idea of, 203

Prophecy of Famine, The (Churchill), 63, 87

Prussia, King, *see* Frederick the Great

Psychical researches, 204

Ramsay, Allan, portraits of Rousseau, 148, and Hume, Frontispiece; 148, 219, 221; Rousseau's resentment, 165 f.; Select Society instituted by, 67, 197

Ramsay, Allan, the elder, 45

Ramsay of Ochtertyre, 51, 217; quoted, 119, 131, 217

Rankenian Club, 107

Rebellion of 1745, Edinburgh during, 40 f., 70

Reid, Thomas, 35, 124

Reimarus, Hermann S., 130

Religion, narrowness and bigotry, 30; morality disassociated from, 170, 180, 181, 193; *see also* Church and clergy

Report . . . [on] the Nature and the Authenticity of the Poems of Ossian (Mackenzie and committee), 100 f.

Reveur, The, 106

Reynolds, Sir Joshua, 36, 200; the Beattie portrait, 196, 221

Richmond, Duke of, 9

Ridpath, George, quoted, 45, 48, 74

Robertson, William, 16, 27, 35, 38, 40, 70, 76, 99, 106, 118, 196, 200, 201, 202; quoted, 92; motto, 199

Roddier, Henri, 218

Rouet, William, quoted, 149

Rousseau, J.-J., 63, 125, 127, 212; dream about Hume, xi, 146, 161, 189; quarrel with Hume, xiv, 132-66; garbled version of the Hume-Wallace controversy, 105; Mirabeau's offer to, 129; quarrel not mentioned in *Confessions*, 132, 165; careers of the two men compared, 133; condemned for impiety: fled from France, 133; overtures of friends in behalf of, 133 ff.; Hume's high opinion of, 134, 135; frank analysis of difference between them, 134; characteristics, 134, 144, 152, 166; asylum in Neuchâtel, 135, 139; refuses pension from Frederick the Great, 136; attitude of French *philosophes* toward, 137, 141, 143, 148; became a man without a country, 138, 139; Hume's efforts to assist, 138 ff., 147, 155, 163; mistress, 139, 140, 149, 153, 160; dog, 140, 146, 150; in Paris, 140, 145; informed about Hume, 144; sanity questioned, 145,

160; the English pension, 146, 154, 155, 159, 163; suspicions of, and campaign against, Hume, 146, 151, 152 ff., 165; in London, 147; Armenian costume, 148; the Ramsay portrait, 148, 165, 219; installed in Davenport's house at Wooton, 150; Walpole's feigned King-of-Prussia letter to, 153, 154, 217 (text, 142); reactions of Hume and others to, 156 ff.; Hume's *Exposé* of, 162; flight from Wooton, 164, 219; Hume's plea for clemency for, because of lunatic condition, 165; Boswell and, 147, 149, 174, 175 f.; Dr. Johnson's condemnation of, 175

Rousseau, Judge of Jean-Jacques (Rousseau), 166

Rover, The (Behn), 58

St. Clair, General, 5

St. James's Chronicle, 154, 155, 163

Salon intime the model for Scottish literati, 197 f.

Savage Man, The (Boswell), 176

Scotland, Dr. Johnson's tour of, and book on, 93; antagonisms against the Scots, 94, 97, 190-92, 220; Hume's reaction, 95, 97

Scots Magazine, 49, 119; excerpts, 44, 54, 80, 118, 202, 210

Scots Prologue for Mr. Sutherland's Benefit-night . . . (Burns), excerpt, 64

Scott, Sir Walter, Golden Age of Burns and, 13, 36, 66; Blacklock and, 36, 37; quoted, 65; attitude toward Macpherson and the Ossianic controversy, 101

Scotticisms, 24, 116

Scottish Bill of Literary Rights, 102

Scottish church, *see* Church and clergy

Scottish Declaration of Literary Independence, 65, 66, 102

Scottish literature, eminent men, 11, 200; philosophic or Augustan Age, 13, 16, 36; Golden Age of Burns

and Scott, 13, 36, 66; literary import of Blacklock, 36 f.; struggle between English and Scottish factions, 64, 191; Hume's influence in the struggle, 64; a banner year, 67; Hume's role as guardian of, in the Ossian affair of Macpherson, 82 ff.; culture and, compared with English, 199 ff.; *see also* Edinburgh literati

Scottish poetry, efforts to raise standards of, 13, 16; ballads occasioned by *Douglas*, with excerpts, 54-58; the Scottish Homers, 67-102; why program sponsored by Hume and his circle not more successful: its valuable by-products, 102

Seal, motto on Hume's, 212

Select Society, Edinburgh, Maclaurin's attacks on, 51, excerpts, 52-54; organization: influence: Hume's part in, 123, 197

Sentimental Journey, A (Sterne), 39

Shaftesbury, Lord, 25, 106; quoted, 199

Shakespeare, Hume on puns of, 52, 215

Shakespeare, the Scottish, 38-66; *see* Home, John

Sharp, L. W., 215

Sharp, Matthew, 21

Shenstone, William, 85; quoted, 79

Sheridan, Thomas, 50, 62

"Shilric, Vinvela" (Macpherson), text, 84

Skepticism and authoritarianism, 204

Smart, Christopher, 70

Smith, Adam, 16, 188, 200, 202; Hume's literary executor, 1, 99; Hume's letters to, 20, 28, 49, 76, 92, 93, 98; letter describing Hume's last days, 184, 208; judgment of, and tribute to, Hume, 184, 211 (text, 208 f.); literary leadership, 199

Smollett, Tobias, 60, 77, 86, 172; quoted, 202

Social Contract (Rousseau), 133

Spence, Joseph, 14, 204; mentality,

Spence, Joseph (*Continued*)
22; relations with Blacklock, 15,
18, 22 ff., 28, 33; with Hume, 22,
23 ff., 42
Spirit of the Laws (Montesquieu),
127
Steevens, George, 200
Sterne, Laurence, quoted, 39, 208
Stevenson, John, 18, 19
Stewart, John, 22, 139, 147
Stone, George, 7, 76
Strahan, William, 1, 74, 89, 127, 211
Strange, Robert, 172
Suppers of Edinburgh literati, 197,
198
Süssmilch, Johann P., 130

Temora, Composed by Ossian (Mac-
pherson), 86
Theatre, antagonism of Scottish clergy,
44 f., 119, 217; redemption by a
Scotsman ardently desired, 48
Thrale, Hester L., 184
Tieman, quoted, 202
Toryism of Hume, 7, 123, 193
Townshend, Charles, quoted, 70
*Tragedy of Douglas Analysed, The
. . .* (anon.), 60
Treatise of Human Nature (Hume),
4, 5
"Treatise on Taste" (Wallace), 126
Tronchin, Louis, 149, 153, 160
*True Account of . . . Archibald
Stewart, Esq., A* (Hume), excerpt,
40-41
"Triumph of Truth over Error"
(Reynolds), 36, 196, 221
Turgot, A.-R.-J., 164, 165
Turin, Hume with embassy at, 5, 194

Vanity of Human Wishes (Johnson),
excerpt, 205 f.
*Various Prospects of Mankind, Nature,
and Providence* (Wallace), 124
Verdelin, Mme de, and the Hume-
Rousseau affair, 136, 137 f., 139,
140, 143, 152, 153, 154, 219
Vesey, Agmondesham, 200

Vesey, Mrs. Agmondesham, 198
Vienna, Hume with embassy at, 5
Voltaire, 14, 46, 52, 62, 63, 157, 167,
174, 176, 211; quoted, 202
Vossius, Isaak, 217

Wallace, George, 127; quoted, 44
Wallace, Robert, xiii, 202; the friendship-in-controversy between Hume
and, 38, 105-31, 201; character
and capabilities, 105-7, 119; the
population controversy, 105, 112-
17, 124, 127-31, 217; papers on
population, 105, 112, 114, 115,
117, 128; other published writings,
106, 119, 120, 123, 124; unpublished writings, 107, 111, 119,
127; refutation of Hume's excoriating analysis of clergymen, excerpts, 108-11; reaction to Presbytery's attack on Hume, 118 ff.;
sympathy for John Home when
persecuted by Highflyers, 119, 217;
called on the carpet by bigots, 119;
other relationships between Hume
and, 123-27, 217; request for ecclesiastical preferment, 125; death,
126
Walpole, Horace, quoted, 101; and
Rousseau, 139, 142, 143, 159, 160,
162, 176; feigned King-of-Prussia
letter to Rousseau, text, 142; resulting reaction, 143, 153, 217; on
Scottish culture, 201
Warburton, William, 6, 35
Wedderburn, Alexander, 118
Wesley, John, on witches, 205
White, Thomas, xii
Wilkes, John, 22, 177, 190, 216;
quoted, 87
Wilkie, William, Scottish Homer, xiii,
40, 68-82, 95, 102, 201, 202;
Hume's account of singularity of,
text, 68-70; the epic *Epigoniad*,
written and published, 71; "a god
and a brute," 70; early life: ministry, 70; attack on Milton and Pope:
resulting retaliation, 72 ff.; Hume's

efforts to interest public in *Epigoniad*, 74-79; epic unfavorably received, 75, 76; its second edition,
76; epic rejected and forgotten,
80, 102; as Professor of Natural
History: brings out *Fables*, 81; composed *Epigoniad* while acting as
scare-pigeon, 69, 216

Wind, Edgar, 221
Witches, 205
Witherspoon, John, 50, 51
Woffington, Peg, 58